Military English

군대생활의
고뇌 추억 지혜

군대
영어

Sir 24

My Dear Readers

When I was in middle school, my dream was to become an English teacher. Fortunately, I managed to achieve my long-cherished dream while I was serving in the Republic of Korea Air Force. During my service years, I earned an MA in English education and had an opportunity to take the English Instructor's Course at the Defense Language Institute in the USA. This book is the end result of that experience and the insight of a long military carrier.

Most Korean males are reborn as real men through the following painful but rewarding process: wandering aimlessly prior to entering military service, parting with girlfriends, having the second attack of measles at boot camp, going on the 100th-day's leave, experiencing private soldiers' sadness, managing trouble with seniors, receiving one's parents' first visit, getting a Dear John letter, taking care of rubber shoes waiting like a Chun-hyang, having a farewell party before discharge, and reporting for discharge, etc.

Here, I have focused mostly on expressing and appreciating memories or recollections about past military life in English and I have included some information about the US military. But some of the contents here are stories or practices from the 1960s to the 1980s in the military, so you may feel that they are a little out of date now.

Finally, I hope that military life will become brighter and will be full of sensitivity as a result of all of the following performing their roles: new recruits, the new recruits' girlfriends, officers, NCOs and military wives.

독자들에게

내가 중학교 다닐 때는 영어교사 되고 싶었다. 어떻게 운이라도 따랐는지 한국 공군에 근무하는 동안 영어교육 석사 학위를 받을 수 있었으며, 미국 국방성언어학교에서 교육받을 기회도 있었다. 이 책은 나의 긴 군생활에서 얻은 경험과 직권의 결과이기도 하다.

한국 남성들은 힘들긴 하지만 해볼 만한 다음의 과정을 겪은 후에 제 2의 남자로 다시 태어난다. 예를 들면 입대 전의 방황, 여자 친구와 이별, 훈련소에서 제 2의 홍역 경험, 100일 휴가, 이등병 때의 서러운 경험, 고참과의 갈등 해소, 부모님의 첫 면회, 애인으로부터 절교편지 받기, 춘향이와 같이 기다리는 고무신 돌보기, 전역회식, 전역신고 등으로.

나는 이 책에서 지난 시절의 병영에 대한 추억을 영어로 표현하고 음미하는데 초점을 두었으며, 또한 미군에 대한 내용도 일부 포함시켰다. 그러나 이 책의 일부 내용은 1960년~1980년대 군대 이야기나 관행으로서 현재와는 다소 거리감이 있을 것이다.

끝으로 입대 장병, 장병의 여자친구, 장교, 부사관 그리고 군인아내들이 각자의 역할에 충실함으로써 군생활이 더욱 밝아지고 감성이 넘치길 기대한다.

Contents (목차)

입대 전 p.16-26

- 도장 가져오세요
- 영장 받았니?
- 해병대 지원* ★: 내용의 흥미 정도
- 친척들에게 작별인사 드려
- 입대 전 파티**
- 총각○○를 떼 주는 관행***
- 여자 친구와 이별
- 고무신 거꾸로 신기***
- 오빠, 걱정 마!
- 아버지의 충고

입대 후 p.28-69

- 입소식 전에
- 입소식*
- 병의 임무
- 입영 선서**
- 엄마는 모르시죠***
- 조디 콜*
- 논산훈련소의 낙서**
- 미군훈련소에서 신송 사항**
- 식사구호!*
- 너의 발을 키워라
- 진짜 사나이(군가)
- 기초군사훈련은 힘들어
- 이렇게 대답하라*
- 미 해병대는 이렇게 대답한다
- "아닙니다!"라고 대답해라**
- 어둠의 자식*
- 러시아인의 불만*
- 침 뱉으면서 군화 닦기
- 내무검사의 목적**
- 팬텀이 지나가겠다
- 너 짝다리 짚는구나!
- 수진*
- 10분 휴식 동안에
- 일석점호에서
- 팬티에 주기 해
- 흰 장갑 점호**
- 사역 중!
- 점화식*
- 오늘밤에 탈영하자**
- 화생방 체험*

- 해병대 쫄따구 헌장★★★
- 한번 해병은 영원한 해병★
- 해병의 또 다른 정의★★
- 사랑하는 아들 훈현에게★
- 너는 무슨 특기 받았냐?
- 훈련병과 스님★★
- 총과 여자★★★
- 일단 군대 가면★★★
- 군인과 애인★★★
- 구령★★
- 계급별 특성★★★

자대생활 p.72-163

- 전입신고
- 너 빽 있지?★★
- 전입 첫날★
- 우리 누나 가슴 빵빵★★★
- 여자친구 있나?★
- 그녀를 어떻게 만났니?
- 그녀 사진 좀 보자
- 너 축구 좀 하냐?★★
- 박물관으로 전속!★★★

- 한국 사람들이 군대에 부정적으로 되는 이유★★
- 고참신상 파악★
- 점호 끝나고 개내무반으로
- 눈물 밥을 먹다★★
- 인상 좀 펴라
- 너 담배 피우냐?
- 홈런 했다★★
- 데이트의 5단계★★★
- 김일병 송★★
- 계급별 이미지★★★
- 이병은 사람이 아니다
- 이등병은 하루에 세 번 운다★★
- 왜 군인들이 4계절을 모두 싫어하나★
- 병사들의 푸념
- 이등병의 맹세★★★
- 이등병 아저씨들에게
- 군바리 애인들에게★★
- 나이 처먹어서 꼽냐?★★★
- 여친을 만나기 위해 탈영
- 누가 먼저 이별을 유도하는가? 여자다!
- 이별 후에 누가 더 괴로운가? 남자다!
- 질문★

- 바퀴벌레와 방위병*
- 군대 업무처리 과정***
- 나는 방공포를 사랑해요***
- 이등병의 슬픔***
- 이등병 수칙***
- 이런 속어를 더 이상 사용하지 말자
- 군대에서 근무 요령***
- 군바리의 기다림에 대한 보상은**
- 군바리 10대 강적***
- 군인의 칠거지악***
- 군바리 하소연**
- 군대 훈련의 유래***
- 휴가신고**
- 저는 부대 식모가 아닙니다!*
- 외출・외박의 목적
- 100일 휴가
- 휴가의 마지막 날**
- 내 여친이 벌써 새 남친을
- 여친에게 말하지 말 것은*
- 나무를 흔들어
- 군대에서 나무가 잘 자라지 않는 이유
- 화생방 경보 발령
- MOPP 4 단계 발령***
- 진급 신고

- 아직도 자고 있어
- 점호만 없어도
- 어떻게 처벌 받을래? I*
- 어떻게 처벌 받을래? II
- 군번줄 보자
- 오늘 일석점호 때 보자
- 점호 끝
- 취침점호
- 천리행군의 기원**
- 패잔병처럼
- 대대장님과의 대화
- 수하 요령**
- 보초 서로 가다
- 수하 I
- 수하 II
- 차량 수하
- 보초수칙
- 근무 중에 건빵 먹기*
- 무좀**
- 부산의 미스 김 일거야*
- 고무신 거꾸로 신었나 봐*
- 자살
- 너무 늦었습니다
- 당신이 누군지 모르겠어!

- 너 군생활 어떠니?
- 사고보고★
- 부적절한 관계★★
- 감점표 내놔!
- 죄수와 군인★★★
- 군생활 3년 후에 ★★
- 허가되지 않은 관물 파손★★★
- 모자에 개구리 마크★
- 전역 회식에서 마지막 한마디★★
- 전역 전날 밤에★
- 전역신고★★★
- 고참 군화의 충고★★★

장교・부사관 p.166-290

- 임관선서★★
- 장교의 책무★
- 부사관의 임무★
- 장교는 시인 같아야★★
- 장교의 존재이유는?
- 부사관은 군대의 척추★
- 장교의 4가지 등급★
- 부하의 4가지 분류★

- 능력있는 장군 밑에★
- 장교의 칠거지악★★★
- 움직이지 못하는 상어
- 야생으로 키우기
- 개인소개★★
- 영외거주
- 잠자러 출근해?
- 꽃밭에 물주기
- 네 부하는 이렇지 않니?
- 초병이 총을 분실★★
- 무장 탈영★★★
- 두 병사가 탈영
- 바람 잘날 없구먼!
- 중위가 초병을 패다★★
- 우리 "군차렷" 걸렸어★★★
- 구타 및 가혹 행위 근절 서약★
- 통화 중이면 1234로
- 장교 바꿔★
- 7사단 근무해봤어?
- 전속신고★
- 대대장님을 떠나기 전에
- 대대장님과 같은 리더가 되겠습니다!★
- 얘기 들었습니다

- 전입신고
- 보직신고
- 너는 운 좋다
- 너 행운이다!
- 그분은 FM이래**
- 미군 벨트
- 교육, 훈련, 잔소리**
- 상사와 시어머니**
- 모기 회식
- 불쌍한 리더십**
- 라면으로 때우다**
- 젊은 장교들을 개xx라고 부르지 마
- 김대위님께 경례하지 말자
- 전투호 2개 파라
- 0-2기가 비행기냐?*
- 내일부터 검열이다
- 너 소설을 썼구나
- 얼음을 다리미로 녹여**
- 가서 좀 자라
- 군대 말뚝 박아라**
- 너 왜 경례 안 해?
- "충성!"해봐!**
- "님"자 빼지 마라***

- 부사관은 항상 중요하다**
- 너 군대 한 번 더 가라
- 보안평가**
- 비인가 디스켓
- 검열 준비해야 돼
- 비인가 전열기
- 화재예방 표어
- 담배 빈대
- 불만 있어
- 금연결의문**
- 비흡연자의 신음소리***
- 골프와 영어 배우기**
- 내기 골프 금지*
- 20번 홀까지 가다***
- 저는 더 이상 골프 안 쳐요*
- 너 없이 검열을 받을 수 있나?
- 토요일 오후에 테니스*
- 테니스 코트에서
- 아부 테니스 게임**
- 나는 그와 한편 하기 싫어
- 삼겹살에 소주**
- 삼겹살
- 마음의 잔*

- 첫 잔은 마셔라**
- 코리안 비아그라***
- 내일은 휴일이나 다름없어
- 이번에는 뭐 내기?***
- 오늘 저녁 회식이야
- 회식 취소
- 어떻게 회식에 안갈 수 있나?
- 10일전에 날 잡았어요
- 너 식사만 해
- 벌주***
- 계급주***
- 우턴하겠습니다*
- 왼쪽으로 두 클릭**
- 이상한 "건배"*
- 음주운전은 살인행위***
- 모두 커피?
- 음주운전
- 음주운전 금지 서약**
- 윤잔과 윤간***
- 퇴근 못해
- 잦은 회식은***
- 느닷없는 "건배"***
- 진급심사

- 위로주***
- 그의 진급은 끝났군!
- 누군가의 큰 짐
- 진급이 모든 것은 아니다*
- 찬물을 끼얹다
- 그는 장군감이 아니다
- 지는 별*
- 장군 될 비전
- 선거와 진급***
- 시체가 일어날지도 몰라**
- 모든 군인은 불평불만 자
- 군인들의 군살
- 청춘을 불살랐다
- 사고보고***
- 이라크 파병 지원***
- 네 얼굴이 분화구 같아
- 나는 찌들었소
- 제대타령**
- 내년에 제대해야지
- 면세양주 한 병 줘
- 중대장님, 저 언제 오프합니까?
- 지휘관의 책무**
- 지휘관의 근무 십계명**

- 지휘관의 의도**
- 지휘관은 결코 잊지 않는다
- 너의 상관은 크고 살찐 늙은 말과 같다
- 세 가지 보고
- 중대장님 지시사항***
- "예, 알겠습니다!" 라고 대답해라
- 미군에서 준수사항***
- 현역에 짐이 되지 말자**
- 늙은 군인의 노래
- 영어의 전략적 능력*

여군훈련소 p.292-301

- 너 뭐 되고 싶어?
- 칠면조 점호
- 내무검사에서**
- 군기가 빠진 김병장
- 너 머리 염색 했구나*
- 립스틱이 너무 진하다***
- 너의 브라는 지급품이 아니구나***
- 누가 또 면회 왔어?
- 면회 전
- 면회 후
- 저 커피타려고 군대 온 거 …

고무신 함성 p.304-337

- 군바리 사랑*
- 제 남친이 곧 군대가는데**
- 상병은 여친을 차버리는가?
- 세상에서 가장 쉬운 일*
- 여자는 언제 우나?
- 세상에서 젤 나쁜 놈**
- 초보 고무신으로부터*
- 너의 소포 받았어**
- 오빠, 나야!*
- 군바리도 인간?***
- 원통엔 어떻게 가져?**
- 치마 입는 게 더 좋은가?**
- 서방님 보시와요~**
- 그의 손잡기도 쉽지 않았어
- 곰신님들~^^*
- 이미 임신 5개월***
- 수잔은 팬티를 잘 내려서**
- 아기가 아직 태어나지 않았어
- 고무신의 맹세***
- 고참 고무신의 맹세*
- 병장에게 보낸 소포*

- 그런 친구가 될게**
- 절교 편지**
- 고참 곰신의 충고***

군인의 아내 p.340-353

- 말없는 계급
- 군인 아내는 연의꼬리
- 슈퍼우먼이 못돼서
- 생각이 깊은 군인의 아내
- 군인 아내의 헌장***
- 군인 마누라는 상팔자
- 여자도 군대 가야 해
- 영진이 엄마 전에*
- 군인 아내의 맹세***
- 유연한 비상대기 명단
- 집시 인생**
- 군인의 아내
- 하나님

최종평가 p.356-365

- Final Test
- 해설 및 정답

Military English

국기에 대한 맹세

나는 자랑스러운 태극기 앞에
자유롭고 정의로운 대한민국의 무궁한
영광을 위하여 충성을 다할 것을
굳게 다짐합니다.

The Pledge of Allegiance to the Flag

*I pledge, in front of proud Taegeukgi, allegiance
to the Republic of Korea
for the eternal glory of the country, liberty and justice.*

Military English

Before Joining the Military
(입대 전)

- 도장 가져오세요
- 영장 받았니?
- 해병대 지원*
- 친척들에게 작별인사 드려
- 입대 전 파티**
- 총각○○를 떼 주는 관행***
- 여자 친구와 이별
- 고무신 거꾸로 신기***
- 오빠, 걱정 마!
- 아버지의 충고

🔵 Bring your seal

"Ding-dong, ding-dong"

"Is Mr. Hong Kil-dong there? I've got a draft notice¹. Bring your seal!" The back of the draft notice says, "Anyone who does not report to the boot camp² after receiving official notification will be sentenced³ to no less than three years' penal servitude⁴ under the regulation of the military service law."

'Once I got my draft notice in my hand, the sky began to look all yellow, though I knew that it would come. I was the only one among my circle of friends who had not yet joined the military. I felt like 'the last leaf' dangling⁵ on a tree. No one was going to give me a farewell party. How can I keep contact with my girlfriend? I wonder if she will change her mind after I have joined the army.' Such mixed feelings lingered⁶ all afternoon.

* **the sky looks all yellow** means "everything looks gloomy or hopeless at the beginning." This expression is inferred from "the bud became yellow."

[해설] ¹draft notice 입영 통지서, 영장. ²boot camp: a training camp for people who have joined the Army, Navy, or Marines (육·해·해병대) 기초군사훈련소: Boot camp can be a tough experience for soldiers. 기초군사훈련소는 군인들에게 힘든 경험이다. ³sentence: to give a punishment 판결을 내리다, 선고하다. ⁴penal servitude 징역: serve a sentence of five years' penal servitude. 5년간 징역을 살다. ⁵dangle [dǽŋɡəl]: to hang or swing loosely 매달리다: The keys are dangling from a chain. 열쇠들이 고리에 걸려 있다. ⁶linger [líŋɡər]: to remain; stay 남다, 머물다: Her perfume lingered even after she had gone. 그녀가 간 후에도 향수가 남아 있었다.

🔸 도장 가져오세요

"딩동—딩동"

"홍길동씨 계십니까? 영장 나왔습니다. 도장 가지고 나오세요!"

입영 통지서 뒤에는 아래와 같이 쓰여 있었다.

"정당한 사유 없이 입영하지 아니한 때에는 병역법 규정에 의하여 3년 이하의 징역형을 받게 됩니다."

'막상 영장을 내 손에 쥐고 보니 하늘이 온통 노랗게 보이기 시작했다. 그것이 올 줄은 알고 있었지만. 나는 내 서클에서 군대 가지 않은 유일한 사람이었으며 내가 나뭇가지의 '마지막 잎새' 처럼 느껴졌다. 내겐 작별 파티를 해 줄 친구가 하나도 없었다. 내 여자친구와 어떻게 연락을 할까? 내가 군대 가고나면 그녀가 변심하지 않을까.' 그런 착잡한 생각이 오후 내내 뇌리에서 떠나지 않았다.

* <u>하늘이 노랗게 보이다</u>는 "처음부터 모든 것이 우울하고 희망이 없음"을 나타낸다. 이것은 "싹수가 노랗다" 에서 온 것으로 추측된다.

제 000004호	현 역 병 입 영		통 지 서
성 명	김철구	주민등록번호	8050537-1731625
세대주 성명	김남철	관 계	자
주 소	광주 광산 소촌(어룡) 602번지 22호 11통 4반		
병 적 지	광주 광산 소촌(어룡) 602번지 22호 11통 4반		
입 영 부 대	○사단		
모이는 장소	광주 북구 오치동		
입 영 일 시	2003년 11월 27일 13:00		
병역법 제 16조 규정에 의하여 위와 같이 현역 입영을 통지합니다. 2003년 10월 9일 광주전남 지방병무청장			

🔸 Did you receive a draft notice?

A: Did you get a draft notice?
B: Yes, I did a week ago.
A: When do you go into the military?
B: Next Monday.
A: Why did you choose the Army?
B: The term is shorter than that of the Air Force.
A: Then, why don't you go into the Marine Corps?
B: I don't think I can make it through Marine training.
A: Then, go into the Air Force, though the term is a little longer.
B: I heard that the basic training in the Air Force is not a piece of cake[1] anymore.
A: Before you join the Army[2], try to keep just one girlfriend and say goodbye to the others[3].

* In Korea in the 1950s, a draft notice was often called "a notice of seizing one's youth."

[해설] [1]be a piece of cake (informal): to be very easy to do 하기 쉬운: That job is so easy; it's a piece of cake! 그 일은 너무 쉬워서 누워 떡먹기이다. [2]join/enter the Army (on 8 July 2006). (2006년 7월 8일) 육군에 입대하다. [3]keep just one girlfriend and say goodbye to the others 여자 친구 하나만 남겨두고 나머지와 헤어지다 → "정리하다"

🔸 영장 받았니?

A: 너 영장 받았어?
B: 일주일 전에 받았어.
A: 언제 입대해?
B: 다음 주 월요일.
A: 왜 육군을 선택했어?
B: 복무기간이 공군보다 짧아서.
A: 그럼 해병대 가지?
B: 해병대 훈련을 견딜 자신 없어.
A: 그럼, 복무기간이 좀 더 길더라도 공군으로 가지.
B: 공군 기초군사훈련도 더 이상 누워서 떡 먹기가 아니라 하더라구.
A: 입대 전에 여자친구 정리도 하구.

* 1950년대 한국에서 징집영장은 종종 "청춘차압장"이라고 불렸다.

Applying for the Marine Corps

[Interviewer : Applicant]

I : What made you apply for the Marine Corps?
A: Because I don't like to lead an ordinary life!
I : Have you heard that a Marine's life is tough?
A: Yes, sir!
I : Don't you think you will regret that you enlisted?
A: No, sir! I want to show how strong I am!
I : Is there anybody in your family who served in the Marine Corps?
A: Yes, my elder brother did.
I : What did he say to you about the Marine Corps?
A: He said, "A marine is not a can that can be crushed, but he is like a soju bottle that can be shattered[1]!"
I : I see. The Marine Corps is not notorious[2] for tough disciplinary punishment[3], but it is famous for tough drills.
OK, go back to your place!

[해설] [1]shatter [ʃǽtəːr]: to break (sth) into very small pieces 박살내다/박살나다: The cup fell to the floor and shattered. 컵이 마루에 떨어져서 박살났다. [2]notorious[noutɔ́ːriəs]: infamous; famous, esp. for sth bad (나쁜 쪽으로) 잘 알려진, 악명 높은 ↔ famous. [3]disciplinary punishment (corrective training) 체벌, 기합(drop, sit-up, push-up, etc.)

해병대 지원

면접관: 해병대엔 왜 지원했나?
지원자: 평범하게 살기 싫어서 입니다!
면접관: 해병대 생활 힘들다는 거 들어봤나?
지원자: 예, 들어봤습니다!
면접관: 지원한 거 후회하지 않겠어?
지원자: 아닙니다! 제가 얼마나 강한지 보여주고 싶습니다.
면접관: 가족 중에 누가 해병대 근무한 사람 있나?
지원자: 예, 저의 형님이 근무했습니다.
면접관: 그가 해병대에 대해서 뭐라고 하더냐?
지원자: "해병은 찌그러지는 깡통이 아니라 박살나는 소주병과 같다!"고 했습니다.
면접관: 알았다. 해병대는 기합으로 악명이 높은 것이 아니라 훈련이 세기로 유명하지. 그럼, 너의 자리로 가봐!

Say goodbye to our relatives

[Son : Father]

F: You should visit all our relatives and say goodbye to them before entering the military.

S: I'm sorry, I don't have the time, father.

F: But you have to, otherwise they'll miss you.
If you visit them, you'll get some pocket money[1].

S: What use is money after I go into the military?

F: Do you think you'll be in the military forever?
You can spend it on your first leave[2].

[해설] [1]pocket money 용돈(child's money) 미국에서는 allowance라고 한다: My pocket money wasn't enough for me so I decided to get a part time job. 나는 용돈이 부족해서 시간제근무로 일하기로 결정했다. [2]leave: a period away from work or the military 휴가: Jane is on sick leave. 제인은 병가 중이다.

친척들에게 작별인사 드려

아버지: 너 입대 전에 친척들 방문해서 인사드려야 한다.

아 들: 그럴만한 시간 없어요, 아빠.

아버지: 인사드려야 해. 그렇지 않으면 섭섭해 하신다.
친척들 방문하면 용돈도 좀 얻을 걸.

아 들: 군대 가고 나면 용돈이 뭔 소용 있어요?

아버지: 너 군대에 평생 있을 거라고 생각하니?
네 첫 휴가 때 쓰면 되잖아.

🔸 Farewell party before being drafted

A: When does Kil-dong go into the military?

B: Next Monday, I think.

A: What kind of farewell party should we hold for him?

B: Let's make him lose his virginity[2] before he gets drafted[1].

A: He is not a virgin, anyway!

B: These days it's really hard to find a virgin at that age.

[해설] [1]draft: to order a person to become a member of the armed forces 징병하다. Jim was drafted into the army. 짐은 육군으로 징병되었다. [2]virginity [vərdʒínəti]: the condition of never having had sex 처녀성, 순결: She was 18 when she lost her virginity (=had sex for the first time). 그녀는 18세에 순결을 잃었다. 〈 virgin [vəːrdʒin]: someone who has never had sex 성경험이 없는 사람

🔸 입대 전 파티

A: 길동이 언제 군대 간데?

B: 다음 주 월요일 부로 갈 걸.

A: 이별 파티 어떻게 해 줘야 하나?

B: 군대 가기 전에 총각○○나 떼 주자.

A: 그는 총각이 아닌데!

B: 요즘엔 그 나이에 총각이 어디 있겠어.

🔵 The practice of making someone lose his virginity

Being drafted into the military often implied death in the past. The friends of the draftees[1] would often hold a special party before their friends were drafted into the military. The party often included liquor and female entertainers.

It is clear that sex has been considered the greatest morale[2] boosting comfort to combat soldiers. For instance, Japanese soldiers were offered sex by comfort women before they were dispatched[3] to the front in World War II. There is also a legend[4] that if a virgin maiden dies without ever putting on a marriage veil, she would become a maiden spirit and harass[5] former neighbors. Similarly, if an adult male dies without ever making love, he becomes a bachelor spirit and hounds his former neighbors.

[해설] [1]draftee 응소병, 징집된 군인. [2]morale [mouræl]: the amount of confidence or hope for the future that people feel (군대 등의) 사기, 풍기. [3]dispatch [dispǽtʃ]: to send sb or sth somewhere (~을 어디로) 급히 보내다, 파병하다. [4]legend [lédʒənd]: an old well-known story from the distant past 전설, 설화: Each country has its legends about the past. 모든 국가는 과거에 대한 전설을 갖고 있다. [5]harass [həræs]: to continue to annoy or upset someone (계속) 괴롭히다: Sgt. Lee harassed me for days about the mistake I made. 이 하사는 내가 실수한 것에 대해서 나를 며칠간 괴롭혔다.

🔵 총각 ○○를 떼 주는 관행

과거에 군대에 징집되는 것은 종종 죽음을 암시했다. 징병된 자들의 친구들은 징병된 자가 입대하기 전에 군대가는 친구에게 특별한 파티를 열어주었다. 그 파티는 종종 술과 여자 접대부도 포함되어 있었다.

섹스는 전투 군인들에게 가장 사기를 높여 주는 것으로 여겨져 왔다. 제2차 세계 대전 때 일본 군인들은 전선으로 배치되기 전에 섹스를 제공받았다. 또한 처녀가 면사포를 한 번도 써보지 못하고 죽으면 처녀 귀신이 되어 주위 사람들을 괴롭힌다는 말이 있다. 이와 마찬가지로 성인 남성이 섹스를 한 번도 해보지 못하고 죽으면 총각 귀신이 되어 그의 예전 이웃 사람들을 괴롭힌다는 말도 있다.

Parting with a girlfriend

[Recruit[1] : Girlfriend]

R: My sweetie[2], take care.

G: Do well in boot camp.

R: Alright. You should not put your rubber shoes on backwards.

G: And you shouldn't change your boots, either.

R: Trust me. I'll write you a letter soon.

* A **rubber shoe** is slang for "a girl whose boyfriend is serving in the military";
  a **boot** is also slang for "a male soldier who is serving in the military."

[해설] [1]recruit: a soldier who has just joined the military 신병. [2]sweetie: (spoken) a way of talking to someone you love (구어) 연인을 칭하는 말

여자 친구와 이별

신병: 자기야, 잘 가.

여친: 훈련 잘 받아.

신병: 알았어. 고무신 절대 거꾸로 신으면 안 돼.

여친: 자기도 군화 바꿔 신으면 안 돼.

신병: 알았어. 내가 곧 편지할게.

* **고무신**이란 "자기의 남자친구가 군복무 중인 여자"; 군화란 "군 복무하는 남자군인"을 가리키는 속어이다.

🔘 Putting on rubber shoes backwards

Until the 1970s, rubber shoes were widely used in Korea. At those times when a woman entered another man's room, she would take off her rubber shoes, placing the toes of the shoes towards the room. But when she was discovered with another man by her husband, she had to hurriedly run out of the room. At that moment, she didn't have enough time to put on the rubber shoes correctly. Therefore "to put on rubber shoes backwards" and "to change one's rubber shoes" means "to change one's mind" or "to dump[1] one's lover" in Korea.

[해설] [1]dump: to suddenly end a romantic relationship (갑자기 애인을) 차버리다, 절교하다: Corporal Kim dumped his girl of five years. 김상병은 5년 동안 사귀어 온 여자를 차버렸다. ‖ I will wait for you to finish your army/military service. 너 제대할 때까지 고무신 거꾸로 신지 않고 기다릴게.

🔘 고무신 거꾸로 신기

1970년대까지 한국에서는 고무신이 널리 사용되었다. 그 당시 여자는 정부(情夫)의 방에 들어갈 때에는 고무신의 코를 방 쪽으로 벗어 놓곤 했다. 하지만 그녀가 정부와 같이 있다가 남편에게 들켰을 때, 그녀는 황급히 방을 빠져 나와야 했다. 그 순간 그녀는 신발을 바로 신을 여유가 없었다. 한국에서 "고무신을 거꾸로 신다"와 "고무신을 바꾼다"는 말은 "변심하다" 또는 "사랑하는 사람을 차 버리다"는 것을 뜻한다.

🔸 Obba, don't worry!

Obba, don't worry!
I will wait for you to the end.
Even though a handsome guy approaches me,
I will proudly say that I already have my sweetheart.
Then I can be honorably embraced[1] by you after your discharge.
And being embraced by you,
I will say that I really had a hard time.
I won't let you leave me ever again.

* **Obba** is a Korean word for a female's elder brother, but it is also used for a female's male friend who is older than she is.

[해설] [1]embrace [imbréis]: to put your arms around sb; hug 껴안다. 포옹하다: He embraces his wife when he comes home from work. 그는 퇴근하면 아내를 포옹한다.

🔸 오빠, 걱정 마!

오빠, 걱정 마!
난 오빠를 끝까지 기다릴 거야.
아무리 멋진 남자가 나에게 다가와도
난 사랑하는 사람이 이미 있다고
자랑스럽게 말 할 거야.
그리고 나중에 오빠가 제대하면
나 당당하게 오빠 품에 안길 수 있잖아.
그리고 오빠 품에 안겨서 말 할 거야,
나 그 동안 정말 힘들었노라고.
이제 다시는 오빠를 보내지 않겠다고…

* **오빠**란 한국어로 여자보다 손위의 남자를 뜻하며, 또한 여자 자신보다 나이가 더 많은 남자친구를 부르는 말이다.

🔸 Father's advice

[Son : Father]

S: Father, I'm going into boot camp now.

F: Take care, my boy.

S: I'll be a good soldier, dad.

F: Be careful of your conduct in boot camp.
Don't let your buddies[1] get punished because of any mistakes you might make.

[해설] [1]buddy: 1) an informal word for a friend 친구: Jack and I have been great buddies for years. 잭과 나는 수년 동안 친구 사이였다. 2) used to address another man 다른 남자를 부르는 말: Drink up and go home, buddy. 다 마시고 집에 가, 친구여.

🔸 아버지의 충고

아들: 아버지, 이제 들어갈게요.

부친: 얘야, 몸조심해라.

아들: 훌륭한 군인이 되겠습니다, 아버지.

부친: 훈련소에서 너의 행동을 조심해라.
너의 잘못으로 인해 네 동료들 벌 받게 하지 마라.

Military English

After Joining the Military
(입대 후)

- 입소식 전에
- 입소식*
- 병의 임무
- 입영 선서**
- 엄마는 모르시죠***
- 조디 콜*
- 논산훈련소의 낙서**
- 미군훈련소에서 신송 사항**
- 식사구호!*
- 너의 발을 키워라
- 진짜 사나이(군가)
- 기초군사훈련은 힘들어
- 이렇게 대답하라*
- 미 해병대는 이렇게 대답한다
- "아닙니다!"라고 대답해라**
- 어둠의 자식*
- 러시아인의 불만*
- 침 뱉으면서 군화 닦기
- 내무검사의 목적**
- 팬텀이 지나가겠다

- 너 짝다리 짚는구나!
- 수진*
- 10분 휴식 동안에
- 일석점호에서
- 팬티에 주기 해
- 흰 장갑 점호**
- 사역 중!
- 점화식*
- 오늘밤에 탈영하자**
- 화생방 체험*
- 해병대 쫄따구 헌장***
- 한번 해병은 영원한 해병*
- 해병의 또 다른 정의**
- 사랑하는 아들 훈현에게*
- 너는 무슨 특기 받았나?
- 훈련병과 스님**
- 총과 여자***
- 일단 군대 가면***
- 군인과 애인***
- 구령**
- 계급별 특성***

Before the entrance ceremony

"May I have your attention, please."
"All recruits report to the drill ground."

"Hey, do you guys think you're still in your own rooms?"
"Sit down, stand up!", "Drop, stand up", "Lie on your stomach, lie on your back!"

The moment I was forced to bend over and touch the ground with the top of my head[1], I took a deep breath thinking over and over again: 'Why does the military exist?', 'Why was I born as a man?', and 'Can I be discharged without having to hurt myself?'

As I lay on my bunk[2], all twenty years of my past life passed through my mind. The first night at boot camp is quite different from a wedding night.

[해설] [1]미군 훈련에서는 drop 엎드려뻗쳐, push-up 팔굽혀펴기, sit-up 윗몸일으키기 등은 있지만 "꼴아 박아(원산폭격/심어)"는 없다. 이처럼 문화적으로 공유되지 않는 것은 "bend over and touch the ground with the top of my head" 등으로 설명해줘야 한다. [2]bunk[bʌŋk]: a narrow bed, often placed one above the other. (2층으로 된) 침상

입소식 전에

"잠시 안내 말씀 드리겠습니다."
"입소 장병 여러분께서는 연병장으로 나와 주시기 바랍니다."

"야, 여기가 아직 너희들 안방인줄 아냐?"
"앉아, 일어서!", "엎드려뻗쳐, 일어서!", "앞으로 취침, 뒤로 취침!"

내가 연병장에 머리를 박아야 하는 순간, '군대란 게 왜 있어야 하는가?', '나는 왜 남자로 태어났을까?', '나는 몸 성히 제대할 수 있을까?' 라는 생각이 하염없이 들었다.

침상에 눕자 지난날 내 인생 20년이 뇌리를 스쳐 지나갔다.

훈련소에서 첫날밤은 결혼 첫날밤과 사뭇 다르다.

The Entrance ceremony

Chung-sung!
Reporting as ordered, sir.
No. 234, Hong Kil Dong and the other 299 trainees ordered to enter basic military training as of July 11, 2003.
Reporting as ordered!

❏ 입 소 식
충-성! 신고합니다.
234번 훈련병 홍길동 외 299명은
2003년 7월 11일부로
기초군사훈련 입소를 명 받았습니다.
이에 신고합니다!

A soldier's duty

As a citizen, a soldier should fill his/her heart with pride for the fact that he/she promotes national defense, and he/she must be faithful to his/her duties. He/she should especially observe[1] the law and be subordinate to seniors' orders. He/she should carry out[2] the mission under any danger or hardship.

[해설] [1]observe [əbzə́ːrv]: to obey a law, agreement, or religious rule (규칙 등을) 준수하다, 따르다: Both sides are observing the cease-fire. 양측은 휴전을 준수하고 있다. [2]carry out: to do sth completely; to accomplish 완성하다: We carried out the mission successfully. 우리는 그 임무를 성공적으로 완성했다.

병의 임무

병은 국민의 한 사람으로서 국방의 의무를 수행하고 있다는 보람과 긍지를 가지고 복무에 충실하여야 한다. 특히, 법규를 준수하고 상관의 명령에 복종하며 직무를 수행함에 있어서 어떠한 위험이나 어려움에 부딪치더라도 맡은 바 임무를 완수하여야 한다.

◯ Oath of enlistment

I, a serving member of the armed services of the Republic of Korea, do solemnly swear that I will render devoted service to our country and people, and will defend my country, and will protect the people and their rights and freedom.

July 11, 2003.

A representative trainee, Hong Kil-dong!

◯ 입영 선서

나는 대한민국의 군인으로서,
국가와 민족을 위하여 충성을 다하며,
국토방위와 국민의 권리 및 자유를
수호할 것을 엄숙히 선서합니다.
2003년 7월 11일
훈련병 대표 홍길동!

🎵 Mama, Mama can't you see 엄마는 모르시죠

Mama, Mama can't you see	엄마, 엄마는 모르시죠
What the Army's done to me	군대가 나에게 어떻게 했는지
Sat me down in a barber's chair	나를 이발소 의자에 앉히고
Spun me around I had no hair	돌리더니 머리가 없어졌어요
Woh-oh-oh-oh, Woh-oh-oh-oh	우-오-오-오, 우-오-오-오-오
Used to wear my faded jeans	나는 빛바랜 청바지를 입곤 했지만
Now I wear my Army greens	이제는 파란 군복을 입고 있지요
Chorus	후렴
Used to date a beauty queen	나는 예쁜 여인과 데이트했지만
Now I date my M-16	이제는 나의 M16과 데이트하지요
Chorus	후렴
Standing tall and looking good	키 크고 멋져 보여서
Ought to be in Hollywood	할리우드에 있어야 마땅한데
Chorus	후렴
Used to drive a Cadillac	나는 캐딜락을 몰았었지만
Now I hump it on my back	이제 등에 짐을 지고 다녀요

* Marching songs in Korea mostly contain sentiments that boost patriotism, but those that are sung in the US military are quite different from those of Korea. Those of the US are sung by the troops in rhythmic fashion after the leader sings them line by line and the contents are very funny and vulgar.
* 한국의 행진곡은 애국심이 치솟는 내용을 담고 있지만, 미군의 행진곡은 한국의 행진곡과 많이 다르다. 미군에서 불리는 행진곡은 리더가 한 소절씩 선창을 하면 음률에 맞춰 후창을 하는데 그 내용이 아주 웃기거나 저질스럽다.

Jody call 조디 콜

Jody this and Jody that	조디는 이런 짓도 저런 짓도 한다네
Jody is a real cool cat	조디는 정말 화끈한 녀석이네
Ain't no use in calling home	집에 전화해도 소용없다네
Jody is on your phone	조디가 니네 전화를 쓰고 있을 텐데 뭘
Ain't no use in going home	집에 가봤자 소용없다네
Jody's got your girl and gone	조디가 네 애인을 낚아채 갔을 텐데 뭘
Ain't no use in feeling blue	우울해 봤자 소용없다네
Jody's got your sister, too	조디가 네 여동생도 해치웠을 텐데 뭘
Ain't no use in looking back	후회해 봤자 소용없다네
Jody's got your Cadillac	조디가 네 캐딜락도 해치웠을 텐데 뭘

* A **Jody call** is troop cadence for marching or running to keep good time, and the word "Jody" means a "civilian who has stolen the affections of the soldier's sweetheart back home."

* 조디 콜은 행진이나 구보할 때 박자를 맞추기 위한 일종의 행진곡으로, "조디"란 "군대 간 사이에 고향에 있는 군인의 애인의 마음을 빼앗은 민간인"을 말한다.

Notes to soldiers at Nonsan boot camp

Prior to Training Camp	I will wait for you for 30 months, or even for 3 years.
In Training Camp	I am going crazy because I want to see you. When do you have your graduation ceremony?
Private	I often see you in my dreams.
Private First Class	I was so busy that I couldn't answer your letters quickly.
Corporal	I am sorry. I had to be introduced to a gentleman by my parents. But don't worry. Maybe you understand.
Sergeant	I went on a date with him once.
Prior to Discharge	I'm sorry. I got engaged to him.
After Discharge	I'm 3 months pregnant. Isn't that life?

논산 훈련소의 낙서

입대 전	당신을 위해서라면 30개월 아니라 3년도 기다리겠어요.
훈련소	미치도록 보고파요. 퇴소식은 언제죠?
이 병	꿈속에서 가끔 당신을 보곤 해요.
일 병	바쁘다 보니 요즘 답장이 늦어져요.
상 병	미안해요. 부모님 권유로 할 수 없이 선을 봤어요. 하지만 염려 마세요. 이해하실 거예요.
병 장	그 사람과 데이트를 한 번 했어요.
전역 전	죄송해요. 그이와 약혼했어요.
전역 후	저 임신 3개월이에요. 뭐 인생이 그런 거 아닌가요?

● Words handed down in the US boot camps

① Say, "yes, sir!"
② Be a wallflower[1]. (∵ It's better if **TIs** don't know your name.)
③ Keep your mouth shut at all times. (Speak only when spoken to.)
④ Don't volunteer for anything. (Unless you just absolutely can't help yourself.)
⑤ Don't bring unnecessary things. (Condoms, toys, etc.)
⑥ Expect to be yelled at. (The **TIs** are going to chew you out for messing up.)
⑦ Do exactly as you are told.
⑧ Never give excuses unless requested.

● TIs(Training instructors) have different titles in the different services in the US.
  • In the Army : Drill Sergeant (DS)
  • In the Marine Corps : Drill Instructor (DI)
  • In the Air Force : Training Instructor (TI)
  • In the Navy : Recruit Division Commander (RDC)

[해설] [1] wallflower: a shy or unpopular person (비유적으로) 수줍어하는/인기 없는 사람: She is a wallflower who does not talk with anyone at a party. 그녀는 파티에서 누구와도 얘기하지 않는 인기 없는 여자다.

● 미군 훈련소에서 신송 사항

① "예, 알겠습니다!"라고 해라.
② 인기 없는 사람이 되라. (교관이 너의 이름을 모르는 게 더 좋다.)
③ 입을 항상 닫고 있어라. (얘기하라고 시키면 말해라.)
④ 무엇이든지 절대 자원하지 마라. (어쩔 수 없는 경우만 제외하고)
⑤ 불필요한 것을 가지고 오지 마라. (콘돔, 장난감 등)
⑥ 야단맞을 각오해라. (교관은 너의 실수에 대해 씹을 것이다.)
⑦ 네가 지시받은 대로 정확히 해라.
⑧ 요청받지 않는 한 변명을 하지 마라.

● 훈련교관(Training instructor)은 각 군에 따라 명칭이 다르다.
  • 미 육군: Drill Sergeant (DS)   • 미 해병대: Drill Instructor (DI)
  • 미 공군: Training Instructor (TI) • 미 해군: Recruit Division Commander (RDC)

Give thanks loudly!   식사구호!

Attention!	차려!
Say grace[1]!	식사에 대한 묵념!
Heads up!	바로!
Give thanks loudly!	식사구호!
I will eat this food prepared with our people's sincere devotion!	국민의 정성어린 이 음식을 감사히 먹겠습니다!

[해설] [1]grace: a short prayer before a meal (식사 전에) 감사기도: Who would like to say grace? Eric, would you like to say grace? 누가 기도할래? 에릭, 네가 기도할래?

Get your feet bigger

[Drill instructor : Private]

D: Any guys whose boots are too big or too small?

T: Yes, mine are too big, sir.

D: Adapt your feet to the boots.
   Grow your feet bigger or put on two pairs of socks.

T: Yes, sir!

너의 발을 키워라

교 관: 전투화가 너무 크거나 너무 작은 사람 있나?

훈련병: 예, 제 전투화가 너무 큽니다.

교 관: 네 발을 전투화에 맞춰라.
   네 발을 키우든지 아니면 양말을 두 켤레 신어라.

훈련병: 예, 알겠습니다!

🔸 A real man (military song)

I was born as a man with lots of things to do
You and I've lived in glory defending our country
We became army buddies in training and in battle
As the sun rises and sets over the peaks of mountains
Our families have a sound sleep counting on us.

🔸 진짜 사나이 (군가)

사나이로 태어나서 할 일도 많다만
너와나 나라 지키며 영광에 살았다
훈련과 전투 속에 맺어진 전우야
산봉우리에 해 뜨고 해가 질 적에
부모형제 나를 믿고 단잠을 이룬다.

🔸 Basic training is tough

　　Basic training is a tough environment! Your sons or daughters may have never been through anything like this before. They must conform[1] to a new set of rules. Training instructors don't allow them to act like they did back home or while in high school.

[해설] [1]conform (to/with): to behave in the way that most other people behave 순응하다: Women must conform to a strict dress code. 여자들은 엄격한 복장규정에 따라야 한다.

🔸 기초 군사훈련은 힘들어

　　기초 군사훈련은 힘든 환경이다! 당신의 아들, 딸은 인생에서 이런 것을 경험해본 적이 없을 것이다. 그들은 새로운 일련의 규칙에 순응해야 한다. 훈련교관들은 그들이 집이나 고등학교에 있을 때처럼 행동하는 것을 허락하지 않는다.

◎ Reply like this

Remember these two responses to questions or orders from your superiors, and you will never go wrong: "I don't know sir, but I'll find out," and "I'll do it or have it done."

◎ 이렇게 대답하라

당신의 상관들로부터 질문이나 명령을 받았을 때, 이 두 가지 대답을 기억하면 당신은 절대로 그릇됨이 없을 것이다. "잘 모르지만, 제가 알아보겠습니다." 그리고 "제가 하겠습니다." 혹은 "그것이 완성되도록 하겠습니다."

◎ The US marines reply like this

Once the US marines receive orders from their seniors, they say "Aye, aye, sir(ma'am)" which means "I understand the orders I have received, and will carry them out."

◎ 미 해병대는 이렇게 대답한다

미 해병이 상관으로부터 명령을 받으면, 그들은 "아이, 아이, 써(맴)"이라고 한다. 이 말은 "나는 내가 방금 지시받은 명령을 이해하며, 그 명령을 수행하겠습니다."라는 뜻이다.

🟡 Say, "No, sir!"

① Are you hot?   No, sir!
② Are you cold?   No, sir!
③ Are you tired?   No, sir!
④ Are you sleepy?   No, sir!
⑤ Are you hungry?   No, sir!
⑥ Do you feel pain?   No, sir!
⑦ Do you feel thirsty?   No, sir!
⑧ Do you feel homesick?   No, sir!
⑨ Do you want to go home?   No, sir!
⑩ Do you hate to eat **jjambab**?   No, sir!
⑪ Do you want a glass of soju?   No, sir!
⑫ Do you want to puff on a cigarette?   No, sir!
⑬ Do you want to eat delicious food?   No, sir!
⑭ Do you want to see your girlfriends?   No, sir!
⑮ Do you find it difficult getting up at 0600?   No, sir!
⑯ Do you feel very disturbed by roll call[1]?   No, sir!
⑰ Do you feel dirty cleaning the toilets?   No-no, sir!
⑱ Do you feel very bored weeding on hot days?   No, never sir!
⑲ Are you going crazy sweeping fallen leaves every day?   No, sir!
⑳ Do you feel that you are freezing to death shoveling snow all morning?   No, never, sir!

* Jjambab is slang for boiled rice served in a mess hall, its literal meaning is leftover boiled rice.

🟡 Remember, boot camp is mostly a mind-game.
　It's designed to tear-down your civilian self and replace it with a military self.
　In boot camp, always tell your instructors what they want to hear!

[해설] [1]roll call: a check to see if anyone has not come 점호: A sergeant did a roll call, asking each soldier to say "Here!" when his or her name was called. 부사관은 병사들이 자기 이름이 불리면 "네"라고 대답을 요구하면서 점호를 했다.

◉ "아닙니다!"라고 대답해라

① 덥냐? 아닙니다!

② 춥냐? 아닙니다!

③ 피곤하냐? 아닙니다!

④ 졸리냐? 아닙니다!

⑤ 배고프냐? 아닙니다!

⑥ 아프냐? 아닙니다!

⑦ 갈증나냐? 아닙니다!

⑧ 집생각 나냐? 아닙니다!

⑨ 집에 가고 싶냐? 아닙니다!

⑩ 짬밥 먹기 싫냐? 아닙니다!

⑪ 소주 한잔 하고 싶냐? 아닙니다!

⑫ 한 모금 빨고 싶냐? 아닙니다!

⑬ 맛있는 음식 먹고 싶냐? 아닙니다!

⑭ 여자친구 보고 싶냐? 아닙니다!

⑮ 06시에 일어나기 힘드냐? 아닙니다!

⑯ 점호 받기 매우 짜증나지?? 아닙니다!

⑰ 화장실 청소하기 더럽냐? 아-아닙니다!

⑱ 더운 여름날 잡초사역 짜증나지? 아닙니다!

⑲ 매일 낙엽 쓸려니 미치겠지? 아닙니다!

⑳ 아침 내내 눈 쓸려니 추워 죽겠지? 아닙니다, 절대 아닙니다!

* **짬밥**이란 군대식당에서 제공되는 밥으로, 글자적인 의미는 남은 밥이다.

◉ 훈련소에서 훈련은 대부분 머리싸움임을 기억하라.
훈련소는 너의 민간인적 자아를 없애고 군인적 자아로 바꾸기 위해 존재한다.
훈련소에서는 너의 교관이 항상 듣기 원하는 대답을 해라!

A son of darkness

① A guy who is exempted[1] from military service is called "the son of God" or "the son of a general."
② A guy who is chosen for reserved service is called "the son of a human being."
③ A guy who is chosen for active duty is called "the son of darkness."

[해설] [1]exempt [igzémpt]: to exclude or free from a duty, restriction, etc (의무 등을) 면제하다: Children from poor families in South Korea are seldom exempted from the obligatory military service. 한국에서 못사는 집의 자식들은 병역의무에서 거의 면제되지 않는다.

어둠의 자식

① 군복무를 면제받은 사람은 "신의 아들" 또는 "장군의 아들"이라고 불린다.
② 보충역으로 선발된 사람은 "인간의 아들"이라고 불린다.
③ 현역으로 선발된 사람은 "어둠의 자식"이라고 불린다.

A Russian's complaint

Nobody is willing to go into the military. I don't think my country deserves to be loved and respected because it doesn't provide a good life for its people. Corruption is everywhere, and people who have no money or connections are stuck on the lowest level, and everyone kicks them around.

러시아인의 불만

아무도 군대 안 가려고 한다. 나는 우리나라가 사랑과 존경을 받을 가치가 없다고 생각한다. 왜냐하면 우리나라가 국민들에게 좋은 삶을 제공하지 못하기 때문이다. 부패가 만연하고 돈이나 인맥이 없는 사람은 최하의 신세에 처하게 되고 사람들로부터 이리저리 차인다.

🔸 Spit-shining shoes

The trainees are busy spit-shining their shoes for tomorrow's barracks inspection. Training instructors often tell the trainees, "Try to produce such a smooth shine that even flies can't walk on your boots."

🔸 침 뱉으면서 군화 닦기

그 훈련병들은 내일의 내무검열에 대비하여 구두에 침을 뱉어가면서 닦느라 바쁘다. 훈련교관들은 훈련병들에게 "너의 구두에 파리가 앉지 못할 정도로 닦아라."라고 종종 말한다.

🔸 The purpose of barracks inspections

The purpose of barracks inspections is to check
whether all the regulations are enforced;
whether soldiers are educated and trained;
whether ordnance[1], facilities, equipment, fixtures[2], and supply are properly maintained; and whether orders and instructions are clearly given and they are carried out properly.

[해설] [1]ordnance [ɔ́:rdnəns]: military weapons and related equipment 화기, 군수품.
[2]fixture [fíkstʃər]: a piece of equipment that is attached inside a house, such as an electric light or a faucet 비품

🔸 내무검사의 목적

내무검사라 함은 제 규정의 이행 여부, 교육 정도, 병기, 시설, 장비 비품 및 보급품의 보존상태, 명령 지시의 숙지 및 실행상태 등을 확인하기 위한 점검을 말한다.

An F-4 Phantom could pass

[Training instructor : Airman basic]

D: Stand straight at attention!
　 The fifth person of the third row.
　 Put your knees together tighter.
　 An F-4 Phantom could pass between your legs.
R: Yes, sir!
D: It's still not enough. Try harder!
R: It's tough to do that, sir!
D: Hey, there is nothing that you can't do in the military.
　 Bind your legs with a taekwondo belt when you go to bed.
R: Yes, sir.

* 오다리: bowed legs: He was born with bowed legs. 그는 오다리로 태어났다. (무릎이 붙지 않는)

팬텀이 지나가겠다

교 관 : 차려 자세 바로 해!
　　　　3오 5번째.
　　　　무릎 붙여라.
　　　　너의 다리 사이로 팬텀이 지나가겠다.
훈련병 : 예, 알겠습니다!
교 관 : 그래도 안 붙는다. 더 붙여봐.
훈련병 : 잘 안됩니다.
교 관 : 임마, 군대에서 안 되는 게 어디 있나.
　　　　잘 때 도복 끈으로 네 다리를 묶고 자라.
훈련병 : 예, 알겠습니다.

🟢 You're standing on one leg!

[Drill instructor : Private]

D: Hey, there in the middle.

P: Me, sir?

D: You're already standing on one leg!

P: I'm sorry, sir.

D: How dare you stand on one leg in front of me?

P: I dislocated[1] my left leg during ranger training yesterday.

D: Return to your position.

P: Recover[2]!

D: "The more you beat trainees and walleyes, the softer they become."

[해설] [1]dislocate [díslouket]: to move sth out of its normal place 잘못 놓다, 삐걱하다: The skier fell and dislocated a shoulder. 그 스키어는 넘어져 어깨를 삐었다. [2]recover: to return to a previously position (이전의 상태/동작으로) 돌아가다. 또한 하던 push-up을 그만하고 일으켜 세우고자 할 때도 recover라고 한다. walleye [wɔ́:lài] 명태

🟢 너 짝 다리 짚는구나!

교 관: 거기, 중간쯤.

훈련병: 저 말입니까?

교 관: 너 벌써 짝다리 짚고 있구나!

훈련병: 죄송합니다.

교 관: 너 감히 내 앞에서 짝다리 짚나?

훈련병: 어제 유격훈련에서 왼쪽다리를 삐었습니다.

교 관: 원위치 해라.

훈련병: 원위치!

교 관: "훈련병과 명태는 패면 팰수록 부드러워진다."

Sick call

[Drill instructor : Private]

D: Any guys who want to go to sick call? Come on over here.

P: Yes, sir. Private Park Kil-dong!

D: Where did you get hurt?

P: I dislocated my left ankle.

D: How did it happen?

P: I fell down while doing bayonet practice[1] yesterday.

D: Let me see.

P: Here, sir.

D: It seems to be okay. Are you malingering[2]?

P: No, I am not, sir!

D: Make a good report to the doctors at the dispensary[3]. Otherwise you will get into trouble again.

[해설] [1]bayonet practice 총검술. [2]malinger [məlíngəːr]: to pretend to be ill in order to avoid having to work (군인 등이) 꾀병을 부리다. malingerer 꾀병부리는 사람. [3]dispensary [dispénsəri]: a place where medical treatment is provided (학교·공장 등의) 의무실, (軍) 의무대

Kinds of Call 집합의 종류

sick call 수진자 집합. mess/chow call 식사 집합. school call 학과 출장 집합. mail call 우편물 수령 집합. drill call 훈련 집합. guard call 초병 집합. church call 교회 참석 집합. fatigue call 사역 집합. First Sergeant's Call 선임 부사관(이 지시하는) 집합 (Signals that the First Sergeant is about to form the company). officer's call 장교 집합 (Signals all officers to assemble at a designated place). 여기서 call은 집합이라는 의미뿐만 아니라 각각의 집합을 뜻하는 약 8소절의 나팔음(sound of bugle)을 뜻하기도 한다. 미군에서의 Mail Call 악보! ⇨

🔸 수진

교 관: 수진(진료 받으러)갈 사람 있나?
　　　　이리 나와라.

훈련병: 예, 박길동 훈련병!

교 관: 너는 어디가 아프냐?

훈련병: 왼쪽발목을 삐었습니다.

교 관: 어쩌다가?

훈련병: 어제 총검술 하다가 넘어졌습니다.

교 관: 한번 보자.

훈련병: 여기요.

교 관: 멀쩡하구먼. 꾀병이지?

훈련병: 아닙니다.

교 관: 그래, 병원에 가서도 군의관들에게 보고 잘 해라.
　　　　안 그러면 또 깨진다.

🔸 미군에서의 mail call 악보

During the ten minute break

[Drill instructor : Private]

D: Hey, do you know I'm still single?

P: Oh, we didn't know that, sir!

D: Do you know a nice girl for me?

P: I have an elder sister, sir!

D: Then, introduce[1] her to me.

P: I'll ask her during my first leave[2], sir.

D: Do you think she will is good match for me?

P: If you really want to meet her, don't give us a hard time!

[해설] [1]introduce는 공식적으로 소개하다는 뜻이다. 위의 대화, 교관의 입장에서 너의 누나와 "엮어 달라"라는 비공식적 표현으로 "Then, fix me up with your elder sister."가 더 적절하다. (fix ~ up: to find a romantic partner for someone) [2]break: a period of time when you stop working or doing sth (짧은) 휴식: Let's break for five minutes and have a drink. 5분간 휴식해서 뭐 좀 마시자. leave: time that you are allowed to spend away from your work (허락이 필요한) 휴가: How much sick leave have you taken? 병가 얼마나 받았니?

10분 휴식 동안에

교 관: 야, 너희들 내가 아직까지 총각인 거 알아?

훈련병: 오, 몰랐습니다.

교 관: 나한테 소개시켜 줄 좋은 여자 없나?

훈련병: 제 누나가 있습니다.

교 관: 그럼 나한테 소개 시켜줘라.

훈련병: 저의 첫 휴가 때 물어 보겠습니다.

교 관: 너의 누나가 나와 잘 어울릴 것 같냐?

훈련병: 제 누나 만나고 싶으면, 저희들 힘들게 하지 마십시오!

🟢 At evening roll call

[Drill instructor : Private]

The first squad totals 10, 7 present.
Count off!
One, two, three, four, five, six, seven, eight, last nine, plus one!
Accidents are: 2 on leave, 1 hospitalized.
Ready for evening roll-call!

D: Hey, let me see your rifle.

P: Here, sir.

D: (Looking at the butt) Did you clean your rifle?

P: Yes, I did, sir.

D: I see several rocks in the butt. Take them out with a needle.

🟢 일석점호에서

제 1분대, 총원 10명, 현재원 7명.
번호!
하나, 둘, 셋, 넷, 다섯, 여섯, 일곱, 여덟, 아홉 번호 끝, 열외1.
사고내용 휴가2, 입원 1.
일석점호 준비 끝!

교 관: 네 총기 좀 보자.

훈련병: 여기 있습니다.

교 관: (개머리판을 보며) 너 총기 청소했나?

훈련병: 예, 그렇습니다.

교 관: 개머리판에 바위가 몇 개 보인다. 그것들을 바늘로 빼내라.

🟢 총기관련 용어

barrel 총열, muzzle 총/포구, front sight 가늠쇠, rear sight 가늠자, sling 멜빵, trigger 방아쇠, stock 개머리, butt 개머리판, hammer 공이치지, cleaning rod 꽂을대, magazine 탄창, ammunition 탄약, ammunition/cartridge belt 탄띠

◉ Mark your name on your underwear

[Drill instructor : Candidate]

D: Let me see your underwear.
C: (Putting his underwear on the desk) Here, sir.
D: Candidate Kim, why didn't you mark your name and number?
C: I did, but it was erased.
D: Write it again in thick letters with a name-pen[1] (permanent marker).
C: Yes, sir.

[해설] [1] name-pen의 영어식 표현은 laundry marker, permanent marker이다.

◉ 팬티에 주기 해

교 관: 너 팬티 좀 보자.
후보생: (팬티를 책상 위에 놓으면서) 여기 있습니다.
교 관: 김 후보생, 너는 왜 팬티에 주기 안 했냐?
후보생: 주기했는데 지워졌습니다.
교 관: 네임펜으로 다시 진하게 주기해라.
후보생: 예, 알겠습니다.

계 급	후보생
군 번	86-38478
성 명	김길동

🔵 White-glove roll call

A: What is your new platoon leader like?

B: He is so fussy about everything.

    We had a **white-glove roll call** last night.

    You'd better make a good first impression[1].

    You never get a second chance to make a first impression.

B: Thanks for your advice.

[해설] [1]make a first impression 첫인상을 주다: It's important to make a good impression at your interview. 인터뷰에서 첫인상을 주는 것은 매우 중요하다.

* **White-glove roll call**
  During roll-calls or barracks inspections, drill instructors wear "white gloves" and feel the surfaces of cabinets or other things in the barracks to check indoor cleanliness status. It's often enforced as it gives a legitimate reason for punishing soldiers and so maintains military discipline.

🔵 흰 장갑 점호

A: 너의 새로 오신 소대장님 어떠시니?

B: 그 분은 모든 면에서 까다로우셔.

    우리는 어젯밤 일석점호에서 "**흰장갑 점호**"를 받았거든.

    좋은 첫인상을 주도록 해.

    첫 인상을 결코 두 번 남길 수는 없다.

B: 충고 고마워.

* **흰장갑 점호**
  점호나 내무검사에서 교관이 "흰장갑"을 낀 손으로 캐비닛 등의 표면을 더듬어 먼지제거 여부를 확인하는 것으로, 가끔 훈련생들의 꼬투리를 잡아서 군기를 잡을 목적으로도 실시된다.

Group attention!

[Officer : Private]

P: Group attention! Resting!

O: Carry on[1]!

You don't need to report while you're working, eating or resting.

P: I will correct my mistake, sir!

O: Who is your drill instructor?

P: Lt. Kim, sir.

O: Did he instruct you that way?

P: No, sir!

[해설] [1]carry on: to continue doing sth: ~을 계속하다: Carry on. You're doing fine. 계속해. 넌 잘하고 있어.

전체 차려!

훈련병: 전체 차려! 휴식 중!

장 교: 계속 해!

　　　작업이나, 식사, 휴식 중일 때는 보고할 필요 없다.

훈련병: 시정하겠습니다!

장 교: 너의 훈련교관은 누구냐?

훈련병: 김중위입니다.

장 교: 그가 그렇게 가르쳤냐?

훈련병: 아닙니다!

🔸 The ceremony of lighting a cigarette

[Training instructor : Trainee]

Ti: Does everybody have a cigarette?

Tr: Yes, sir!

Ti: Lie down on the ground!

Tr: Action!

Ti: Load[1] one cigarette into your mouth!

Tr: Load one cigarette into your mouth. Action!

Ti: Ready to fire?

Tr: Yes, sir!

Ti: Fire!

Tr: Fire!

* Korean Air Force trainees were prohibited from smoking once they started their basic military training. After three or four weeks of basic training, "the ceremony of igniting a cigarette" was held. But this was abolished in the 1990s.

[해설] [1]load: to put bullets into a gun or film into a camera (총에 총알을, 카메라에 필름을) 장전하다/넣다.

🔸 점화식

교 관: 모두들 담배 가지고 있나?
훈련병: 예, 있습니다!
교 관: 지면에 누워!
훈련병: 실시!
교 관: 담배 일발 장전!
훈련병: 담배 일발 장전. 실시!
교 관: 발사 준비되었나?
훈련병: 예, 준비되었습니다!
교 관: 발사!
훈련병: 발사!

* 한국공군의 피교육생들은 기초 군사훈련과정에 입과 하면 흡연이 금지되었다. 3~4주간의 기초교육 후에는 "점화식"이 거행되었다. 하지만 이것은 1990년대에 폐지되었다.

Let's go AWOL tonight

A: Tom, let's go AWOL tonight.
B: Why? Our training is almost over!
A: I can't stand this training anymore.
B: How can you escape[1] from this garrison?
A: Most sentries[2] are almost asleep at dawn.

[해설] [1]escape [iskéip]: to succeed in going away from a place 도망가다, 탈출하다: The tiger escaped from its cage. 호랑이가 우리에서 도망을 갔다. [2]sentry [séntri]: a soldier standing outside a building as a guard 초병, 보초

오늘 밤에 탈영하자

A: 탐, 오늘밤에 탈영하자.
B: 왜? 이제 우리 훈련도 거의 끝났어!
A: 나 이 훈련 더 이상 못 참겠어.
B: 부대를 어떻게 빠져나가?
A: 대부분의 초병이 새벽에는 거의 잠들거든.

❏ Running cadence	구보행진곡
AWOL, AWOL, where've you been? Down in the bars, drinking gin. What you going to do when you get back? Sweat it all out on the PT track.	탈영, 탈영, 너 어디 있었니? 술집에서 진을 마시고 있었지. 너 돌아오면 어떻게 되는지 알아? PT트랙에서 땀을 진하게 빼겠구나.

* AWOL[éiwɔːl]: Absent Without Official Leave
  공식적인 휴가를 얻지 않고 무단이탈/결근하는 것
* PT: Physical Training 육체적인 훈련
* This is often sung in the U.S. Army when on training runs.
  이것은 미 육군에서 구보할 때 종종 불린다.

At the gas training chamber

"Take off your gas mask!"
"Now you are going to sing the national anthem.[1]"

After we sang the song, everybody coughed, sneezed and had runny eyes and noses. The experience at the gas training chamber was the most horrible thing during basic training.

[해설] [1]anthem [ǽnθəm]: a song of devotion or admiration 축가, nation anthem 애국가: The national anthem is sung before every baseball game. 매 야구 경기 전에 애국가를 부른다.

화생방 체험

"방독면 벗어!"
"이제 애국가를 부른다."

우리가 애국가를 부른 뒤에 모든 병사들은 기침과 재채기를 했고 눈물과 콧물을 흘렸다. 화생방 실험실에서의 경험은 기초 군사훈련 동안 가장 혹독했다.

🔵 The Marine private's charter

I entered boot camp with full realization that the marine privates' missions are perilous[1]. Carrying on the brilliant spirit of the senior members of the Marine Corps, I will establish in myself the attitude of invincibility[2] of the Marines and contribute to the protection and unification of my motherland.

Hereupon as a private of the Marine Corps, I take the following path; I will endure being battered and slapped with my iron backside and iron-clad face[3], I will develop my intuition and I will enhance my volubility[4] and ferociousness[5] in the true spirit of the Marine Corps using my reckless[6] courage as a stepping-stone.

[해설] [1]perilous [pérələs]: very dangerous 매우 위험한. [2]invincibility [invìnsəbíləti] 무적, 불패 〈 invincible [invínsəbəl]: too strong to be defeated 이길 수 없는, 무적의. [3]iron-clad face 철면피한 얼굴, 뻔뻔한. [4]volubility [vàljəbíləti] (말의) 유창함 〈 voluble [váljəbəl]: talking a lot with great energy and enthusiasm 말 잘하는, 능변인. [5]ferocious [fəróuʃəs]: extremely violent or severe 잔인한, 지독한 [6]reckless [réklis]: doing sth dangerous without thinking; foolish 무모한, 분별없는: He is a reckless driver. 그는 무모한 운전사다.

🔵 해병대 쫄다구 헌장

우리는 해병대 쫄다구의 아찔한 사명을 띠고 훈련소에 입소했다. 선배 해병의 빛난 얼을 되살려 무적해병의 자세를 확립하고 조국수호와 통일에 이바지한다.

이에 해병 쫄다구의 나아갈 바를 밝혀 튼튼한 히프와 뻔뻔한 면상으로 빠따와 따귀를 맞고도 참아내며, 타고난 통밥을 개발하고 우리의 깡다구를 약진의 발판으로 삼아 수준 높은 이빨과 개병대의 곤조를 드높인다.

● Once a marine, always a marine 한번 해병은 영원한 해병

Once a marine, always a marine	한번 해병은 영원한 해병
Once a senior, always a senior	한번 고참은 영원한 고참
Once a junior, always a junior	한번 졸병은 영원한 졸병
Once an officer, always an officer	한번 장교는 영원한 장교
Once a marine's gf, always a marine's gf	한번 해순은 영원한 해순

● If anybody can be a marine, I would never have applied for the Marine Corps.
누구나 해병이 될 수 있다면 나는 결코 해병대를 선택하지 않았을 것이다.

● Redefinition of Marine 해병의 재 정의

ARMY: Another Retarded[1] Misguided Youth or Ain't Ready to be a Marine Yet

MARINE: Muscles Are Required, Intelligence Not Expected

NAVY: Never Again Volunteer Yourself

　육　군: 지능이 떨어지고 잘못 인도된 또 다른 젊은이 혹은 해병대가 되기엔 아직 준비되지 않은 젊은이
　해병대: 근육만 요구되고 지능은 기대되지 않은(군인)
　해　군: 다시는 스스로 자원하지 마라(해군에)

[해설] [1]retarded [ritάːrdid]: less mentally developed 지능이 떨어지는 〈 retard: to delay the development of sth 성장을 늦추다: Cold weather can retard the plants' growth. 추운 날씨가 식물의 성장을 늦출 수 있다.

● The Air Force is like Cinderella
The Air Force seems to be quite similar to Cinderella in the USA because the Cinderella has two ugly and greedy sisters (the Army and the Navy). Similar to this, the Ministry of National Defense of the Republic of Korea is often called "the Ministry of the Army" because most of the key positions for the Ministry of National Defense of the Republic of Korea are usually filled with army generals.

● 공군은 신데렐라
미국에서 공군은 신데렐라와 매우 유사해 보인다. 왜냐하면 신데렐라는 추하고 탐욕스러운 두 누이(육군과 해군)가 있기 때문이다. 이와 유사하게도 한국의 국방부는 종종 "육방부"라고 불린다. 그 이유는 한국 국방부의 대다수의 주요한 보직들은 육군 장군들로 충원되기 때문이다.

My Dear son, Hun-hyun

I've been looking at your empty room for two weeks now. Your mother dusts and cleans your photo, desk, and bed every day. She can't stand to see even one speck of dust on them. Isn't that a clear sign that she misses you? The clothes you wore before you went into the military came back in a parcel yesterday. Your mother cried over the clothes all afternoon and fell asleep holding them in her hands. That scene broke my heart.

How are you getting along in boot camp? As nothing is easy in this life, you may feel very uneasy in the military because you have not experienced it before.

Remember that your father passed through basic military training too. During basic training you will go through the same training as I did. I don't think you are so weak that you can't survive the training. I hope you can put up with the daily hardships. Your parents are waiting for you with warm hearts. I think the more you endure hardship, the more you grow. Responsibility, courage, courtesy, etc. cannot be covered by any other educational institution. The military life will be a valuable asset guiding your social life after you get discharged. In the military you will probably meet colleagues and military instructors who have different opinions or views of life, but don't complain about it. Try to accept them for what they are.

Try to dress warmly. You may feel that the wind in the military area is much colder than it is here. Be a great trainee who can appreciate the food, though it doesn't suit your taste. Try to endure it a little longer, thinking that you can see us soon. Try to be faithful from day to day!

– From your loving father

사랑하는 아들, 훈현에게

　네가 없는 텅 빈 방을 본 지도 2주가 다 되어 간다. 네 엄마는 너의 사진, 책상, 침대를 매일 같이 청소한단다. 그것에 먼지가 조금이라도 묻는 것을 못 본다. 그것은 너에 대한 그리움의 표시 아니겠니? 어제는 네가 입고 갔던 속옷이 소포로 되돌아 왔더라. 네 엄마는 그걸 보고 오후 내내 울다가 안고 잠들었다. 그 모습을 보니 내 마음이 찢어지는 구나.

　훈련소 생활은 할 만하냐? 세상의 일이 쉬운 게 하나도 없듯이, 특히 군대라는 곳에서 처음 느껴본 불안감이 매우 클 줄 안다.

　아버지도 기초군사훈련을 마쳤다는 것을 명심해라. 기초군사훈련 동안 너는 내가 경험한 훈련을 겪을 것이다. 나는 네가 훈련을 마치지 못할 정도로 허약하다고 생각하지 않는다. 네가 하루하루의 고생을 헤쳐 나가길 바란다. 너의 부모님은 따뜻한 마음으로 너를 기다리고 있단다. 네가 고난을 많이 겪을수록 그만큼 성장하는 법이다. 책임감, 예절, 용기 등은 다른 교육기관에서 커버 될 수 없다. 군생활은 전역 후에도 소중한 자산이 될 것이다. 군대에서 너는 아마도 너와 다른 견해나 인생관을 지닌 동료나 교관을 만나게 될 것이다. 하지만 그것에 대해서 불평하지 마라. 있는 그대로 수용해라.

　옷을 따뜻하게 입어라. 군대에서 부는 바람은 여기서의 바람과 사뭇 다르게 느껴질 것이다. 음식이 너의 입맛에 맞지 않더라도 감사하게 먹을 줄 아는 멋있는 훈병이 되어라. 우리가 곧 만날 수 있다는 생각을 하면서 조금만 더 참아라. 하루하루를 충실하도록 해라!

- 사랑하는 아버지로부터

● What specialty did you get?

A: What specialty[1] did you get?
B: Air defense artillery (ADA).
A: Now you are going to die!
B: Why?
A: Military discipline is severely enforced in the ADA.
　　It's often called "the Marine Corps" of the Air Force.
B: Why is it so tough to serve there?
A: The ADA was originally part of the Army.
　　Then, in 1990 it came under the command of[2] the Air Force.
　　But its commanders are still Army-minded.
B: Once I've got my specialty, there is no choice.
　　I will do my best to be the number one artilleryman.

[해설] [1]specialty [spéʃəlti]: a particular type of work or job 전공, (군대) 주특기/병과(branch of service). 미 육군과 해병대에서는 Military Occupational Specialty (MOS), 미 공군에서는 Air Force Specialty Codes(AFSC), 미 해군에서는 Navy Enlisted Classification(NEC)라는 용어를 사용한다. [2]under the command of A: A의 지휘 하에

● 너는 무슨 특기 받았냐?

A: 너는 무슨 특기 받았냐?
B: 방공포.
A: 너 이제 죽었다!
B: 왜?
A: 방공포는 군기가 빡세.
　　방공포는 종종 "공군의 해병대"라고 불리지.
B: 방공포에서 근무하기 왜 힘들까?
A: 방공포가 원래 육군이었지.
　　1990년 육군에서 공군으로 전군 되었다.
　　아직도 지휘관들이 육군 마인드를 가지고 있지.
B: 이왕 받은 거 별 도리가 있냐.
　　나는 최고의 방공포병이 되기 위해 최선을 다할 거야.

🟢 Recruits and Buddhist priests

① They have to get their hair chopped off.
② They have to put on a uniform.
③ They have to be early risers.
④ They have to memorize lots of rules and regulations.
⑤ They have to discipline their bodies and their minds.
⑥ They are advised against eating aphrodisiac[1] foods.
⑦ They have to do everything by themselves.
⑧ They have three taboos: liquor, cigarettes, and women.
⑨ They have to be secluded[2] from the world.
⑩ They have to control their passions[3].

[해설] [1]aphrodisiac[æ̀froudíziæ̀k]: a food or drug that makes sb feel sexual excitement 성욕을 촉진하는 음식/약, 최음제(催淫劑). [2]seclude [siklúːd]: to keep sb apart from the other people 분리/격리하다. [3]passion: a very strong feeling of sexual love 정욕(sexual desire; lust)

🟢 훈련병과 스님

① 그들은 삭발해야 한다.
② 그들은 유니폼을 입어야 한다.
③ 그들은 일찍 일어나야 한다.
④ 그들은 많은 규칙을 암기해야 한다.
⑤ 그들은 심신을 수련해야 한다.
⑥ 그들은 정력음식을 먹지 말아야 한다.
⑦ 그들은 모든 것을 스스로 해야 한다.
⑧ 그들은 삼 금이 있다: 술, 담배, 여자.
⑨ 그들은 격리된 사회에 살아야 한다.
⑩ 그들은 정욕을 억제해야 한다.

🟢 우리나라 사관학교 생도들의 三禁은 禁酒, 禁煙, 禁婚이다.

A rifle and a woman

① Most of them are secondhand.

② They are often called sweetheart.

③ They have to be handled carefully.

④ They need lubricating[1] periodically.

⑤ They should be polished after using.

⑥ It takes some time to break them in[2].

⑦ It's easy to identify mine from others.

⑧ It's sometimes annoying to carry them.

⑨ They are not necessary during a vacation.

⑩ They will become obsolete[3] in the long run[4].

⑪ They have to be used by the authorized person.

⑫ They are very convenient once you get a good one.

⑬ It's not easy to hit the bull's eye[5] with the first shot.

⑭ Their appearance doesn't tell how long they have been used.

⑮ Brand-new[6] ones don't always guarantee good performance.

[해설] [1]lubricate [lúːbrikèit]: to put a lubricant on sth: ~에 기름을 치다. [2]break sb in: to get sb used to a new job or situation 적응시키다, 익숙하지다. [3]obsolete [àbsəlíːt]: no longer used, replaced by sth better 쓸모없는, 폐물. [4]in the long run: from now far into the future; in the end 나중엔, 결국에는 [5]hit the bull's-eye: to hit the center of the target 명중시키다. [6]brand-new: new and never used before 새것의, 사용된 적이 없는: That is a brand-new television, not secondhand. 이것은 새 텔레비전이지 중고가 아니다.

총과 여자

① 대부분이 중고다.

② 흔히 애인이라 불린다.

③ 조심스럽게 다뤄져야 한다.

④ 주기적으로 기름칠이 필요하다.

⑤ 쓰고 나면 닦아줘야 한다.

⑥ 길들이는데 시간이 좀 걸린다.

⑦ 내 것은 다른 것과 섞여도 금방 찾는다.

⑧ 휴대하기에 때때로 귀찮다.

⑨ 휴가 때 꼭 필요하지는 않다.

⑩ 언젠가는 쓸모없게 된다.

⑪ 인가된 사람만 사용해야 한다.

⑫ 좋은 것을 만나면 아주 편하다.

⑬ 첫발로 명중하기란 쉽지 않다.

⑭ 외관상 얼마나 사용되었는지 알 수 없다.

⑮ 새 것이라고 항상 훌륭한 성능을 보장하지 않는다.

🔴 Once you go into the military,

① you become healthy.
② you can walk straight.
③ you eat a balanced diet.
④ you become an early riser.
⑤ you have a positive attitude.
⑥ you become self confident.
⑦ you can arrange things in order.
⑧ you can appreciate trivial things.
⑨ you become popular with the girls.
⑩ you become considerate to others.
⑪ you set a good example[1] to others.
⑫ you learn to appreciate your family.
⑬ you can acquire a sense of justice.
⑭ you can handle emergency situations.
⑮ you can cultivate the spirit of frugality[2].
⑯ you can enhance your leadership skills.
⑰ you can obtain a blackbelt in Taekwondo.
⑱ you can cultivate a sense of responsibility.
⑲ you get one military occupational specialty.
⑳ you can take the initiative[3] any time, anywhere.
㉑ you can protect the weak, the old, and females.
㉒ you can build a house with an entrenching shovel[4].
㉓ you get the courage to sing a song in front of others.
㉔ you can fully recognize that you should defend your country.
㉕ you can understand all kinds of four-letter words[5] from the 8 provinces.

[해설] [1]set an example: to behave in the way others should 모범을 보이다. [2]frugality [fruːgǽləti] 검소 〈 frugal[frúːgəl]: be careful about spending money 검소한. [3]take the initiative 솔선하다, 주도권을 쥐다. [4]entrenching shovel 야전삽: A weapon, a broom, a mop, and an entrenching shovel are soldier's best friends. 총, 빗자루, 밀대걸래와 야전삽은 병사들의 가장 좋은 친구들이다. [5]four-letter word 욕 (cunt, fuck, shit, etc.)

🔸 일단 군대가면,

① 건강해질 수 있고
② 똑바로 걸을 수 있고
③ 가리는 음식이 없어지고
④ 일찍 일어나게 되고
⑤ 긍정적인 태도를 갖게 되고
⑥ 자신감을 갖게 되고
⑦ 물건을 제자리에 정리할 수 있고
⑧ 사소한 것에 감사할 수 있고
⑨ 여자들에게 인기를 얻을 수 있고
⑩ 다른 사람을 배려하게 되고
⑪ 다른 사람에게 모범을 보이게 되고
⑫ 가족의 소중함을 알게 되며
⑬ 정의감을 배양할 수 있고
⑭ 비상 상황을 처리할 수 있고
⑮ 절약정신을 배양할 수 있고
⑯ 리더십 스킬을 배양할 수 있고
⑰ 태권도에서 검은 띠를 딸 수 있고
⑱ 책임감을 배양할 수 있고
⑲ 하나의 주특기가 생기고
⑳ 언제 어디서나 주도권을 잡을 수 있고
㉑ 약자, 노인과 여성을 보호할 수 있고
㉒ 야전삽 하나로 집을 지을 수 있고
㉓ 용기를 가지고 타인 앞에서 노래를 부를 수 있고
㉔ 내 나라를 스스로 지켜야겠다는 것을 완전히 알게 되고
㉕ 8도의 욕을 다 이해할 수 있다.

🔸 아들이 해병대 훈련을 받은 뒤 변한 모습에 감탄하는 미국의 한 아버지

He looks different, he walks different, he talks different, he has such a sense of bearing and pride all I could do was look at him in awe. Oh yes, the training is hard, what he went through is unimaginable to any one that has not been there. Let me tell you the surprise of what else they are taught. My Marine son has better values, better morals, better manners than any one I know. It is so much more than Yes Sir, Yes Ma'am...so much more. He cares about how he looks, he cares about what he does, and its not a boastful, bad ass thing. He is a true gentleman. I saw patience, and a calmness in him that I have never seen...

🟢 A soldier and his sweetheart

① When you served your parents, I was called up[1] by my motherland.
② When you expected sunny days, I prayed to have rain.
③ When you got up by the alarm clock, I was woken up from an uneasy sleep by a bugle.
④ When you used shampoo, I washed my hair with laundry soap[2].
⑤ When you drank chilled beer, I drank water from the faucet in the restroom.
⑥ When you complained about food, I finished my jjambab in two minutes.
⑦ When you ate ice cream, I ate salt to keep from fainting[3].
⑧ When you became bored with eating bread, I donated blood to get a piece of bread.
⑨ When you put on cosmetics, I put on camouflage cream[4].
⑩ When you kidded around in the playground, I received punishment.
⑪ When you talked about Plato's philosophy, I criticized Communism.
⑫ When you danced at a nightclub, I struggled in the gas training chamber.
⑬ When you strolled on a college campus, I crawled on grave mounds[5].
⑭ When you breathed air from air conditioners, I put my head down on the ground under the hot sun.
⑮ When you sang a pop song to sober up after drinking, I sang a military song loudly.
⑯ When you tilted a cocktail glass at a cafe, I tilted my canteen[6] at a stream.
⑰ When you traveled on a train, I went on maneuvers[7] in a military truck.
⑱ When you read today's horoscope[8], I read one that was 10 days' old at the garbage dump.
⑲ When you enjoyed drama on TV at 22:00, I couldn't roll even my eyeballs at evening roll call.
⑳ When you were lost in meditation[9] looking at the evening stars, I left for the sentry box looking at the dawn stars.
㉑ When you saw another man to overcome loneliness, I scratched your name, three letters, on the parade ground.
㉒ When you were glad to receive a gold necklace from another man, I cried to receive my dog tags.
㉓ When you were delighted to see another man, I took a deep sigh looking at a middle aged woman serving at the mess hall.
㉔ When you were embraced by another man, I embraced a cold blanket thinking of you.
㉕ When you pledged your love to another man, I pledged that I'd dedicate my life to my country.

[해설] [1]called up 소환하다. [2]laundry soap 빨래비누. [3]faint 실신한. [4]camouflage cream 위장 크림. [5]grave mound 흙무덤. [6]canteen [kæntíːn]: a container for liquid 수통. [7]go on maneuvers: to do a military exercise 기동하다. [8]horoscope 점성, 운세. [9]meditation [mèdətéiʃən]: the act of remaining in a silent and calm state 묵상, 명상

🔸 군인과 애인

① 너 부모님께 효도할 때, 나 조국의 부름 받았다.

② 너 화창한 날 기다릴 때, 나 비 내리길 기도 했다.

③ 너 자명종에 일어날 때, 나 기상나팔에 선잠 깼다.

④ 너 샴푸로 머리 감을 때, 나 빨래 비누로 머리 감았다.

⑤ 너 시원한 맥주 마실 때, 나 화장실에서 수돗물 마셨다.

⑥ 너 음식 투정할 때, 나 짬밥 2분 만에 해치웠다.

⑦ 너 아이스크림 먹을 때, 나 쓰러질까 소금 먹었다.

⑧ 너 빵에 싫증났을 때, 나 빵 한 봉지 받으려고 피 뺐다.

⑨ 너 화장품 바를 때, 나 위장크림 발랐다.

⑩ 너 운동장에서 뛰놀 때, 나 뺑뺑이 돌았다.

⑪ 너 플라톤 철학을 논할 때, 나 공산당을 비판했다.

⑫ 너 나이트에서 춤출 때, 나 가스실에서 몸부림쳤다.

⑬ 너 캠퍼스 거닐 때, 나 흙무덤에서 낮은 포복했다.

⑭ 너 에어컨 바람 쐴 때, 나 뜨거운 태양 아래 머리 박았다.

⑮ 너 술 깨려고 노래 부를 때, 나 목이 터지도록 군가 불렀다.

⑯ 너 카페에서 칵테일 잔 기울일 때, 나 개울가에 수통 기울였다.

⑰ 너 열차로 여행 할 때, 나 군용트럭 타고 작전 나섰다.

⑱ 너 오늘의 운세 볼 때, 나 쓰레기장에서 열흘 지난 운세 보았다.

⑲ 너 밤 10시에 드라마 볼 때, 나 점호 받느라 눈동자도 못 굴렸다.

⑳ 너 저녁별 보며 사색에 잠길 때, 나 새벽별 보며 초소로 나섰다.

㉑ 너 외롭다고 딴 남자 만날 때, 나 연병장에 너의 이름 석 자 새겼다.

㉒ 너 다른 남자에게 금목걸이 받고 기뻐할 때, 나 개 목걸이 받고 울었다.

㉓ 너 다른 남자 만나 즐거워할 때, 나 식당 아줌마 보고 한숨지었다.

㉔ 너 다른 남자 품에 안길 때, 나 당신 생각하면서 찬 모포를 끌어안았다.

㉕ 너 다른 남자에게 사랑을 맹세할 때, 나 조국에 목숨 바칠 것을 맹세했다.

Orders for Command 구령

1. Platoon attention!　소대 차려!
2. Parade rest　열중 쉬어!
3. At ease!　쉬어!
4. Rest!　편히 쉬어!
5. Sit down!　앉아!
6. Stand up!　일어서!
7. Listen!(Attention!, Pay attention!)　주목!
8. Private Kim!　김이병!
9. Here, sir!　네!
10. On hats!　착모!
11. Off hats!　탈모!
12. Hand salute!　경례!
13. Ready two!　바로!
14. Fall in!　집합!
15. Fall out! (Dismissed!)　헤쳐!
16. Count off!　번호!
17. Roll left (right)!　좌(우)로 굴러!
18. Lie down on your stomach!　앞으로 취침!
19. Lie down on your back!　뒤로 취침!
20. Put head down on the ground　머리 박아!
21. Left (Right) face!　좌(우)향 좌(우)!
22. Left (Right)…, As you were!　좌(우)로…, 다시!
23. About face!　뒤로 돌아!
24. Squad halt!　분대 섯!
25. Read back! (Repeat back!)　복창!
26. Out of ranks!　열외!
27. Guide on me!　본관(本官) 기준!
28. Guide on PFC Kim, dress right, dress!　김일병 기준, 우로 나란히!
29. Fall in according to height!　신장 순 집합!
30. Company in column of four, fall in!　중대 4열 종대 집합!
31. Dress left (right), dress!　좌(우)로 나란히!
32. Eyes right!　우로 봐!
33. Ready front!　바로!
34. Close interval dress right, dress!　좁은 간격 우로 나란히!
35. Close interval dress left, dress!　좁은 간격 좌로 나란히!
36. Normal interval dress right, dress!　정식 간격 우로 나란히!
37. Double interval dress right, dress!　양팔 간격 우로 나란히!
38. Private Kim, forward 5 centimeters!　김이병 5센티미터 앞으로!
39. Corporal Park, little bit to the left!　박상병 약간 좌로!
40. Forward march!　앞으로 갓!
41. Half step march!　반보 앞으로 갓!

42. Two steps backward, march!
    뒤로 2보 갓!
43. Count cadence march!
    번호 맞춰 갓!
44. Mark time march!
    제자리 걸음으로 갓!
45. To the rear march!
    뒤로 돌아 갓!
46. Right flank march!
    우향 앞으로 갓!
47. Left flank march!
    좌향 앞으로 갓!
48. Right oblique flank march!
    반우향 앞으로 갓!
49. At ease march! 제자리 걸어 갓!
50. Left (Right) wheel!
    줄줄이 좌(우)로 갓!
51. Column left (right) march!
    줄줄이 좌(우)로 갓!
52. Double time march! 뛰어 갓!
53. Quick time march!
    바른 걸음으로 갓!
54. Route step march!
    길 걸음으로 갓!
55. Keep step! 발 맞춰!
56. Sir, the parade is formed!
    분열 준비 끝!
57. We are prepared for inspection!
    열병 준비 끝!
58. Persons to be honored to center, march! 수상자 앞으로!
59. First Squad all present!
    제 1분대 집합 끝!
60. PT formation move!
    체조대형으로 벌려!
61. Port arms! 앞에 총!
62. Present arms! 받들어 총!
63. Order arms! 세워 총!
64. Trail arms! 허리에 총!
65. Stack arms! (Pile arms!)
    걸어 총!
66. Take arms! (Unpile arms!)
    풀어 총!
67. Left (Right) shoulder arms!
    좌(우)로 어깨 총!
68. Adjust slings! 멜빵 조여!
69. Raise pistol! 권총 빼어!
70. Insert magazine! 탄창 끼어!
71. Withdraw magazine! 탄창 빼어!
72. Open chamber! 노리쇠 후퇴!
73. Load one round!
    실탄 일발 장전!
74. Close chamber! 노리쇠 전진!
75. Commence fire! 사격 개시!
76. Cease fire! 사격 중지!
77. Are there any alibis?
    이상 있는 사수 손들어?
78. At close interval, fall in!
    좁은 간격으로 모여!
79. Fix bayonets! 꽂아 칼!
80. Unfix bayonets! 빼어 칼!

● Each rank and its characteristics

PVT	The new private soldiers who just moved into a new location are nothing but pupils in a kindergarten. They receive lots of disciplinary punishment and they lead a tense life. They have to learn new things as much as possible in a short time. While privates, they should not laugh at comedy programs on TV. It is clear that while they are privates, it's as if they are having a "second attack of measles."
PFC	After two or three months, the new private soldiers become privates first class. They become accustomed to barracks life so they have more leisure time than they were privates, but they still have to run and shout out their ranks and names. The main difference between privates and privates first class is that privates first class can do their jobs by themselves. Once they become privates first class, they are told that they have become "human beings."
CPL	The corporal's primary mission is to direct and supervise privates and privates first class and to serve sergeants. Corporals are often "sandwiched" between privates, privates first class and sergeants. While they are corporal, their girlfriends graduate from colleges and get a job and this may lead some of them to send their boyfriend a Dear John letter.
SGT	Sergeants always look lazy and as if they are doing nothing, but they finally supervise soldiers' work and make a harmonious relationship with both NCOs and officers. Sergeants are the driving force that gets things done in the military. They will show their potential during operations. Considering their job performance and prospect of discharge, they are often called "one among the five ranks of star," i.e., one of those who wear stars on their shoulders.

계급별 특성

이병
자대에 배치된 이병은 갓 입학한 유치원생이나 다름없다. 이병은 긴장된 생활의 연속으로 얼 차례도 가장 많이 받으며 단기간 내에 할 수 있는 한 새로운 것을 많이 배워야 한다. 이병 때는 TV의 코미디 프로를 보면서 함부로 웃어서도 안 된다. 이병 때는 "제 2의 홍역"임이 분명하다.

일병
일병은 2~3개월이 지나면 일병이 된다. 일병은 내무생활에도 익숙하고 이병보다는 여유가 있지만 아직도 뛰어다니고 관등성명도 크게 대어야 한다. 일병과 이병의 중요한 차이점은 일병은 고참들이 일을 시키지 않아도 일을 할 수 있다는 것이다. 일병이 되면 겨우 "사람"이 되었다고 한다.

상병
상병의 주 임무는 일・이병을 지도, 감독하고 병장을 모시는 일이다. 상병은 일・이병과 병장 사이에서 가끔 "샌드위치"가 되곤 한다. 상병 때에 병사들의 여자 친구는 대학을 졸업하고 취직을 해서 새로운 환경에 접하게 되므로 여자 친구로부터 대다수 절교 편지를 받는다.

병장
병장은 겉으로 보기에는 게으르고 아무것도 안 하는 것처럼 보이지만 병사들의 업무를 최종 감독하며 장교 및 부사관들과의 인간관계도 조화롭게 한다. 병장은 군대를 움직이는 원동력으로 훈련 시에 잠재력을 발휘한다. 업무 수행 능력이나 전역의 희망으로 볼 때 그들은 종종 "5대 장성 중의 하나"라고 불린다.

군대영어

군대생활의 고뇌 추억 지에

Military English

Serving at a New Location
(자대 생활)

- 전입신고
- 너 빽 있지?★★
- 전입 첫날★
- 우리 누나 가슴 빵빵★★★
- 여자친구 있냐?★
- 그녀를 어떻게 만났니?
- 그녀 사진 좀 보자
- 너 축구 좀 하냐?★★
- 박물관으로 전속!★★★
- 한국 사람들이 군대에 부정적으로 되는 이유★★
- 고참신상 파악★
- 점호 끝나고 개무반으로
- 눈물 밥을 먹다★★
- 인상 좀 펴라
- 너 담배 피우냐?
- 홈런 했다★★
- 데이트의 5단계★★★
- 김일병 송★★
- 계급별 이미지★★★
- 이병은 사람이 아니다
- 이등병은 하루에 세 번 운다★★
- 왜 군인들이 4계절을 모두 싫어하나★
- 병사들의 푸념

- 이등병의 맹세★★★
- 이등병 아저씨들에게
- 군바리 애인들에게★★
- 나이 처먹어서 꼽나?★★★
- 여친을 만나기 위해 탈영
- 누가 먼저 이별을 유도하는가? 여자다!
- 이별 후에 누가 더 괴로운가? 남자다!
- 질문★
- 바퀴벌레와 방위병
- 군대 업무처리 과정★★★
- 나는 방공포를 사랑해요★★★
- 이등병의 슬픔★★★
- 이등병 수칙★★★
- 이런 속어를 더 이상 사용하지 말자
- 군대에서 근무 요령★★★
- 군바리의 기다림에 대한 보상은★★
- 군바리 10대 강적★★★
- 군인의 칠거지악★★★
- 군바리 하소연★★
- 군대 훈련의 유래★★★
- 휴가신고★★
- 저는 부대 식모가 아닙니다!★
- 외출·외박의 목적

Military English

Serving at a New Location
(자대 생활)

- 100일 휴가
- 휴가의 마지막 날★★
- 내 여친이 벌써 새 남친을
- 여친에게 말하지 말 것은★
- 나무를 흔들어
- 군대에서 나무가 잘 자라지 않는 이유
- 화생방 경보 발령
- MOPP 4 단계 발령★★★
- 진급 신고
- 아직도 자고 있어
- 점호만 없어도
- 어떻게 처벌 받을래? I★
- 어떻게 처벌 받을래? II
- 군번줄 보자
- 오늘 일석점호 때 보자
- 점호 끝
- 취침점호
- 천리행군의 기원★★
- 패잔병처럼
- 대대장님과의 대화
- 수하 요령★★
- 보초 서로 가다
- 수하 I
- 수하 II
- 차량 수하
- 보초수칙
- 근무 중에 건빵 먹기★
- 무좀★★
- 부산의 미스 김 일거야★
- 고무신 거꾸로 신었나 봐★
- 자살
- 너무 늦었습니다
- 당신이 누군지 모르겠어!
- 너 군생활 어떠니?
- 사고보고★
- 부적절한 관계★★
- 감점표 내놔!
- 죄수와 군인★★★
- 군생활 3년 후에★★
- 허가되지 않은 관물 파손★★★
- 모자에 개구리 마크★
- 전역 회식에서 마지막 한마디★★
- 전역 전날 밤에★
- 전역신고★★★
- 고참 군화의 충고★★★

🔵 Move-in report

[New Soldier : Senior]

N: Pilsung! Reporting as ordered, sir.

　　Private Hong Kil-dong ordered to move into…

S: Hey, haven't you had breakfast this morning?

　　Are you whispering? Spit it out[1]!

N: Yes, sir!

S: Hey, close your eyes.

N: Yes, sir. Action!

S: Can you see anything?

N: No, everything is dark.

S: Bingo[2]! That's your future in the military.

[해설] [1]spit sth out: to send sth from the mouth: (침·음식·피 따위를) 뱉다: used to tell sb to say more quickly/loudly 빨리/큰소리로 말하라고 재촉할 때 사용된다. Come on, spit it out. Who told you about this? 야, 말해봐. 누가 너에게 여기에 대해 말해줬어? [2]bingo: used to say sb that s/he has guessed sth correctly 누가 추측한 것이 맞았을 때 하는 말, 맞았(혔)어!

🔵 전입신고

신병: 필승! 신고합니다. 이병 홍 길동은 전입을….

병장: 야, 오늘 아침 안 먹었어?

　　　속삭이냐? 큰 소리로 해!

신병: 예, 알겠습니다.

고참: 임마, 눈 감아 봐.

신병: 예, 알겠습니다. 실시!

고참: 뭐가 보이냐?

신병: 아닙니다. 그냥 깜깜합니다.

고참: 빙고! 그게 앞으로 너의 군생활이다.

Hey, do you have pull?

[Senior : New Soldier]

S: Hey, do you have pull[1]?

N: No, sir.

S: Look at this guy. You came to this unit without pull?

You really don't have a powerful supporter?

N: No, I don't sir.

S: I'm going to find out and you'll be sorry.

[해설] [1]pull: power or influence 영향력, 빽, 연줄 : She has pull with the police. 그녀는 경찰과 연줄이 있다.

너 빽 있지?

고참: 야, 너 빽 있지?

신병: 아닙니다.

고참: 이 놈 봐. 너 빽 없이 이 부대로 왔다고?

너 정말 빽 없단 말이야?

신병: 예, 없습니다.

고참: 너 발각되면 안 좋아.

🔵 The first day at the new location

[Senior : New soldier 1 ~ New solider 4]
[A group of new soldiers came into the barrack room and each soldier is being asked the following questions.]

S: Where is your home?

N1: My home is Seoul, sir!

S: Is the whole of Seoul your home?
Are you the only guy who lives in Seoul?

N1: My home is in Seoul Gangnam-gu Gaepo-dong~.

S: Did I ask you to tell me your address? You fuck.

S: Do you have an elder sister?

N2: Yes, I have, sir!

S: Hand her over to me! I'll guarantee a smooth military life for you.

S: Do you have younger sisters?

N3: No, I don't, sir!

S: Read back. "My military life went completely wrong." Action!

N3: Action! "My military life went completely wrong[1]."

S: How many days are left until your discharge day?

N4: I don't know, sir!

S: Do you think it will ever come?

N4: In about 2 years.

S: If I were you, I would commit suicide[2]!

[해설] [1]go wrong: 잘못되다, 꼬이다. [2]commit suicide: to kill yourself deliberately 자살하다. commit adultery 간통하다. commit는 옳지 않은/불법인 것을 행하다 (to do sth wrong or illegal) 뜻이 있다. If a man commits adultery with another man's wife, both the adulterer and the adulteress must be put to death. 한 남자가 유부녀와 바람을 피우면 모두 사형에 처해져야 한다.

🔸 전입 첫날

[한 무리의 신병이 내무반으로 들어오자 다음의 질문을 받는다.]

고 참: 너의 집이 어디냐?

신병1: 네, 저의 집은 서울입니다.

고 참: 서울이 다 느그 집이냐?
　　　서울에 너만 살어?

신병1: 저의 집은 서울 강남구 개포동~.

고 참: 누가 주소 대랬나, 새꺄?

고 참: 누나 있냐?

신병2: 예, 있습니다!

고 참: 나한테 넘겨! 너의 편안한 군생활 보장한다.

고 참: 여동생 있냐?

신병3: 없습니다!

고 참: 복창한다. "내 군대생활 완전히 꼬였다." 실시!

신병3: 실시! "내 군대생활 완전히 꼬였다."

고 참: 너 제대 며칠 남았냐?

신병4: 모르겠습니다!

고 참: 그날이 오냐?

신병4: 한 2년 남았습니다.

고 참: 나 너 같으면 자살한다!

🔸 My elder sister has large breasts

[New soldier : Corporal : Sergeant]

[A new soldier came into the barrack room and he is being asked by his seniors.]

C: Hey, do you have a younger sister or an elder sister?

N: Yes, Private Hong Kil-dong! I have just one elder sister, sir!

C: Oh, really? How old is she?

N: Twenty four, sir!

C: Are you serious? Is she beautiful?

N: Yes, she is.

C: How tall is she?

N: About 167 cm, sir!

C: What about her body shape and face?

N: She exceeds Miss Korea. (A sergeant overheard the conversation and he cuts in.)

S: Hey, just a moment. Attention! You guys, don't touch this new soldier, otherwise you shall die! New soldier, let's have a serious talk. I will let you have a comfortable military life.

N: Yes, sir!

S: But does your elder sister have large breasts?

N: Yes, she does.

S: Is she as well endowed[1] as the actress, Queen of Buxom?

N: Yes, sir!

S: Oh, how do you know? Have you ever seen them?

N: (hesitating to answer) I saw her breasts when she was breast-feeding[2] my cousin!

S: Are you kidding me? Are you going to die?

N: No, I answered your question truthfully, sir!

[해설] [1]endowed: 재산/능력을 물려받은 뜻이지만, 비유적으로 여자가 큰 가슴을, 남자가 큰 성기를 물려받은 것을 뜻한다. (Typically used for a guy to mean he's got a big penis, and for a girl to mean she has big breasts.): Man, that Lisa chick is well endowed, she's got the biggest tits in school. 와, 저 리자는 가슴이 크다. 그녀는 학교에서 가슴이 제일 크다.
[2]breast-feed: to feed a baby with milk from her breasts 모유를 먹이다.

우리 누나 가슴 빵빵[1]

[한 신병이 내무반에 들어오자 고참으로부터 질문을 받는다.]

상병: 야, 너 여동생이나 누나 있냐?

신병: 예, 이병 홍길동! 누나가 한 명 있습니다!

상병: 그래? 몇 살인데?

신병: 24살입니다!

상병: 정말이냐? 예뻐?

신병: 예, 예쁩니다.

상병: 그래, 키가 얼마냐?

신병: 167 cm 정도 됩니다!

상병: 몸매와 얼굴은?

신병: 미스 코리아 뺨칩니다!

　　　(엿 듣던 한 병장이 대화에 끼어든다.)

병장: 야, 잠시 주목! 너희들 오늘부터 이 신병 건들지 마. 건드리면 죽어!
　　　신병, 넌 나와 진지한 대화 좀 하자. 네 군생활 편하게 해줄게.

신병: 예, 알겠습니다.

병장: 근데, 네 누나 가슴은 크냐?

신병: 예, 큽니다!

병장: 가슴의 왕자인 그 여배우 정도 되냐?

신병: 예, 그렇습니다.

병장: 그래. 니가 어떻게 알아? 보기라도 했어?

신병: (머뭇거리다가) 조카 젖줄 때 봤습니다!

병장: 너 날 놀리지? 너 죽고 싶냐?

신병: 아닙니다. 묻는 말에 그냥 대답했을 따름입니다!

[해설] [1]가슴이 빵빵한 의 자세한 설명 → p. 315

🔵 Do you have a girlfriend?

[New soldier : Senior]

S: What did you do before coming into the Army?

N: I just spent time doing nothing.

S: Were you a robber doing nothing?

N: No, I attended university.

S: Which university?

N: The chemical engineering department at Korea University.

S: Oh, Korea University? I guess you're bright.
   Hey, do you have a girlfriend?

N: Yes, sir.

S: Then do you have an elder or younger sister?

N: I have no younger sister, but my elder sister is married.

S: I see a dark cloud[1] coming over your military life!

[해설] [1]cloud는 가산 명사로 사용되어 a가 붙었다. "하늘에 구름 한 점 없다."라고 강조할 때는 조수사인 "a speck of"를 사용하여 "There was not a speck of cloud in the sky."로 표현한다. 또한 "먹구름이 몰려온다."에서 come 대신 cast를 사용해도 된다.

🔵 여자 친구 있나?

고참: 군대오기 전에 뭐했니?

신병: 놀다 왔습니다.

고참: 노는 깡패였나?

신병: 아닙니다. 학교 다녔습니다.

고참: 어디 다니는데?

신병: 고려대 화학과 다닙니다.

고참: 오, 고대? 머리는 좋은가 보다.
      야, 너 여자 친구 있나?

신병: 예, 그렇습니다.

고참: 그럼 누나 여동생은?

신병: 여동생은 없고 누나는 시집갔습니다.

고참: 너 군생활에 먹구름이 팍 끼는 구나!

How did you meet her?

[New soldier : Senior]

S: Wipe the sweat[1] from your face.

N: Thank you, sir!

S: Do you have a girlfriend?

N: Yes, I do, sir.

S: How did you meet her?

N: I got acquainted with her after chasing after her for one year.

S: Does she attend Korea University, too?

N: Yes, she majors in[2] English linguistics and literature.
   She has had a hard time since I joined the army.

S: Oh, that's too bad!

[해설] [1]sweat [swet]: n. a salty liquid comes out through your skin 땀. v. to have liquid coming out through your skin 땀을 흘리다. [2]major in sth: to study sth as your main subject at a college or university 전공하다: She is majoring in biology. 그녀는 생물학을 전공한다.

그녀를 어떻게 만났니?

고참: 얼굴에 땀 좀 닦아라.

신병: 감사합니다!

고참: 너 여자친구 있냐?

신병: 예, 있습니다.

고참: 그래, 어떻게 만났냐?

신병: 학교에서 1년 동안 따라다니다 사귀게 되었습니다.

고참: 네 애인도 고대 다니냐?

신병: 고대 영문학과에 다닙니다.
      제가 군대 온 뒤에 많이 힘들어 하고 있습니다.

고참: 정말 안됐구나!

● Let me see her photos

[New soldier : Sergeant]

S: Do you have a girlfriend?

N: Yes, sir!

S: Let me see her photos.

N: Here you go, sir.

S: (Surprisingly) Where did you make a pass[1] at such a cool chick[2]?
   (Kissing one of the photos) Introduce her to me.

N: Oh, I haven't kissed her yet, sir.
   Pleases give them back to me right now.

S: Just wait a little longer.
   Do you think I'm such an easy person to handle?
   The moment you meet me, your happiness ends and unhappiness begins.

[해설] [1]make a pass at sb: to make a bold attempt to attract sb's sexual interest; hit on sb (성적 호기심에서) 접근하다, 꼬시다: He made a pass at her during the party. [2]chick: (slang) a young woman (속어) 젊은 여자: She is a cool chick! 그녀는 끝내주는 영계다. (관련속담: An old he-goat still likes a greenleaf 늙은 숫염소도 새싹을 좋아한다(Frisian). An old cat likes young mice. 늙은 고양이도 어린 생쥐를 좋아한다. (Spanish, Chile, Cuba, Mexico)

● 그녀 사진 좀 보자

병장: 너 애인 있냐?
신병: 예, 있습니다.
병장: 사진 좀 보자.
신병: 여기 있습니다.
병장: (놀라면서) 와! 너 어디서 이렇게 예쁜 아가씨를 꼬셨어?
      (사진 한 장에 뽀뽀하면서) 나 소개 시켜줘라.
신병: 저도 아직 키스도 못해봤습니다.
      당장 사진 돌려주십시오.
병장: 좀 더 기다려 봐.
      너 내가 만만한 사람으로 생각하는 모양이지?
      너 나 만나는 순간, 행복 끝 불행 시작이다.

Are you a good soccer player?

[New soldier : Senior]

S: Hey, Private Hong?

N: Yes, Private Hong Kil-dong, sir!

S: Are you a good soccer player?

N: Yes, I was a member of a morning soccer team before I joined the army.

S: Then, what's your position?

N: Right wing, sir!

S: Oh, good. I'm glad to have you!

N: Don't expect too much, sir!

Some tips about playing soccer in the military.
Don't attempt to dribble while you're a private.
Keep running on the soccer ground until you become a corporal.
Keep in mind that soccer in the military is "combat soccer."
Anyway, reply "I'm good at soccer." to the question, "Are you good at soccer?"

너 축구 좀 하냐?

고참 야, 홍일병?
신병 예, 홍길동 이병!
고참 너 축구 좀 하냐?
신병 예, 군대오기 전에 조기축구회에 다녔습니다.
고참 그럼, 네 포지션이 어디니?
신병 라이트윙이었습니다.
고참 너 같은 사람 받아서 좋구나.
신병 너무 큰 기대는 마십시오.

군대에서 축구에 관한 조언
이병 때는 드리블하지마라.
축구할 때 상병 때까지는 계속 뛰어라.
군대에서 축구는 "전투축구"임을 명심해라.
"축구를 잘 하느냐?"라는 질문에 "잘 한다."고 일단 대답해라.

Be transferred to a museum!

[New soldier : Senior]

S: Do you have a girlfriend?

N: Yes, I do, sir!

S: How many times did you have…?

N: No, I have never…, sir!

S: You mean that you're a virgin[1]?

N: Yes, sir!

S: You're a treasure that might be found once in a thousand years!
   Be prepared to be transferred to a museum as of next Monday.

N: Yes, sir!

[해설] [1]virgin: someone who has never had sex, especially a girl or young woman (특히, 여성) 성경험이 전혀 없는 사람: I wanted to remain a virgin until I got married, but …. 난 결혼할 때까지 보물로 남아 있으려 했건만 ….

박물관으로 전속!

고참: 여자친구 있냐?

신병: 예, 있습니다.

고참: 몇 번이나 해…?

신병: 한 번도….

고참: 너 숫총각이란 말이야?

신병: 네, 그렇습니다.

고참: 너는 천 년에 한 번 발견될지도 모르는 보물이구나!
   너 다음 주 월요일 부로 박물관으로 전속 갈 준비해라.

신병: 네, 알겠습니다!

◎ Why Koreans become negative towards the military

① They worry for 20 years before enlistment.
② They've been forced to write morale boosting letters for soldiers at school.
③ They have to be yelled at and disciplined in the military.
④ They have to go through a second attack of measles at basic training.
⑤ Nine out of ten soldiers get a **Dear John letter** in the military.
⑥ They have to receive homeland reserve training after their military service.
⑦ They have to be a member of Civil Defense Corps until the age of 55.
⑧ They have to send their sons to do obligatory[1] military service.
⑨ They have to reply to their sons' letters.
⑩ They have to visit their sons after their sons' first relocation[2].

[해설] [1]obligatory [əblígətɔ̀:ri]: required by law, custom, rules, etc. 의무적인. [2]relocation 재배치 〈 relocate: to (cause a person or company to) move to a new place (사람·회사를) 새로운 장소로 이동/배치하다: My company relocated me to Paris. 나의 회사는 나를 파리로 배치했다.

◎ 한국 사람들이 군대에 부정적이게 되는 이유

① 그들은 입대 전 20년간 걱정한다.
② 그들은 학교에서 위문편지 쓰라고 강요받는다.
③ 그들은 군대에서 야단맞고 군기 잡혀야 한다.
④ 그들은 기초군사훈련에서 제 2의 홍역을 겪어야 한다.
⑤ 그들의 10명 중 9명은 군대에서 절교편지를 받는다.
⑥ 그들은 전역 후에도 예비군 훈련을 받아야 한다.
⑦ 그들은 55세까지는 민방위 요원이 되어야 한다.
⑧ 그들은 자기 아들을 군복무 하러 보내야 한다.
⑨ 그들은 자기 아들의 편지에 답장해 주어야 한다.
⑩ 그들은 아지 아들이 첫 배치를 받으면 면회를 가야 한다.

◎ Dear John letter

Dear John letter란 여자가 자신의 남친/남편에게 보내는 절교 편지로 2차 세계 대전 중 미군들이 해외에 장기간 주둔하면서 이 용어가 생겼다. 군인들이 여친·아내에게서 받는 편지는 보통 "Dear Johnny", "My dearest John", "Darling" 등의 친근한 말로 시작되지만, 절교편지는 무뚝뚝한 "Dear John"으로 시작함에서 비롯되었다. 남자가 여자에게 보내는 절교편지는 Dear Jane letter 라고 한다. (John 과 Jane는 각각 남자와 여자를 대표하는 흔한 이름에서 연유되었음)

◎ Grasping seniors' details

[Senior : New Soldier]

S: What do you know about me, Chel-soo.

N: Your name is Hong Kil-dong.

You were born in Mokpo and raised in Seoul.

You graduated from Seoul High School with honors.

Your DOB(Date of Birth) is February 20, 1986.

Your citizen number is 860220-2804315.

Your serial number is 86-38478.

Your height is 176 centimeters.

Your weight is 65 kilograms.

Your religion is Gibulick.

Your hobby is making passes at girls.

Your girlfriend's name is Kim Young-suk.

She is beautiful and sexy.

Your ex's name is Kong Sun-hee.

S: I see. You have a good memory.

Now eat your meal.

* Gibulick or Gibulchun means either a blended religion of Christianity, Buddhism, and Catholicism and/or a multi-religious person who participates in the various practices of the three religious beliefs.
  • Memorizing facts about superiors does not help us to do our job.
  • Let's not ask junior soldiers to memorize these things anymore.
  • Members of the US military are not required to memorize these things.

고참신상 파악

고참: 철수, 나에 대해서 이야기 해봐라.

신병: 선배님의 이름은 홍길동입니다.

선배님께서는 목포에서 출생하여 서울에서 자랐으며,

서울고등학교를 우수한 성적으로 졸업하셨습니다.

생일은 1986년 2월 20일이며,

주민등록번호는 860220-2804315이며,

군번은 86-384780이며,

키는 176 cm,

몸무게는 65 Kg,

종교는 기불릭,

취미는 여자 꼬시기,

여자친구의 이름은 김영숙,

그녀는 매우 예쁘고 섹시하며,

예전 여자 친구의 이름은 공순희였습니다.

고참: 알았다. 넌 기억력이 좋구나.

이제 밥 먹어라.

* **기불릭** 또는 **기불천**이란 기독교, 불교, 천주교가 혼합된 종교 또는/그리고 세가지 종교(기독교, 불교, 천주교) 행사에 모두 참석하는 다종교적인 사람을 말한다.
  - 상관에 관한 사실을 암기한다는 것은 임무에 도움을 주지 않는다.
  - 너의 부하 군인들에게 이런 것을 더 이상 암기하지 말도록 하자.
  - 미군들도 이런 것을 암기하라고 강요받지 않는다.

🔸 Come to barracks numner 7 after roll call

[Senior : New Soldier]

S: Newcomer, your duty starts tomorrow, doesn't it?

N: Yes, sir!

S: You memorized our unit roster[1], didn't you?

N: Yes, I did, sir.

S: Hey, who is the 3rd highest ranking person in our company?

N: Park, Lee, Hmm…, Maybe Kim?

S: Are you playing me around because I cut you some slack[2]? Come to barracks number 7 after roll call. I'm going to discipline you.

[해설] [1]roster[rɑ́stəːr]: a list of people's names 명부: The teacher checked the roster to see whom he would teach this year. 그 교사는 금년에 누구를 가르칠 지 명부를 확인했다. [2]cut/give sb some slack: to give sb the right to be wrong (~에게) 실수할 기회를 주다, 빡세게 굴지 않다: You're too strict with your trainees; cut them some slack. 넌 훈련병들에게 너무 엄격해, 좀 풀어줘라. After a severe barracks inspection, our platoon leader gave us some slack. 혹독한 내무검사 후에 우리 소대장님은 군기를 좀 풀어 주었다.

🔸 점호 끝나고 7내무반으로

고참: 막내, 내일부터 근무 투입이지?

신병: 네, 그렇습니다.

고참: 중대 서열은 다 외웠겠지?

신병: 네, 그렇습니다.

고참: 야, 우리 중대에서 서열 세 번째는 누구냐?

신병: 박, 이, 흠…, 김인가?

고참: 내가 잘 해주니 고참을 놀리는구나?
점호 끝나고 7내무반에 와라. 군기 좀 잡아야겠다.

◎ Eating lunch in tears

[Sergeant : New Soldier]

S: Chel-soo, what's my profile?

N: Your name is Hong Kil-dong.

　Your hometown is Gwangju in Jella-do.

S: What? I'm from Jella-do?

　You didn't even remember my hometown yet.

　I'm from Gwangju in Gyeonggi-do, not in Jella-do.

N: I'm sorry, sir. I just got confused.

S: After lunch, come to barracks number 7.

N: Yes, sir. (and the new soldier begins to eat lunch in tears)

◎ 눈물 밥을 먹다

병장: 철수, 나에 대해서 이야기 해볼래?

신병: 선배님의 이름은 홍길동입니다.

　　　선배님의 고향은 전라도 광주입니다.

병장: 뭐? 내 고향이 전라도 광주라고?

　　　넌 내 고향도 아직 기억 못하는 구나.

　　　내 고향은 전라도 광주가 아니라 경기도 광주다.

신병: 죄송합니다. 헷갈렸습니다.

병장: 밥 먹고 7내무반으로 튀어와.

신병: 알겠습니다. (그리고 그 신병은 눈물 밥을 먹기 시작했다.)

🔸 Stop frowning

[Sgt. First Class : Corporal]

S: Corporal Kim, stop frowning[1].

C: I'm sorry, sir.

S: What's the matter with you?

C: I broke up[2] with my girlfriend during my last leave.

S: Oh, really.

C: I have been dating her for 5 years.

S: Try to find another fish[3].

[해설] [1]frown [fraun]: n. a look of disapproval (얼굴의) 찡그림, v. to have a frown on one's face 얼굴을 찡그리다: She frowned when she heard the bad news. [2]break up: to end a marriage or romantic relationship 절교하다: Troy and I broke up last month. 트로이와 나는 지난달 헤어졌다. [3]fish: term for biological women used primarily by gay men (동성애 남자들에 의해 주로 표현되는) 여자: Ugh! Why are there so many fish in the club tonight? 어! 오늘밤 클럽에 웬 여자들이 그렇게도 많은가?

🔸 인상 좀 펴라

중사: 김상병, 인상 좀 펴라.

상병: 죄송합니다.

중사: 뭐 문제 있나?

상병: 지난번 휴가 때 제 여자친구와 깨졌습니다.

중사: 오, 그래.

상병: 5년간 사귀었습니다.

중사: 여자가 한 둘인가.

Do you smoke?

[Private : Corporal]

C: Do you smoke?

P: Private Lee Won-young! No, I don't, sir!

C: You don't?

P: No, sir!

C: You haven't tasted how delicious **a military pine tree** is!

P: I heard that the military pine tree is stronger!

* **Military pine tree** was a brand of cigarette formerly provided in the military.

너 담배 피우냐?

상병: 너 담배 피우냐?

이병: 이병, 이, 원, 영! 저는 담배 피우지 않습니다!

상병: 그러냐?

이병: 네! 그렇습니다!

상병: 너, "군대솔"이 얼마나 맛있는지 모르는구나.

이병: 군대솔이 더 독하다고 들었습니다.

* 군대 솔(소나무)이란 군대에서 지급되었던 담배의 상표이름이다.

🔵 I got a homerun

[Sergeant : Corporal 1 ~ Corporal 4]

S : How far did you go with your girlfriend?

C1: I only got to first base. (to kiss on the lips)

C2: I got to second base. (to touch breasts)

C3: I got to third base. (to touch 'down there')

C4: I got a homerun. (to have sex)

* David got to first base last night with Laura. (kiss someone on a romantic date)
* Tom and Mary got to second base behind the gym!
* We went all the way. (homerun)
* We met two months ago, but we're still only on first base!
* How far did you get with her? - Only first base, I might lose her if we don't get any farther.

🔵 홈런 했다

병 장: 넌 여자 친구와 진도 어디까지 나갔니?

상병1: 겨우 퍼스트 베이스. (키스까지만)

상병2: 세컨드 베이스. (가슴을 만지는 단계)

상병3: 서드 베이스. ('아래 거기'를 만지는 단계)

상병4: 홈런 했다. (섹스까지 한 단계)

* 데이비드는 지난밤 로라와 일루까지 갔다. (키스)
* 탐과 메어리는 체육관 뒤로 가서 이루까지 갔다.
* 우리는 진도 다 나갔다. (홈런)
* 우리는 두 달 전에 만났지만 아직도 일루에 있어!
* 그녀와 진도는 어디까지 나갔니? - 일루, 진도를 더 나가지 않으면 그녀를 잃을 지도 모르겠어.

● The five stages of dating

When a couple begin dating they have to go through 5 stages of the dating process.

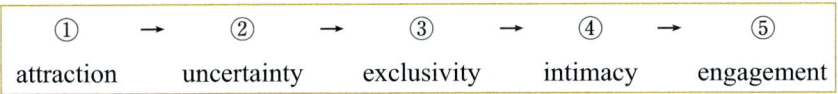

① Attraction: a stage of attracting a partner or being attracted by a partner
② Uncertainty: a stage of deciding whether he or she is compatible with me
③ Exclusivity: a stage of ruling out others except for one's final partner
④ Intimacy: a stage of building a close, affectionate and intimate relationship
⑤ Engagement: a stage of vowing to others that we're engaged

* If a stage is missed or a couple has a problem in the fifth stage, then they move back to stage two.

● 데이트의 5 단계

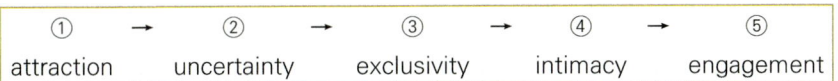

① 매력교환 단계: 상대방에게 매력을 주고받는 단계
② 불확실한 단계: 상대방이 나에게 맞는지 결정하는 단계
③ 독점권 형성 단계: 상대자를 마지막 애인이 되도록 다른 사람을 배제시키는 단계
④ 친밀감 형성 단계: 가깝고 사랑스러운 친밀감을 형성하는 단계
⑤ 약혼 형성 단계: 우리가 약혼했다고 공언하는 단계

* 5단계에서 한 과정을 빠트리거나 문제가 발생하면 ② 단계로 되돌아간다.

🔴 Private Kim's Song 김일병 송

MAJs, LTCs and COLs are jeep thieves
2nd LTs, 1st LTs and CPTs are gun thieves
SSGs, SFCs and MSGs are food thieves
Poor PVTs and PFCs are hardtack thieves

소령 중령 대령은 짚차 도둑놈
소위 중위 대위는 권총 도둑놈
하사 중사 상사는 부식 도둑놈
불쌍한 일·이병은 건빵도둑놈

MAJs, LTCs and COLs drink whiskey
2nd LTs, 1st LTs and CPTs drink beer
SSGs, SFCs and MSGs drink soju
Poor PVTs and PFCs drink **makkolli**
(Yeah, yeah, yeah, yeah)

소령 중령 대령은 양주 마시고
소위 중위 대위는 맥주 마시고
하사 중사 상사는 소주 마시고
불쌍한 일·이병은 막걸리 마시고
(예, 예, 예, 예)

* COL(Colonel) 대령, LTC(Lieutenant Colonel) 중령, MAJ(Major) 소령, CPT(Captain) 대위, 1st LT(First Lieutenant) 중위, 2nd LT(Second Lieutenant) 소위, MSG(Master Sergeant) 상사, SFC(Sergeant First Class) 중사, SSG(Staff Sergeant) 하사, PFC(Private First Class) 일병, PVT(Private) 이병

* makkolli is wine made from unrefined rice 막걸리란 쌀로 만든 정제되지 않은 술

Image of each rank 계급별 이미지

uneasy	Private	불안한	이병
quick-witted	Private First Class	눈치 빠른	일병
shrewd	Corporal	요령꾼	상병
sleepyhead	Sergeant	잠꾸러기	병장
talkative	Staff Sergeant	말 많은	하사
guider of all	Sergeant First Class	짜리도사	중사
most soldierly	Master Sergeant	군대체질	상사
matured	Sergeant Major	원숙한	원사
old-timer	Warrant Officer	노숙한	준위
disciplined	Second Lieutenant	똥기합 든	소위
dandy	First Lieutenant	멋을 아는	중위
master of the miscellaneous	Captain	잡합의 명수	대위
lazy	Major	할 일 없는	소령
cunning	Lieutenant Colonel	간사한	중령
potbellied president	Colonel	배 나온 사장	대령
arrogant	Brigadier General	거만한	준장
dignified	Major General	무게 있는	소장
jealous of Four Star General	Lieutenant General	대장 꼬와하는	중장
visionless	General	희망 없는	대장

* This is seen through the eyes of army privates. 육군병사에 의한 관찰임

◉ A private is not a human being

A private is not a human being.
A private first class is a human-being.
A corporal is a soldier.
A sergeant is half a civilian.

◉ 이병은 사람이 아니다

이병은 사람이 아니다.
일병은 사람이다.
상병은 군인이다.
병장은 반 민간인이다.

◉ Private soldiers cry three times a day

"A man cries three times in his life."
Which crazy guy said that?
He must not be a Korean man.
Private soldiers of the ROK cry three times a day.

◉ 이등병은 하루에 세 번 운다

"남자는 태어나서 세 번 운다."
어떤 미친 자식이 그 말을 했나?
그는 분명 대한민국 남자가 아닐 것이다.
대한민국의 이등병은 하루에 세 번 운다.

◎ Why soldiers hate the four seasons

They hate Spring because they have to plant trees.
They hate Summer because they have to cut or weed.
They hate Autumn because they have to sweep fallen leaves.
They hate Winter because they have to shovel snow.

◎ 왜 군인들이 4계절을 모두 싫어하나

봄은 나무 심어서 싫고.
여름은 잡초 사역으로 싫고.
가을은 낙엽 청소로 싫고.
겨울은 눈 치우기 싫고.

◎ Soldiers' grumbling

During boot camp: just drawing a deep sigh.
While a private: fed up[1] with the drill of running with a pack.
While a private 1st class: fed up with marching at night.
While a corporal: fed up with falling in.
While a sergeant: the military is like an X.
On discharge day: nothing to say.

[해설] [1]fed up: frustrated; disgusted 짜증나다, 신물 나다: I am completely fed up with all of the false promises. 나는 거짓 약속에 신물이 난다.

◎ 병사들의 푸념

훈련소 시절: 한숨만 나온다.
이등병 시절: 무장 구보에 질려버렸다.
일   병 시절: 야간 행군에 질렸다.
상   병 시절: 집합에 질렸다.
병   장 시절: 군대 X 같다.
전   역 당일: 할 말이 없다.

◯ The private soldier's oath

First, however sad I am, I won't cry in a toilet cubicle.
Second, however hungry I am, I won't eat in a toilet cubicle.
Third, however tired I am, I won't nod off[1] in a toilet cubicle.

[해설] [1]nod off: to fall asleep 졸다: I nodded off during class. 나는 수업 시간에 졸았다.

◯ 이등병의 맹세

첫째, 아무리 슬퍼도 화장실에서 울지 않겠다.
둘째, 아무리 배고파도 화장실에서 먹지 않겠다.
셋째, 아무리 피곤해도 화장실에서 졸지 않겠다.

◯ Dear private soldiers

Living from day to day is hard enough,
you don't have time to worry about future problems or regretting past mistakes. Leave the past in its place and let the future come as it will.
Private soldiers, way to go!

◯ 이등병 아저씨들에게

하루하루의 삶이 매우 고단해서,
너는 미래의 문제와 지난 실수를 고민할 시간이 없다.
과거는 과거의 자리에 내버려두고 미래는 그대로 다가오도록 해라.
이등병 아저씨 파이팅!

🔸 Dear gunbaries' sweethearts

The hardest and busiest time for soldiers is when they are privates because they have to adapt themselves to a new environment. They sweat profusely[1] doing chores: cleaning toilets, weeding, sweeping fallen leaves, shoveling snow, and cramming all the regulations into their mind. They do not have enough time to write a letter to you.

When they are privates, soldiers are like in a second period of measles. The suicide rate for private soldiers is higher than for other ranks. Women in Korea, if you have a boyfriend or lover who joined the military, please don't jilt[2] him until he becomes a corporal. That is one of the contributions you can make for our country. True love waits!

[해설] [1]profuse [prəfjúːs]: excessive 아낌없는 과도한. cram [kræm]: to study quickly and hard 주입식 공부를 하다: He crammed all night for the exam the next day. [2]jilt [dʒilt]: to desert a friend or loved one without warning (애인을 갑자기) 차버리다: She saw him every day, then jilted him. 그녀는 그를 매일 만났지만 그를 차버렸다.

🔸 군바리 애인들에게

군인들은 이병 때가 새로운 환경에 적응해야 하느라고 가장 힘들고 바쁩니다. 그들은 화장실 청소, 잡초제거, 낙엽 쓸기, 제설작업 등의 자질구레한 것들과 모든 규정을 암기하느라 땀을 많이 흘립니다. 그들은 당신에게 편지 쓸 충분한 시간도 없습니다.

군인에게 이병 시절은 인생에서 제 2의 홍역기간이나 다름없습니다. 이등병들의 자살률이 타 계급의 자살률보다 높습니다. 한국의 여자분들이여, 그대의 남친이 군대 갔다면 그가 상병 될 때까지는 제발 차 버리지 마세요. 그것은 당신이 국가에 헌신할 수 있는 방법 중의 하나입니다. 진실한 사랑은 참고 기다립니다!

Are you getting your revenge because you are older?

While a private at OO unit was being instructed by his senior, a corporal, behind their barracks at 1850~1900 Tuesday July 25, 2000. The private was told "You motherfucker, are you getting your revenge because you are older than me?" And the private got instantly furious at his senior's words. He struck the corporal in the face and the corporal struck him back.

나이 처먹어서 꼽냐?

OO부대 이병이 2000. 7. 25(화) 18:50~19:00 내무반 뒤에서 선임 상병으로부터 교육을 받고 있던 중 "OO놈아, 나이 처먹어서 꼽냐"라는 욕설을 듣자 순간적으로 격분하여 주먹으로 상병의 얼굴을 폭행하는 등 상호 폭행하였음.

Went AWOL to see his girlfriend

A sergeant at OO unit has been keeping company with a female staff sergeant at the same unit since around June of 2000 and she recently told him that she wanted to break up with him. Hearing this he became depressed and deserted from the military in order to see her on vacation at around 22:30, Tuesday, 7th of September 2000. However, he was caught by Military Police who were on surveillance[1] duty after he had been absent for 11 hours and 30 minutes.

[해설] [1]surveillance [sərvéiləns]: the act of watching a particular person or place carefully 감시: Police have the suspect under surveillance. 경찰은 그 용의자를 감시하고 있다.

여친을 만나기 위해 탈영

OO부대 병장이 2000년 6월경부터 같은 부대 여군 하사와 교제해 오던 중 최근 여군 하사로부터 헤어지자는 말을 듣고 이를 고민, 2000. 9. 7(화) 22:30경 휴가 중이던 그녀를 만날 목적으로 무단이탈 하였다가 11시간 30분 만에 잠복 중인 헌병에게 검거됨.

🔵 Who usually initiates the breakup? Women!

A group of Harvard scientists vigilantly[1] followed the affairs of 231 Boston couples. Of those who split up, usually it was the woman who suggested the separation. The man wanted to stick it out to the bitter end.

[해설] [1]vigilant [vídʒələnt]: watchful 방심하지 않는, 주의 깊은

🔵 보통 누가 먼저 이별을 유도하는가? 여자다!

일단의 하버드 대학 과학자들은 보스턴 커플 231명의 애정 사건을 주의 깊게 추적했다. 이별한 사람들 중에서 이별을 하자고 한 것은 대개 여자였다. 남자는 끝까지 집착을 보였다.

🔵 Who suffers more from the breakup? Men!

The men felt lonelier, more depressed, unloved, and least free after a split. The men reported that they found it extremely hard to accept that they were no longer loved and that she had really gone. What disturbed them most is that they could do nothing about it in the military.

In fact, three times as many men commit suicide after a disastrous love affair as women. How can your boyfriend say to his first sergeant or platoon leader, "I got dumped by my girlfriend?" He will get faint!

🔵 이별 후에 누가 더 괴로워하는가? 남자다!

이별 후에 남자가 외로움, 침울함, 사랑받지 못하는 느낌을 더 느끼며 이별의 아픔에서 자유롭지 못하다. 남자들은 그들이 더 이상 사랑받지 못하고 그녀가 가버렸다는 것을 정말 받아들이기 힘들다는 보고가 있다. 남자들을 가장 괴롭히는 것은 군대에서 어떻게 할 수 없다는 것이다. 비참한 사랑의 실패 후에 자살은 남자가 여자보다 3배나 많이 한다. 당신의 남자친구가 그의 선임부사관이나 소대장에게 "저 여자 친구한테 차였습니다."라고 어떻게 말할 수 있을까? 그는 까무러칠 거다!

Questions

	Men	Women
① Who falls in love faster?	☑	☐
② Who is more idealistic about love?	☑	☐
③ Who usually initiates a breakup?	☐	☑
④ Who suffers more from a breakup?	☑	☐
⑤ Who loves their lovers more?	☑	☐

질문

	남자	여자
① 누가 먼저 사랑에 빠지는가?	☑	☐
② 누가 사랑에 더 이상주의인가?	☑	☐
③ 보통 누가 먼저 이별을 제안하는가?	☐	☑
④ 이별 후에 누가 더 괴로워하는가?	☑	☐
⑤ 누가 애인을 더 사랑하는가?	☑	☐

Cockroaches and conscripted reservists

① Women hate them.

② They hang around in groups.

③ They crawl out mostly at night.

④ They pretend they aren't what they are.

⑤ They are more numerous than expected.

⑥ They eventually show their true colors.

바퀴벌레와 방위병

① 여자들이 싫어한다.

② 떼를 지어 다닌다.

③ 밤에 주로 기어 나온다.

④ 아닌 척 한다.

⑤ 의외로 쪽수가 많다.

⑥ 결국엔 티를 낸다.

The way things get done in the army 군대 업무처리 과정

A special insight into the way things get done in the army
군대에서 어떤 일이 완성되는 특별한 통찰

The Colonel calls the Major	중령은 소령을 부른다.
When something must be done.	무슨 일을 해야 할 때.
The Major calls the Captain	소령은 대위를 불러서
And starts him on the run.	그에게 일을 착수시킨다.
The Captain then gets busy	대위는 바쁘게 되고
And strives to make things suit	일을 상황에 맞추어 보고는
By shifting all the baggage[1]	모든 짐(책임)은
On a "shavetail[2]" Second Lieut.	신참 소위에게 맡겨진다.
The said Lieutenant ponders	지시받은 소위는 곰곰이 생각하고
And strokes a beardless jaw,	수염도 없는 턱을 쓰다듬고 나서는
Then calls the trusty Sergeant	믿음직한 병장을 불러서는
And to him lays down the law[3].	규정을 환기시킨다.
The Sergeant calls the Corporal	병장은 상병을 불러서
And explains how things must be,	일이 어떻게 되어야 하는지 설명한다.
And the Corporal calls the Private-	그리고 그 상병은 이병을 부른다.
And that, my friends, is ME[4].	친구들아, 그 이병이 바로 "나"다.

[해설] [1]baggage: burdensome task or responsibility 일, 책임. [2]shavetail: (a slang term in the U. S. Army) a brand new second lieutenant (미· 군대속어) 신임 육군 소위. [3]lay down the law: to state the rules 규정을 강조하다. [4]And that, my friends, is ME란 이등병은 지휘계통(the chain of command)에서 최하에 처해있어서 모든 것을 스스로 해야 하는 심정을 독자들에게 호소하고 있다. (I am the private at the bottom of the chain of command who has to do things for everyone else above me .)

◉ I love the air defense artillery

When my specialty was decided as air defense artillery(ADA), my father completely stopped eating and went to his bed. I can't tell you how devastated I was at that time.

Now I have become a high spirited airman first class in an ADA unit. My ADA unit's position overlooks the sea and our unit is filled with good comradeship. The commander and NCOs are all considerate. All my senior enlisted men are very humane. I thank all of them.

Let's admire our ADA from now on.
Serving in the ADA is interesting.
We can enjoy good clean air.
We play basketball, volleyball, and jogku.
Inspectors rarely visit here.
We have enough time to prepare for inspections
after being informed of the day they plan to visit.

We enjoy clear TV reception.
We have a reliable electrical supply.
It's much better than you think.
But we are more lonely here than on the base.
Now let's look up to the ADA.
My Commander, NCOs, and seniors, thank you very much.

* **Jokgu** is a game played between two teams of four people, where each team tries to win by kicking a football over the net into the other team's playing area until they are unable to return the ball. This is mostly favored by soldiers who have limited space.

🔵 나는 방공포를 사랑해요

내가 방공포 특기를 받았을 때 아버지는 식음을 전폐하고

몸져누웠습니다. 그 당시의 절망감은 이루 말할 수 없었지요.

지금은 방공포병 부대에서 늠름한 일병이 되었지요.

바다가 내려다보이는 방공포, 인간의 정이 넘치는 곳입니다.

포대장님, 부사관님들 모두 자상하십니다.

고참들 또한 인간미가 넘칩니다.

정말 고마울 따름입니다.

이제 우리 방공포를 우러러 봅시다.

방공포 재미있습니다.

공기 좋지요.

농구, 배구, 족구 하지요.

검열관 잘 안 오지요.

온다고 연락 오면

그때부터 준비해도 안 늦지요.

TV 잘 나오지요.

전기 잘 들어오지요.

생각보다 좋아요.

하지만 비행장보다는 외롭지요.

이제 방공포를 존경합시다.

포대장님, 부사관님, 선임들 너무너무 고맙습니다.

* **족구**란 4명씩으로 구성된 2개 팀에 의한 경기로, 각 팀은 상대방이 공을 받아 넘길 수 없을 때까지 네트 위로 상대방 편으로 축구공을 차서 점수를 얻는 게임이다. 주로 군인들에 의해서 제한된 공간에서 많이 애용된다.

● A private soldier's sorrow

① Why can't I watch TV?
② Why can't I read the newspaper?
③ Why do I have to gulp[1] down soup?
④ Why can't I take a nap on holiday?
⑤ Why do I have to sleep at attention?
⑥ Why do I have to look at the wall at attention?
⑦ Why can't I use the public telephones and the PX.
⑧ Why do I have to keep running during soccer games?
⑨ Why do I have to sleep under fur blankets in summer?
⑩ Why do I have to sing and dance in front of my seniors?
⑪ Why do I have to sing and dance wearing a gas mask?
⑫ Why do I have to confess my sexual experiences to my seniors?
⑬ Why do I have to eat raw garlic and onion when I do something wrong?
⑭ Why do I have to say that "I will correct myself." without accepting that I have made a mistake?
⑮ Why do I have to be awakened and move to other places because I snored a little during my sleep?

[해설] [1]gulp (down): to swallow whole mouthfuls, usu. quickly (얼른) 마시다, 삼켜버리다: The thirsty man gulped (down) the water. 갈증 난 남자는 그 물을 얼른 마셨다. (cf.) chug-a-lug [tʃʌgəlʌg 처갈럭]: to drink all of sth without stopping (속어) 단숨에 마시다: He's chug-a-lugged an entire bottle of beer/soju. 그는 맥주/소주 한 병을 나발 불었다.

● Don't say these things to anybody

① You're stupider than private soldiers.
② I wonder if your children will be like you.
③ Did you receive a proper primary school education?
④ You mess up everything you do. You short and fat guy!

🔸 이등병의 슬픔

① 왜 나는 TV를 볼 수 없는가?
② 왜 나는 신문을 볼 수 없는가?
③ 왜 나는 국을 마셔야 하는가?
④ 왜 나는 휴일에 낮잠을 잘 수 없는가?
⑤ 왜 나는 차려 자세로 잠을 자야 하는가?
⑥ 왜 나는 차려 자세에서 벽을 쳐다봐야 하는가?
⑦ 왜 나는 공중전화와 PX를 사용할 수 없는가?
⑧ 왜 나는 축구 경기 때 계속 뛰어야 하는가?
⑨ 왜 나는 여름에 모포를 덥고 자야 하는가?
⑩ 왜 나는 내 고참 앞에서 가무를 해야 하는가?
⑪ 왜 나는 방독면을 착용하고 가무를 해야 하는가?
⑫ 왜 나는 성경험을 고참에게 고백해야 하는가?
⑬ 왜 나는 잘못을 했을 때 생마늘과 양파를 먹어야 하는가?
⑭ 왜 나는 잘못한 줄도 모르면서 "시정하겠습니다."라고 해야 하는가?
⑮ 왜 나는 자다가 코를 좀 곯았다고 잠에서 깨워져서 다른 데로 가야하는가?

🔸 누구에게도 이런 말을 하지 마라

① 너는 이등병보다 못하다.
② 너의 자식들이 너 닮을까 걱정된다.
③ 너는 초등학교나 제대로 나왔냐?
④ 너는 일마다 망치는구나. 이 짜리몽땅한 것이!

Rules for privates

① I'll eat what I am given.

② I'll do just as I am told.

③ I'll be beaten whenever my seniors beat me.

④ I'll serve my seniors as I would serve God.

⑤ I'll always say what my seniors want to hear.

⑥ I'll be beaten to death when I defy[1] my seniors.

⑦ I'll shell[2] chestnuts with an X when I'm asked to by my seniors.

⑧ Restrooms are eternal oases for privates soldiers.

⑨ Harassing a senior is like raping a senior's wife.

⑩ Beating is a remedy for private soldiers who talk nonsense.

⑪ Juniors should shed tears whenever seniors feel sorrow.

⑫ A senior's breath is like a typhoon to private soldiers.

⑬ I'll toss my seniors shoulder-high[3] until my wrists break.

⑭ Seniors are alumni with God and drinking buddies with Buddha.

⑮ Although seniors make mistakes, all the responsibilities and consequences fall on private soldiers.

[해설] [1]defy [difái]: to refuse to obey sb or sth 거절하다, 무시하다: My son defied my wishes and joined the navy. 내 아들은 나의 바람을 거절하고 해군에 입대했다. [2]shell: to remove the shell or covering 까다, 벗기다: We shelled peanuts and put them in a bowl. 우리는 땅콩을 까서 사발에 담았다. [3]toss sb shoulder-high 헹가래 치다.

🔸 이등병 수칙

① 주면 주는 대로 먹는다.

② 시키면 시키는 대로 한다.

③ 때리면 때리는 대로 맞는다.

④ 고참을 하나님처럼 모신다.

⑤ 고참의 귀를 늘 즐겁게 한다.

⑥ 고참에게 대들면 피살(被殺)이다.

⑦ 고참이 X로 밤송이를 까래도 깐다.

⑧ 화장실은 이등병의 영원한 안식처이다.

⑨ 고참 희롱은 고참부인 강간과 동일하다.

⑩ 이등병의 헛소리에는 몽둥이가 약이다.

⑪ 고참이 슬플 때 쫄따구는 눈물을 흘려야 한다.

⑫ 고참의 숨소리는 이등병에겐 태풍이다.

⑬ 내 손목이 부러지도록 고참을 헹가래쳐주겠다.

⑭ 고참은 하나님과 동창이며 부처님과 술친구이다.

⑮ 고참이 잘못해도 책임은 이등병에게 있다.

◉ Let's not use these slang terms anymore

① a eola or byeongari (a baby or a baby chicken implying a new soldier)

② a wanggocham, a galcham or a peacham (a sergeant who is about to be discharged)

③ a ssogari (a mandarin fish implying a platoon leader)

④ a malddong (a horse dung implying the badge of a field grade officer[1])

⑤ a hobagssi (a pumpkin seed implying the badge of a warrant officer)

⑥ a babpulddeggi (boiled rice implying the badge of a company grade officer[2])

⑦ a judori (a sergeant major)

⑧ a gunbari (a derogatory word for a private soldier)

⑨ jjambab (food for soldiers at a mess hall in the military)

⑩ a gaemokgeri (a dog tag)

[해설] [1]field/mid grade officer 영관장교 (소령~대령). [2]company grade officer 위관장교. general officer 장관급 장교

◉ 이런 속어를 더 이상 사용하지 말자

① 얼라 혹은 병아리 (신병)

② 왕고참 혹은 갈참, 폐참 (전역 예정 병장)

③ 쏘가리 (쏘가리는 물고기로 소대장을 의미)

④ 말똥 (말똥으로 영관장교 계급장을 의미)

⑤ 호박씨 (호박씨로 준위 계급장을 의미)

⑥ 밥풀떼기 (삶은 쌀로 위관 장교 계급장을 의미)

⑦ 주도리 (주임 상사)

⑧ 군바리 (사병을 뜻하는 경멸적인 말)

⑨ 짬밥 (군대 식당에서 병사들의 식사)

⑩ 개목걸이 (군번줄)

Tips for serving in the military

① Be faithful to your direct senior.
② Get complete control over your direct juniors.
③ Try to always fit in with[1] your fellow soldiers.
④ Think of girls when you are having a tough time.
⑤ Officers and NCOs are internal enemies to their men.
⑥ Pretend that you're going to die if you get hurt slightly.
⑦ Playing soccer, singing and dancing are fundamental[2].
⑧ Never be the one punished to set examples for correct behavior[3].

[해설] [1]fit in (with) sb or sth: to be in harmony (with sb or sth) ~와 조화를 이루다: I'm not sure how she'll fit in with the other staff. 그녀가 다른 직원들과 잘 어울릴지 모르겠다. [2]fundamental [fʌndəméntl]: relating to the most important; basic; primary 중요한, 근본적인: Honesty is NOT a fundamental principle in a corrupt society. 부패한 사회에서 정직은 근본적인 원리가 못된다. [3]be punished to set examples for correct behavior 올바른 행동을 하도록 본보기(본데)로 처벌받다 → 시범케이스에 걸리다.

군대에서 근무요령

① 바로 윗 고참에게 엄청 잘해라.
② 바로 아랫 쫄다구를 확 잡아라.
③ 뭐든지 중간만 해라.
④ 힘들 때일수록 여자 생각을 해라.
⑤ 간부들은 병들에겐 내부의 적이다.
⑥ 쫌만 다치면 무조건 죽는 시늉해라.
⑦ 축구, 노래와 춤은 기본이다.
⑧ 시범케이스가 되지 마라.

🟠 Gunbaries' reward for,

① one hour's waiting is to get a 10 minute break.
② half a day's waiting is to eat jjambab.
③ one day's waiting is to go to bed.
④ two days' waiting is to get a pack of cigarettes.
⑤ one week's waiting is to get a pack of hardtack biscuits.
⑥ one month's waiting is to receive a month's pay.
⑦ one and a half months' waiting is to get an overnight pass.
⑧ three months' waiting is to get a bonus.
⑨ nine months' waiting is to get leave.
⑩ three years' waiting is to get a discharge.

* Gunbaries' lives are a continuation of waiting to the end!

🟠 군바리의 기다림에 대한 보상은,

① 한 시간의 기다림은 10분간 휴식이요.
② 한나절의 기다림은 짬밥이요.
③ 하루의 기다림은 취침이요.
④ 이틀의 기다림은 담배요.
⑤ 한 주의 기다림은 건빵이요.
⑥ 한 달의 기다림은 월급이요.
⑦ 달 반의 기다림은 외박이요.
⑧ 석 달의 기다림은 보너스요.
⑨ 아홉 달의 기다림은 휴가요.
⑩ 삼 년의 기다림은 전역이다.

* 군바리의 삶은 끝까지 기다림의 연속이다!

◐ Gunbaries' 10 deadly enemies

① Waking up when it's time to fall asleep.
② Break is over when it's time to take a rest.
③ Meal time is over when it's time to eat.
④ Lights out when it's time to write a letter.
⑤ Fatigue begins when it's time to study.
⑥ Emergency calls when it's time to take leave.
⑦ Surprise roll calls when it's time to go to the PX.
⑧ The stopping or curtailing[1] of daily passes and overnight passes whenever visited.
⑨ Wearing full combat gear[2] in the summer.
⑩ Eating ice cream in the winter.

[해설] [1]curtail [kəːrtéil]: to cut back; shorten: 박탈/삭감하다: He had to curtail his speech when time ran out. 그는 시간이 없어서 연설을 줄여야 했다. [2]gear: special equipment, clothing, etc. that you need for a particular activity: (특정 목적을 위해 사용되는) 옷/장비: Don't forget to bring hiking/camping gear. 하이킹/등산 장비 가지고 오는 것을 잊지 말라. full combat gear 완전군장: Lebanese army troops in full combat gear and armored cars are deployed…. 완전무장한 레바논 군인과 장갑차들이 전개되고 ….

◐ 군바리 10대 강적

① 잠들 만하면 기상
② 쉴 만하면 휴식 끝
③ 먹을 만하면 식사 끝
④ 편지 쓸 만하면 소등
⑤ 공부 할 만하면 작업
⑥ 휴가 갈 만하면 비상
⑦ PX 가려고 하면 불시 인원파악
⑧ 면회만 오면 외출·외박 통제
⑨ 여름에 완전 무장
⑩ 겨울에 아이스크림 먹기

● A soldier's seven evils[1]

① He who doesn't salute his seniors.

② He who isn't faithful to his seniors.

③ He who gives a false report.

④ He who is poor at marksmanship[2].

⑤ He who can't carry out his duties successfully.

⑥ He who emphasizes his age rather than his ability.

⑦ He who is sullen[3] all day after being scolded for something once.

[해설] [1]evil: extremely bad, wicked 매우 나쁜, 악: He tries to hurt people; he's evil. [2]marksmanship: the ability to shoot skillfully 사격술. [3]sullen [sʌlən]: showing that you are in a bad mood by being silent and looking unhappy 부루퉁한, 실쭉한

● Enlisted personnel are required to salute all commissioned officers. Even a brand-new second lieutenant "officially" outranks the highest-ranking enlisted member, the Sergeant Major of the Army.

● 군인의 칠거지악

① 상관에게 경례를 하지 않는 자

② 상관에 충성하지 않는 자

③ 허위 보고하는 자

④ 사격을 못하는 자

⑤ 자신의 직무를 성공적으로 수행하지 못하는 자

⑥ 자신의 능력보다는 나이를 내세우는 자

⑦ 한번 혼났다고 종일 시무룩한 자

● 모든 사병은 장교들에게 경례를 해야 한다. 심지어 갓 임관한 신임 소위도 사병에서 가장 높은 육군 주임원사보다 공식적으로는 계급이 더 높다.

🟢 A soldier's complaints

If I go home on a starlit night, that's AWOL.
If I fall asleep, that's neglect of duty.
If I act cheerful, that's a violation of military discipline.
If I talk back, they say I'm poorly disciplined.
If I drink, I would be confined in military prison.
What kind of human beings do they want soldiers to be?
However, the last hope is that the clock in the Ministry of National Defense never stops ticking.

🟢 군바리 하소연

별이 빛나는 밤 집에 가자니, 탈영이요.
잠을 자자니, 근무 태만이요.
기분 내자니, 군기 위반이요.
말대꾸하자니, 군기 빠졌다지.
술을 마시자니, 영창이라.
도대체 군바리는 어떠한 인간이라는 말인가?
하지만 마지막 희망이 있다면 국방부 시계는
쉼 없이 돌아가고 있다는 것이다.

◯ The origins of military training

① Wire entanglements came into existence because of Seoul gunbaries trying to escape from boot camp.

② First-come-first-served came into existence because of slow Chungchung-do gunbaries.

③ **Julbbadda** came into existence because of disobedient Gyeongsang -do gunbaries.

④ River-crossing training came into existence because of Jeju-do gunbaries living in the water.

⑤ Ranger training came into existence because of Gangwon-do gunbaries living in the mountains.

⑥ Two hundred kilometer marching came into existence because of Ulleung-do gunbaries living on an island.

⑦ Checking personnel came into existence because of sly Gyeonggi-do gunbaries.

⑧ Night guard duty came into existence because of cunning Jella-do gunbaries.

* **Julbbadda** means that a soldier beats lower ranking soldiers with a bat, and this continues down to the lowest rank.

* "do" stands for "province" or "island."

🔹 군대 훈련의 유래

① 탈영하는 서울 군바리 때문에 철조망이 생겼고

② 동작 느린 충청도 군바리 때문에 선착순이 생겼고

③ 말 안 듣는 경상도 군바리 때문에 줄빠따가 생겼고

④ 물에 사는 제주 군바리 때문에 도하훈련이 생겼고

⑤ 산에 사는 강원도 군바리 때문에 유격훈련이 생겼고

⑥ 섬에 사는 울릉도 군바리 때문에 200Km 행군이 생겼고

⑦ 뺀질거리는 경기도 군바리 때문에 인원파악이 생겼고

⑧ 약삭빠른 전라도 군바리 때문에 불침번이 생겼다.

＊ **줄빠따**는 군인이 자기보다 낮은 계급의 군인을 방망이로 엉덩이를 때리는 것으로, 이것이 가장 낮은 계급까지 계속된다.

Reporting for one's leave

[Master Sgt.: Private]

Reporting as ordered, sir.
Private First Class Kim Kil-dong,
ordered to go on leave
from July 28 through August 2, 2002.
Reporting as ordered!

M: Is this your first leave since you joined the military?

P : Yes, the **100th-day's leave**, sir!

M: What are you going to do on your leave?

P : I'm going to visit my parents and relatives.

M: You don't have a girlfriend, do you?

P : No, not yet. sir!

M: When you're out on your first leave, every female who wears a skirt looks beautiful. Be careful! Even a small snake[1] has some poison!

* Five days and four nights leave is allowed to the enlisted soldiers on the 100th day after they entered the military.

* Leave is authorized absence from the military and is of longer duration than a one-day pass or an overnight pass. The duration of a leave is from one day to about 20 days. Kinds of leave are: annual leave, leave on official reason, petitionary leave, leave after arduous duty, prize furlough, parental leave, sick leave, etc.

[해설] [1]snake: a bad, dishonest person 음흉한 사람, 배신자: That snake never paid me the money he owed me. 저놈은 나한테 빌린 돈을 한 번도 갚지 않았다.

휴가신고

신고합니다. 일병 김길동은
2002년 7월 28일부터 8월 2일까지
휴가를 명 받았습니다.
이에 신고합니다!

상사: 이번이 네가 군대 와서 첫 휴가지?
일병: 예, 100일 휴가입니다.
상사: 휴가 때 뭐할 거냐?
일병: 부모님과 친척들을 방문할 예정입니다.
상사: 너 여자 친구는 없지, 그렇지?
일병: 예, 아직 없습니다.
상사: 100일 만에 밖으로 나가면 치마를 입은 여자는 모두 예뻐 보일 거다.
　　　조심해! 작은 뱀이라도 조금의 독은 가지고 있다.

* 병사들은 입대 후 100일째 4박5일간의 휴가를 받는다.

* 휴가란 직무에서 공적으로 면제되는 것으로 외출이나 외박보다 길다. 휴가 기간은 하루에서 약 20일 정도 된다. 그 종류는 연가, 공가(公暇), 청원휴가, 위로휴가, 포상휴가, 출산휴가, 병가 등이 있다.

🔸 I am not the unit's kitchen maid!

Get me some water. Yes, sir!
Make some coffee. Yes, sir!
Get me a cigarette. Yes, sir!
Get me a lighter. Yes, sir!
Clean up the table. Yes, sir!
I am sorry. I am not the unit's kitchen maid, sir!

🔸 저는 부대 식모가 아닙니다!

물 좀 가져와라. 예, 알겠습니다!
커피 좀 타 와라. 예, 알겠습니다!
담배 좀 가져와라. 예, 알겠습니다!
라이터 좀 가져와라. 예, 알겠습니다!
테이블 좀 치워라. 예, 알겠습니다!
죄송합니다. 저는 부대 식모가 아닙니다!

◎ The purpose of taking a one-day pass, an overnight pass, etc.

The purpose of taking a one-day pass, an overnight pass and going on leave is to let soldiers leave their barracks life temporarily, settle their private and/or family business, relieve their fatigue so that they can lead a cheerful barracks life, and be highly motivated for military duty.

◎ 외출·외박의 목적

외출·외박 및 휴가의 목적은 군인으로 하여금 병영으로부터 일시적으로 떠나 영외에서 각종 용무를 해결하거나 집안일을 돕고 심신의 피로를 회복하게 함으로써 사기를 높여 병영 생활의 명랑 화를 기하고 나아가 군복무에 대한 의욕을 북돋우는데 있다.

◎ On the 100th-day's Leave 100일 휴가

A: Look! Who's this?	이게 누구냐?
B: How's it hanging?	그 동안 잘 지냈어?
A: I'm doing great. Are you on leave now?	잘 지냈지. 너는 휴가야?
B: Yes, I'm on the 100th-day's leave.	그래, 100일 휴가 나왔어.
A: When are you going back?	언제 복귀해?
B: Next Saturday.	다음 주 토요일.
A: Then let's have a drink next week.	다음 주 한잔하자.
B: OK. I'll call you tonight.	알았어. 오늘밤 전화할게.

🔸 The last day of leave

At the moment I am going to go back after a lightning leave,
I am shaking at the thought of going back into the military, it's worse than dying.

If I had felt this earlier, I would have slept an hour less and seen her face once more before coming back[1].
I would have slept an hour less and eaten more chicken and delicious food[2].

Oh ~, how happy I would be if this were a mere nightmare[3].
Now I can understand the guys who go AWOL.
I wish I could disappear like smoke after a deep sigh[4].

↱ would, could, should, might

[해설] [1, 2]는 "If + S + had + pp, S + **wcsm** + have + pp."는 가정법 과거완료 형태로 병사가 휴가를 다녀온 뒤 휴가 기간 중에 잠을 덜자고 좀 더 알차게 보냈어야 하는 후회, 미련, 아쉬움을 표현하고 있다. [3, 4]는 가정법 과거(I would be ~. I wish I could disappear ~ .) 로서 현재에서 어찌할 수 없는 심정을 표현하고 있다.

🔸 휴가의 마지막 날

휴가가 번개같이 흘러가고 군대로 복귀하는 순간
다시 들어가기가 죽기보다 더 싫어 몸서리치네요.

이럴 줄 알았으면
잠 한 시간 덜 자고 그녀 얼굴 한 번 더 보고 오는 건데.
잠 한 시간 덜 자고 치킨과 맛난 것 많이 좀 먹는 건데.

오~, 이것이 악몽이라면 얼마나 좋겠어요.
탈영하는 녀석들의 심정이 이제 이해가 가네요.
제가 긴 한숨과 담배연기처럼 사라졌으면 좋겠어요.

🔵 My gf has already found a new bf

I am on my 100th-day's leave now.
But my gf has already found a new bf.
Her new bf is my senior classmate,
a member of the social circle I joined in the same college.

Before I joined the army he said
"I will take good care of your gf."
Are there any guys we can trust?
Now I've got back the ring and photos from her.

My footsteps on my way to the base are heavy.
You are a bitch.
A girl who changes her rubber shoes should be punished by Heaven!

🔵 내 여친이 벌써 새 남친을

100일 휴가를 나왔져.
벌써 여친에게는 남친이 생겼더라구여.
그녀의 새 남친은 나의 선배로
나와 같은 학교 서클 회원이었죠.

내가 군대 가기 전에 그는
"내가 네 여친 잘 돌봐줄게" 라고 했는데.
세상에 믿을 넘이 있을까?
이제 반지, 사진도 다 돌려 받았어요.

부대로 복귀하는 발이 무겁군요.
개 같은 눈.
곰신 바꿔 신는 여자는 천벌을 받아야 한다!

What you don't talk about to your girlfriend

① Talking about the military.
② Talking about soccer.
③ Talking about having played soccer in the military.

* It is known that young men in England were encouraged to play soccer in order to make them tired and weaken their sexual desire. And this is one of the factors which led to England becoming a strong soccer nation. Then is soccer encouraged to reduce sex crimes in the military?

여친에게 말하지 말 것은

① 군대 얘기.
② 축구 얘기.
③ 군대에서 축구 한 얘기.

* 영국에서는 청소년들의 신체를 피곤하게 만들어 성욕을 감퇴시킬 목적으로 축구가 권장되었던 것으로 알려졌다. 이것이 영국을 축구 강국으로 만든 요인 중의 하나다. 그럼, 군대에서는 성범죄를 줄일 목적으로 축구를 권장하는 것일까?

🍂 Shake the trees

A: I'm tired of sweeping the leaves every day.

B: Let's shake the trees until all the leaves fall.

A: If we're noticed by the command sergeant major, we'll get into big trouble.

B: It's better to be punished, though.

A: How can we sweep fallen leaves every morning! Don't the streets covered with recently fallen leaves look very romantic?

B: Yeah, I don't understand what we gain from sweeping leaves every day. Anyway we are not living on a university campus.

A: Maybe our command sergeant major knows a deeper meaning.

🍂 The definition of "fallen leaves" in the military
Fallen leaves are objects that are of almost no value as compost to trees but they mess up the environment and cause forest fires, so they have to be eliminated immediately after they fall.

🍂 나무를 흔들어

A: 매일 낙엽 쓰는데 지쳤다.

B: 잎들이 다 떨어질 때까지 나무를 흔들자.

A: 그러다 주임원사님에게 들키면 혼나.

B: 그래도 벌 받는 게 낳다.

A: 어떻게 매일 아침마다 낙엽을 쓸어? 낙엽으로 덮인 거리가 매우 낭만적이지 않아?

B: 맞아. 매일 우리가 낙엽을 쓸어서 얻는 게 뭔지 모르겠어. 어쨌든 우리는 대학 캠퍼스에 사는 게 아니야.

A: 우리 주임원사님은 더 깊은 의미를 아시겠지.

🍂 군대에서 "낙엽"에 대한 정의
낙엽은 나무의 거름으로서도 거의 가치가 없으며 주위만 어지럽히고 산불을 유발하는 존재로서 떨어지는 즉시 제거되어야 할 대상이다.

◎ Why trees don't grow well in the military

① They have to get up too early. (∵ morning roll-call)
② They are sleepless at night. (∵ emergency training)
③ They have cold feet. (∵ all fallen leaves are swept off)
④ They are often transferred. (∵ by order of the Commander)
⑤ They are often shaken. (∵ the last leaf is the soldiers' enemy)
⑥ They have to breathe salty dust. (∵ during soldiers' formation drills)
⑦ Their skins are often taken off. (∵ objects of practicing a tug-of-war)
⑧ They are often cursed by instructors. (∵ "shout until all the leaves fall!")
⑨ They are often kicked. (∵ objects of kicking when practicing taekwondo)
⑩ They often have to "stand like statues." (∵ regular inspections and frequent visits by VIPs)

◎ 군대에서 나무가 잘 자라지 않는 이유

① 너무 일찍 일어나야 한다. (∵ 일조점호)
② 밤에 잠을 설친다. (∵ 비상 훈련)
③ 발이 시리다. (∵ 낙엽을 다 쓸어간다)
④ 전속을 가끔 다닌다. (∵ 지휘관의 명령에 의해)
⑤ 종종 흔들린다. (∵ 마지막 잎새는 병사의 적이다)
⑥ 짠 먼지를 마셔야 한다. (∵ 병사들의 제식훈련 기간)
⑦ 껍질이 가끔 벗겨진다. (∵ 체육대회 때 줄다리기 연습 대상)
⑧ 종종 교관들의 저주를 받는다. (∵ "나뭇잎이 다 떨어지도록 큰 소리로 외쳐!")
⑨ 종종 발에 차인다. (∵ 태권도에서 발차기 연습의 대상)
⑩ 종종 "동상처럼" 서 있어야 한다. (∵ 정기 검열과 잦은 VIP방문)

🟢 CBR warfare is declared

A: What a smell! CBR warfare is declared!

B: It smells like rotten eggs or potatoes.

A: Was it you, Sgt. Park? Surrender[1].

B: No, don't be suspicious[2] of an innocent person.

A: Wasn't it you, Sgt. Kim?

C: Oh, I'm sorry. This morning I ate boiled barley.

A: Please, go out and fart[3]!

∗ CBR: Chemical, Biological and Radiological (warfare) (군사) 화생방(전)

[해설] [1]surrender [səréndər]: to give into the demands of sb: ~의 요구에 응하다, 항복하다. [2]suspicious[səspíʃəs]: feeling that you do not like or trust sb or sth 의심스러운. [3]fart [fɑːrt]: gas coming from the anus 방귀, 방귀뀌다(=break wind)

🟢 화생방 경보 발령

A: 어 냄새! 화생방 경보 발령!

B: 계란이나 감자 썩은 냄새 같군.

A: 박병장, 너지? 자수해.

B: 아니, 생사람 잡지마!

A: 김병장 너 아냐?

C: 오, 미안. 오늘 아침에 보리밥을 먹어서.

A: 제발 좀 나가서 뀌어라.

Announcement of MOPP 4

[Senior : Junior]

S: What's the siren for?

J: It's the announcement for MOPP[1] 4.

S: What's MOPP 4?

J: At this phase, we have to put on a gas mask, the ground crew ensemble(GCE)[2], rubber boots and rubber gloves.

S: Let's put them on quickly. I think my gas mask is leaking.

J: Mine is okay, sir.

S: You make sure that mine is fixed next time.

J: Yes, sir.

* [1] MOPP: Mission Oriented Protective Posture (임무형 보호 태세)
  [2] GCE(Ground Crew Ensemble, 침투보호의; 浸透保護衣)

MOPP 4단계 발령

고참: 무슨 사이렌이냐?

신참: MOPP 4단계 발령입니다

고참: MOPP 4단계가 뭐야?

신참: 예, MOPP 4단계에서는 방독면, 보호의, 덧신, 장갑을 착용해야 합니다.

고참: 그래, 빨리 착용하자. 내 방독면은 새는 것 같다.

신참: 제 것은 괜찮은 것 같습니다.

고참: 다음에 내 것 좀 수리해 놓아라.

신참: 알겠습니다.

Reporting one's promotion

[Private Kim : First Sgt.]

Reporting as ordered, sir.
Private First Class Kim, Kil-dong,
ordered to be promoted to Corporal
as of January 3, 2002.
Reporting as ordered!

FS: Congratulations! Now you're a corporal!
PK: No reward for my promotion, sir?
FS: Have an extra tray of lunch at the mess hall.
PK: That's very heartless of you, sir!

진급신고

신고합니다. 일병 김길동은
2002년 1월 3일부로
상병으로 진급을 명 받았습니다.
이에 신고합니다!

부사관: 축하해! 너 이제 상병 되었구나!
이 병: 제 진급에 뭐 없습니까?
부사관: 식당에서 점심 더블 츄라이 해라.
이 병: 선임 부사관님, 너무 하십니다!

◎ He is still sleeping

[Senior : Junior]

S: Hey, wake up Corporal Kim.

J: Yes, sir!

S: It's been a long time since the morning bugle[1].
   How come he is still sleeping?

[해설] [1]bugle: a musical instrument like a trumpet, which is used in the army to call soldiers (군대) 나팔

◎ 아직도 자고 있어

고참: 야, 저기 김상병 깨워라.

후참: 예 알겠습니다.

고참: 기상나팔이 울린 지 언젠데.
   어떻게 아직도 자고 있나?

◎ If it were not for a roll call…

A: It's almost roll call time. Let's go clean our rooms.

B: Can't roll-call be abolished? It's annoying to have it every day.

A: We keep our barracks clean only because of roll call.

B: In the military, a day begins and ends with roll call.

◎ 점호만 없어도

A: 야, 점호시간 다됐다. 청소하러 가자.

B: 점호 좀 안 없어지나? 매일 점호 받기 짜증나.

A: 점호라도 있기에 숙소가 깨끗이 유지되지.

B: 군대에서의 하루는 점호로 시작해서 점호로 끝나지.

How are you going to be punished?

[Platoon leader : Corporal Kim]

PL: Do you admit your misconduct[1] today?

CK: Yes, sir.

PL: How are you going to be punished?

CK: I will just accept your decision.

PL: Would you write a separate letter of regret every day for five days or would you like to receive ten strokes with a baseball bat?

CK: I prefer to get ten strokes.

[해설] [1]misconduct: misbehavior; wrongdoing 비행, 나쁜 짓: Jack fought with other students and was expelled from school for misconduct. 잭은 다른 학생과 싸워서 나쁜 행위로 퇴학되었다.

어떻게 처벌 받을래?

소대장: 너 오늘 잘못을 인정하지?

김상병: 예, 그렇습니다.

소대장: 어떻게 처벌 받을 거야?

김상병: 결정에 따르겠습니다.

소대장: 반성문을 5일간 계속 쓸래, 아니면 야구 빠따로 10대 맞을래?

김상병: 10대 맞는 게 더 좋습니다.

How will you be punished?

You admit your wrongdoing, don't you?
How will you be punished? You have four choices.
First, would you like to be punished according to the regulations?
Second, would you like to hand in[1] 10 separate letters of apology?
Third, would you like to receive 10 strokes with a baseball bat?
Or fourth, would you fix me up with a beautiful girl?

[해설] [1]hand in: to submit; to present 제출하다: The student handed in her term paper right on time. 그 학생은 정시에 시험지를 제출했다.

어떻게 처벌 받을래?

너는 너의 잘못을 인정하지?
어떻게 처벌 받을래? 네 가지 방법이 있다.
첫째, 규정에 따라 처벌 받을래?
둘째, 반성문을 10회 제출할래?
셋째, 야구 배트로 10대 맞을래?
넷째, 나에게 예쁜 여자 하나 소개시켜 줄래?

● Show me your dog tags

[Platoon leader : Sergeant Kim]

P: Sgt. Kim, where are your dog tags[1]?

S: They are in a desk drawer back in the office.

P: You should hang them around your neck according to regulations.

S: I wish I could wear them only during operational training.

P: Nobody knows when accidents will happen.

[해설] [1]dog tag: a small piece of metal marked with one's name and service number 군번줄 (a soldier's identification tag)

● 군번줄 보자

소대장: 김병장, 너는 인식표 어디 있나?

김병장: 사무실 책상 서랍 안에 있습니다.

소대장: 규정에 항상 목에 차게 되어 있잖아?

김병장: 작전에 나갈 때만 착용했으면 좋겠습니다.

소대장: 언제 무슨 일이 일어날 줄 아나.

🔸 Let's see at tonight's roll-call

    Seniors are sweating repairing the fox holes, but you rookies are smoking there! Let's see at tonight's roll call. You will pay for[1] that. Once unexploded bombs, mines, bullets are found, report them immediately. Bear in mind[2] that handling unexploded bombs and misfired ammunition may lead to tragic consequences for yourself and your comrades.

[해설] [1]pay for: suffer or be punished for doing something 대가를 치루다, 보복하다: If you drink any more, you'll be paying for it in the morning. 술을 더 마신다면 내일 아침에 대가를 치룰 것이다. [2]bear in mind: to remember 기억하다, 명심하다: Bear in mind that he was only 19 years old when he was drafted into the army. 그가 징병되었을 때는 오직 19세이었음을 기억하라.

🔸 오늘 일석점호 때 보자

    고참들은 전투호 보수한다고 땀을 뻘뻘 흘리는데, 너희 신병 녀석들은 거기서 담배나 피우고 있어! 오늘 점호시간에 보자. 그에 대한 대가를 치르게 될 거다. 불발탄, 지뢰, 실탄이 발견되면 발견 즉시 보고해라. 불발탄을 함부로 다룬다는 것은 나와 전우의 생명을 앗아갈 수 있다는 것을 명심해라.

🔵 Roll-call is over

[Duty officer : Barracks leader]

DO: Physical harassment is not happening these days, huh?

BL: No, it's not happening anymore, sir.

DO: I see, roll call is over.

BL: Pilsung!

DO: Go to bed early.

Watching TV isn't allowed tonight because you guys are going on a thousand-ri march tomorrow.

* Pilsung (loyalty), Chungsung (fidelity), Dangyul (unity) and other catchphrases are used in giving and receiving hand salutes in the Korean military. These are different from unit to unit and between different sections of the armed forces.

🔵 점호 끝

당직사관: 요즘은 구타 같은 거 없지?

내무반장: 예, 더 이상 없습니다.

당직사관: 그래, 점호 끝.

내무반장: 필승!

당직사관: 일찍 자라.

금일 TV 시청은 없다.

왜냐하면 내일 너희들 천리행군을 떠나기 때문이다.

* 필승, 충성, 단결 그리고 다른 구호들은 한국 군대에서 거수경례를 주고받을 때 사용된다. 이는 부대 및 각 군에 따라 다르다.

To take a bed-check

[Squad leader : Corporal Kim]

SL: You guys need to square things away[1] tonight.

CK: Who is the DO(duty officer)[2] tonight?

SL: Lt. Kim. Why do you ask?

CK: Isn't he somewhat easygoing?

SL: Do the basics, though.

　　　Shine the boots and square away the bed.

CK: I think we have a bed-check.

　　　All day, today, we broke our back[3] helping farmers on the farm.

SL: I'll ask the DO to take a bed-check.

[해설] [1]square ~ away; to put things away or in order 치우다/정리하다: Make sure your room is squared away. 방 정리 잘 해 놓아라. [2]DO(Duty Officer) 당직사관. Field Officer of the Day(FOD) 당직사령. Charge of Quarters(CQ)당직부사관(부사관 1명, 병사1명으로 구성되어 점호 등 점검). [3]broke one's back: 뼈 빠지게 고생하다. For the first few years after I came to the States, I had to break my back. 미국에 와서 처음 2, 3년 동안 뼈 빠지게 일해야 했다.

취침점호

분대장: 너희들 오늘밤 정리 잘해라.

김상병: 오늘 당직사관 누구시죠?

분대장: 김중위님. 왜?

김상병: 그분은 좀 널널하지 않습니까?

분대장: 그래도 기본은 해라.

　　　군화 손질과 침구 각도 잡고.

김상병: 오늘 취침점호 하겠지.

　　　오늘 하루 종일 대민지원 가서 뼈 빠지게 고생했는데.

분대장: 내가 당직사관님께 취침점호 하자고 말씀 드려볼게.

◎ The origin of the one thousand-ri march

A: Do you happen to know when the one thousand-ri march began?
B: After Kim Shin-Jo's group came over here in 1975.
A: How come people call it "one thousand-ri march?"
B: Because it's one thousand-ri from Seoul to Pyongyang.

◎ 천리 행군의 기원

A: 너, 천리행군이 언제부터 생겼는지 아니?
B: 1975년 김신조 일당이 넘어온 뒤로부터요.
A: 왜 천리행군이라 하지?
B: 그야 서울부터 평양까지가 천리니까 그렇지.

◎ Like a defeated troop

A: Who are those guys, walking like a defeated[1] troop?
B: They are the Homeland Reserve Forces.
A: I don't know why people act like that when they put on a reserve forces uniform.

[해설] [1]defeat [difí:t]: to beat, win a victory over 쳐부수다, 이기다: They defeated the enemy after a long war. 그들은 오랜 전쟁 후에 적을 이겼다.

◎ 패잔병처럼

A: 패잔병처럼 걸어가는 사람 누구냐?
B: 예비군들입니다.
A: 사람들이 예비군복만 입으면 왜 저렇게 행동하는지 모르겠어.

◯ Conversation with the commander

[Commander : Enlisted soldier]

C: What do you do on weekends or holidays?

E: We do sports most of the time, sir.

C: How often do you get a pass?

E: Every 6 weeks we go on overnight pass for 3 days and 2 nights.

C: How often do you receive hardtack biscuits?

E: Once a week, sir.

C: How about ramon noodles?

E: We get them 6 times a month.

C: While you're in the military, learn English and computers. It'll be a big help when you're discharged[1].

[해설] [1]discharge: to officially allow sb to go or to send him/her away from a place (어디로 공식적으로) 보내다: After his discharge from the army, he got married. 그는 전역 후 결혼했다.

◯ 대대장님과 대화

대대장: 주말과 휴일은 어떻게 보내나?
병　사: 주로 운동을 합니다.
대대장: 외박은 자주 나가나?
병　사: 6주마다 2박3일씩 나갑니다.
대대장: 건빵은 얼마나 자주 나오나?
병　사: 일주일에 한 번씩 나옵니다.
대대장: 라면은?
병　사: 한 달에 6회 받습니다.
대대장: 군대 있을 때 영어와 컴퓨터를 배워둬라.
　　　　제대하면 큰 도움이 될 거야.

🔸 The gist of challenges[1]   수하 요령

- Halt! 　　　　　　　　　　정지!
- Hands up! 　　　　　　　　손들어!
- If you move, I will fire! 　움직이면, 쏜다!
- Password! 　　　　　　　　암호!
- Who goes there? 　　　　　누구냐?
- What's your business? 　　용무는?
- Proceed three steps! 　　　3보 앞으로!

[해설] [1]challenge: to question 질문하다, 수하(誰何) 하다: "Who goes there?/Who's there?" challenged a soldier on guard. "누구냐"하고 근무 중인 초병이 수하했다. "Hands up or we will shoot!" "손들어, 들지 않으면 쏜다!"

🔸 Going on sentry duty   보초 서로 가다

A: Sgt. Kim, have a beer. 　　　　　　　김병장, 맥주 한잔해.
B: I have to go on sentry duty. 　　　　저 보초 서러 가야 합니다.
A: I thought you came off sentry duty. 나는 네가 보초서고 온 줄 알았다.
B: Enjoy the beer, sir. 　　　　　　　　맥주 드십시오.
A: Take care, Sgt. Kim. 　　　　　　　　김병장 수고해.

Challenge I

[Company commander : Sentry guard]

SG: Hands up!

CC: (puts his hands up)

SG: Turn around!

CC: (turns around)

SG: (in a low voice) Seoul.

CC: (in a low voice) Potato.

SG: What's your business?

CC: On patrol.

GS: Chung Sung! On duty, sir!

CC: The wind cuts like a knife[1]. Be careful not to catch a cold.

SG: Chung Sung! I'll keep on[2] doing my duty, sir!

[해설] [1]cut like a knife: (바람 등이) 살을 에듯이 차다. [2]keep on: to continue to do sth 계속하다: Even after I asked her to shut up, she kept on talking. 내가 그녀에게 말을 그만하라고 했지만 그녀는 계속 말했다.

수하 I

초 병: 손들어!
중대장: (손을 든다)
초 병: 뒤로 돌아!
중대장: (뒤로 돈다)
초 병: (작은 목소리로) 서울.
중대장: (작은 목소리로) 감자.
초 병: 용무는?
중대장: 순찰 중이다.
초 병: 충성! 근무 중!
중대장: 바람이 살을 에듯이 차다. 추운데 감기 조심해라.
초 병: 충성! 계속 근무!

Challenge II

[Company commander : Sentry guard]

SG: Halt[1]!
CC: I'm company commander.
GS: Halt!
CC: Hey, I'm your company commander!
SG: I know, but you have to be challenged, sir! Hands up! Show me your back!
CC: (puts his hands up and turns around)
SG: (in a whispering voice) F-15.
CC: (in a whispering voice) Linda.
SG: Pil-Sung! I'm doing my duty, sir!
CC: You're doing a good job. Take care.
SG: Pil-Sung! I'll keep on doing my duty, sir!

[해설] [1]halt: to stop or make sth stop 중지하다, 중지시키다. Do you remember that one of the former defense ministers had an inappropriate relationship with a female lobbyist named Linda? 너는 전 국방부 장관 중의 한 사람이 린다라는 여자 로비스트와 부적절한 관계를 가졌다는 것을 기억하니?

수하 II

초 병: 정지!
중대장: 나 중대장이다.
초 병: 정지!
중대장: 야, 중대장이라니까!
초 병: 하지만, 중대장님도 수하를 받아야 합니다.
      손들어! 뒤로 돌아!
중대장: (손을 들고 뒤로 돈다)
초 병: (속삭이는 목소리로) F-15.
중대장: (속삭이는 목소리로) 린다.
초 병: 필승! 근무 중!
중대장: 너, 근무 잘 서는구나. 수고해라.
초 병: 필승! 계속 근무!

⬤ Challenging an unidentified car

[Sentry guard : Patrolling officer]

SG: Stop!

PO: (after the car stops)

SG: Headlights off!

PO: (after the headlights are off)

SG: Get out of the car.

PO: (after getting out of the car)

SG: Turn around and raise your hands.

PO: (after raising his hands)

SG: (after advancing and whispering) Widow.

PO: (answering in a whispering voice) Cucumber.

SG: Pil-Sung! No, problems, sir!

PO: Let me take your rifle.

SG: No, sir. My rifle is another me!

PO: OK, take care. Corporal Kim.

SG: Pil-sung! I'll carry on, sir!

🔶 차량 수하

초 병: 정지!

순찰장교: (차가 멈춘 뒤에)

초 병: 헤드라이트 꺼!

순찰장교: (헤드라이트 꺼진 뒤에)

초 병: 차에서 하차.

순찰장교: (하차 후에)

초 병: 뒤로 돌아, 손들어.

순찰장교: (손을 든 후에)

초 병: (다가가서 속삭이는 목소리로) 과부.

순찰장교: (속삭이는 대답으로) 오이.

초 병: 필승! 근무 중 이상 무!

순찰장교: 네 총 좀 보자.

초 병: 안됩니다. 총기는 제2의 생명입니다!

순찰장교: 알았다. 김상병 수고해.

초 병: 필승! 계속 근무!

The codes of sentry duty

[Senior : New soldier]

S: How long has it been since you were assigned here?

N: Three weeks, sir!

S: Then you have memorized all the codes of sentry duty?

N: Yes, sir!

S: Then what's number three in the code?

N: Well, uh…

S: Didn't you memorize it yet?

N: Yes, sir!

S: Then why didn't you answer me immediately?

N: I memorized it, but I'm too nervous to…

S: I'll check again tomorrow night.

보초수칙

고참: 너, 여기 배속된 지 얼마나 됐냐?

신병: 3주 됐습니다.

고참: 그럼 근무수칙 다 암기할 수 있지?

신병: 예, 그렇습니다.

고참: 그럼 보초 수칙 3번이 뭐냐?

신병: 저….

고참: 아직도 암기 못했어?

신병: 아닙니다.

고참: 그럼 왜 바로 대답 못해.

신병: 외웠습니다만, 너무 긴장해서….

고참: 내일 밤에 다시 확인하겠다.

● Eating hardtack biscuits on guard

A: Do you have some hardtack left?

B: Hardtack at midnight?

A: I'm starving[1]!

B: You shouldn't eat on guard duty.

A: Nobody can see us now.

B: Who is tonight's DO?

A: Capt. Kim.

B: He is not the kind of person to patrol at this time.

A: Yes, if he comes here now, that would be strange.

* A Marine on duty has no friends. - Marine Corps proverb-

[해설] [1]starve [stɑːrv]: to be very hungry 매우 배고픈: I'm starving; let's have a big dinner. 배고파 죽겠다. 저녁 많이 먹자.

● 근무 중에 건빵 먹기

A: 건빵 남은 거 있나?

B: 이 밤에 웬 건빵?

A: 배고파 죽겠어!

B: 근무 중에 취식하면 안 돼.

A: 아무도 보는 사람 없어.

B: 오늘밤 당직사관은 누구야?

A: 김 대위님.

B: 그는 이 시간에 순찰할 사람이 아니야.

A: 맞아, 지금 그가 여기 오면 비정상이지.

*해병대는 근무 중에 친구가 없다. - 해병대 격언-

◎ Athlete's foot

A: I go crazy every summer.

B: Why?

A: Because of athlete's foot[1].

B: Dry out your boots.

A: Do you have some ointment[2] for athlete's foot?

B: Use this medicine. A U.S. soldier gave me.
   It seems to be making me better.

A: I heard that after having served in the military, only athlete's foot and dandruff[3] remain. Athlete's foot is the result of going on a 1,000-ri march and dandruff is due to being punished by being made to put your head down.

B: Once you are infected[4] with athlete's foot in the military, it stays with you until your 60th birthday.

[해설] [1]athlete's foot: a type of skin disease that causes itching in the skin between the toes 무좀. [2]ointment [ɔ́intmənt]: a soft oily substance that you rub into your skin 연고, 고약. [3]dandruff [dǽndrəf]: small white pieces of dead skin from your head 비듬 [4]infect [inférkt]: to give sb a sickness or disease 전염시키다: A flu virus has infected everyone in the office. 감기 바이러스가 사무실 전원에게 전염되었다.

◎ 무좀

A: 여름만 되면 미치겠어.

B: 왜?

A: 무좀 때문에.

B: 구두를 바짝 말려.

A: 무좀에 바를 약 좀 없니?

B: 이거 발라봐. 한 미군 병사가 주던데. 나는 좀 나은 것 같아.

A: 군대 갔다 오면 남는 게 무좀과 비듬뿐이래. 천리행군으로 무좀이, 원산폭격으로 비듬이 생기지.

B: 군대에서 걸린 무좀은 환갑까지 간다.

Maybe Miss Kim from Busan

[Corporal : Sergeant]

C: Sgt Kim, you've got a call from the visiting center.

S: Who could it be at this time?

   Maybe Miss Kim from Busan again.

   Hey, Corporal Kim? Could you see her instead of me?

C: Why do you ask me to see her?

S: You go see her.

C: She came from Busan, a thousand-ri from here.

S: She has no sense.

   She's mistaken in her belief that I love her dearly.

부산의 미스 김 일거야

상병: 김병장님, 면회실에서 전화 왔습니다.

병장: 이번엔 누굴까?

   아마 또 부산의 미스 김 일거야.

   야, 김상병? 나대신 그녀를 만나줄래?

상병: 왜 저보고 그녀를 만나라고 하십니까?

병장: 네가 한번 만나 봐라.

상병: 그녀는 천리나 되는 부산에서 왔다구요.

병장: 그녀는 눈치가 없어.

   그녀는 내가 그녀를 되게 사랑하는 줄로 착각하고 있어.

🔸 Put on her rubber shoes backwards

A: I think she put on her rubber shoes backwards.

B: Why do you think so?

A: I haven't had any news from her since last month.

B: "We can't predict the direction that crayfish and women will go."

A: Didn't you mark her before coming into the military?

B: Up to the '80s, taking her virginity away was enough to make sure of her, but not now.

A: "A boat passes through the Han River, it doesn't leave any mark."

＊ In Korea, a woman before marriage used to be called an immaculate virgin whether she was a real virgin or not. A woman before marriage was often compared to a "blank paper" that can be marked by her future husband on the wedding night. Here, **mark** (sometimes, **stamp**) means "to have sex" or "to pop her cherry" so that other men won't approach the marked woman.

🔸 고무신 거꾸로 신었나 봐

A: 그녀는 고무신 거꾸로 신었나 봐.

B: 왜 그렇게 생각해?

A: 지난달부터 소식이 전혀 없으니 말이지.

B: "가재와 여자는 가는 방향을 알 수 없어."

A: 군대오기 전에 주기 안했어?

B: 80년대는 한번 주기하면 끝났는데 요즘은 아니야.

A: "한강에 배 지나가도 표 안 난다."

＊한국에서 결혼 전에 여자는 그녀가 정말 처녀이든 아니든 간에 처녀라 불리곤 했다. 결혼 전에 여자는 결혼 첫날밤에 자기 남편에게 주기 되는 "백지"로 종종 간주되었다. 여기서 **주기하다**(때때로, **도장 찍다**)라는 말은 다른 남자들이 주기 된 여자에게 접근하지 못하도록 "섹스를 하거나" 혹은 "처녀 딱지를 뗀다."는 말을 의미 한다.

Blow one's brains out

A: One of the enlisted men blew his brains out[1].

B: When did it happen?

A: Last night.

B: Who was it?

A: Park Hong-il.

He's been gloomy[2] since his girlfriend left him.

B: Poor guy! She's not the only fish in the sea!

[해설] [1]blow someone's brains out: to kill someone by shooting them in the head (권총으로 머리를 쏘아) 죽이다: He threatened to blow my brains out if I didn't hand over the money. 그는 내가 그 돈을 건네주지 않으면 머리에 총을 쏘겠다고 위협했다. [2]gloomy [glúːmi]: feeling sad and without hope 우울한: She became very gloomy after her divorce.

자살

A: 사병 중에 한 명이 총으로 자살했다.

B: 언제 일어났는데?

A: 지난밤에.

B: 누군데?

A: 박홍일.

B: 왜 자살했을까?

A: 여자 친구가 떠난 후 비관해 왔대.

B: 불쌍한 놈! 세상에 여자가 한둘인가!

It's too late

[Lt. Park : Sgt. Kim]

LP: Sgt. Kim, how is it going with your girlfriend?

SK: We went to an obstetrician[1], but it's too late for an abortion.

LP: Aren't you going to marry her, anyway?

SK: Yes, but we're ashamed of ourselves for "exceeding the speed limit.[2]"

LP: Then marry her and have a baby.
Time cures all wounds. A woman cries all her life after she aborts[3] her first child.

SK: Yes, sir.

[해설] [1]obstetrician[ὰbstətríʃən]: a doctor with special training in how to care for pregnant women and help in the birth of babies 산과의(産科醫), [2]exceed the speed limit 속도위반 즉 뜻하지 않은 임신 "to be pregnant before marriage, usually a surprise, not planned"에 대한 영어식 표현은 "knocked up"또는 "up the duff"가 있다: I really should've used a condom with her... I knocked her up! 그녀와 할 때 콘돔을 사용했어야 했는데... 그만 그녀를 임신시켰네. She's up the duff and really confused right now. 그녀는 느닷없는 임신으로 혼란에 빠졌다. [3]abort: to end a pregnancy before the normal time of birth 임신중절 하다: The doctor aborted the baby to save the mother's life. 의사는 엄마의 생명을 위해서 아이를 낙태했다.

너무 늦었습니다

박중위: 김병장, 네 여자 친구와 그 일은 잘 되어 가니?

김병장: 산부인과 갔는데, 시기가 지났답니다.

박중위: 어차피 그녀와 결혼할 거 아닌가?

김병장: 예, 맞습니다만, "속도위반"해서 부끄럽습니다.

박중위: 그녀와 결혼해서 애를 낳아라.
시간이 모든 것을 해결해 준다.
첫 아이를 잃은 여자는 평생 운다.

김병장: 알겠습니다.

◎ I don't remember who you are!

A man went far into a frontline boot camp. Several months later, the man received a letter from his girlfriend, saying, "Let's break up. Now return my photos to me." The soldier got angry and he asked his fellow soldiers if he could borrow their girlfriends' photos. He sent all the pictures to his girl friend saying, "I don't remember who you are. Keep yours and return the others to me."

◎ 당신이 누군지 모르겠어!

한 남자가 멀리 전방에 있는 훈련소로 입소했다. 몇 달 후에 그 남자는 그의 여자 친구에게서 "우리 헤어져요. 이제 내 사진은 돌려주세요."라는 편지를 받았다. 그 군인은 화가 나서 자기 동료 친구들에게 그들의 여자 친구들의 사진을 빌려달라고 했다. 그는 모든 여자들의 사진을 그의 여자 친구에게 "난 당신이 누군지 기억이 없어요. 당신의 사진만 빼놓고 나머지는 돌려주세요."라는 편지를 보냈다.

● How's your military life going?

How's your military life going?
↳ Very well. I wish I could extend my service period.
↳ Just so-so.
↳ I'm counting off the days.
↳ I feel one day is longer than 10 days.
↳ Time drags.
↳ A watched pot never boils.
↳ A day seems to be three autumns long.

● 너 군생활 어떠니?

너 군대 생활 어떠니?
↳ 매우 좋아. 군복무를 연장했으면 좋겠어.
↳ 그저 그래.
↳ 날을 하루하루 지우고 있어.
↳ 하루가 열흘보다 긴 것 같아.
↳ 시간이 되게 안가.
↳ 지켜보고 있는 냄비는 잘 안 끓어.
↳ 일일여삼추 (一日如三秋).

● Reporting a fault

[Company commander : Cadet Hong]

CH: Sir, Cadet Hong Kil-dong reporting as ordered!

CC: Do you know why I called you?

CH: Yes, sir! Because I was put on report by the 2nd Company Commander.

CC: For what?

CH: I chewed gum in uniform while I was on vacation.

CC: Where were you noticed?

CH: In front of Seoul station.

CC: How could you chew gum when wearing cadet dress uniform? It looks ugly.

CH I am really sorry, sir!

CC: You should wear ordinary clothes if you can't keep your proper bearing[1] as a cadet.

CH: I am sorry, sir!

[해설] [1]bearing: the way sb moves or stands 태도: an elderly man with a military bearing 군인 같은 태도를 지닌 나이든 남자

● 사고보고

홍생도: 홍길동 생도, 중대장님께 부르심 받고 왔습니다!
중대장: 너 내가 왜 불렀는지 아니?
홍생도: 예, 압니다! 2중대장님으로부터 지적을 받았기 때문입니다.
중대장: 무엇 때문에?
홍생도: 휴가 중에 제복을 입고 껌을 씹었습니다.
중대장: 어디서?
홍생도: 서울역 앞에서 그랬습니다.
중대장: 생도들이 정복을 입고 왜 껌을 씹나? 보기 추하게.
홍생도: 정말 죄송합니다.
중대장: 생도 복장을 하고 품위를 지킬 자신이 없으면 사복을 입어야지.
홍생도: 죄송합니다.

An Inappropriate relationship

[Company commander : Cadet Hong]

CC: Cadet Hong Kil-dong. It's you again!
CH: Yes, sir!
CC: What did you get blacklisted[1] for this time?
CH: I was caught having an inappropriate relationship with my girlfriend.
CC: An inappropriate relationship like "Clinton and Lewinsky?"
CH: No, I just I walked arm in arm with my girlfriend.
CC: How can that be an inappropriate relationship?
That is going too far.
CH: I am sorry.
CC: Our regulations state that you have to maintain a gap measuring at least one-step between you and your girlfriend while you are out walking together.
CH: Yes, sir!
CC: Don't use the words "inappropriate relationship[2]."

[해설] [1]blacklist: to put people's names on a list (좋지 않은 것으로) 명단에 올리다, (좋지 않은 것의) 명단. [2]inappropriate relationship: illegal sexual contact 부적절한 관계: The president publicly denied having had a relationship with Lewinsky. 대통령은 르윈스키와 부적절한 관계를 가졌다는 것을 공개적으로 거부했다.

부적절한 관계

중대장: 홍길동 생도 너 또 왔구나!
홍생도: 예, 그렇습니다!
중대장: 이번에 또 무슨 지적을 받았나?
홍생도: 여자 친구와 부적절한 관계로 지적을 받았습니다.
중대장: 부적절한 관계라니? "클린턴과 르윈스키"같은 그런?
홍생도: 아닙니다. 여자 친구와 팔짱을 하고 걸었습니다.
중대장: 그게 뭐 부적절한 관계야. 표현이 너무 심하다.
홍생도: 죄송합니다.
중대장: 우리 규정에는 애인과 동행 시 1보 거리를 유지하는 것으로 되어 있다.
홍생도: 예, 그렇습니다!
중대장: "부적절한 관계" 라는 말을 쓰지 마라.

Give me a demerit card!

[Company commander : Cadet Hong]

CC: Cadet, Hong, Why do you doze[1] off in class again and again?

CA: I burned the midnight oil[2] until 2 a.m., well after lights out.

CC: Burning the midnight oil is a waste of time if you doze off in class.

CA: I am sorry, sir.

CC: Bad learning attitude! Give me a demerit[3] card!

∗ After lights out at 2200, soldiers should not move around for 30 minutes so that their comrades can get to sleep.

[해설] [1]doze (off): to sleep lightly for a short time 졸다. [2]burn the midnight oil: to work, study until late at night 밤늦게까지 일/공부하다: I had to burn the midnight oil before final exams. 나는 기말고사 전에 열심히 공부해야 했다. [3]demerit [di:mérit]: a bad mark against a person's record (학교·훈련소의) 벌점: The sergeant gave a soldier 10 demerits for not cleaning his rifle properly. 부사관은 한 사병이 총기를 청소하지 않아서 벌점 10점을 주었다.

감점표 내놔

중대장: 홍생도, 너 수업시간에 왜 자꾸 졸아?

홍생도: 새벽 2시까지 연등을 했습니다.

중대장: 연등하고 수업시간에 졸면 무슨 소용 있나?

홍생도: 죄송합니다.

중대장: 수업태도 불량! 감점표 내놔!

∗ 22시 소등 후에 군인들은 30분 동안 동료들이 잠들도록 돌아다녀서는 안 된다.

Prisoners & private soldiers

① They have to wear a uniform.
② They have a serial number.
③ They have to have a roll call.
④ They're watched for 24 hours.
⑤ They're counting off the days.
⑥ They are often beaten to death.
⑦ They have no freedom of speech.
⑧ They are mostly under privileged[1].
⑨ They need to get a pass to go out.
⑩ They are often punished as a group.
⑪ They have dorm inspection regularly.
⑫ They're confined to a designated area.
⑬ They can't drink whenever they want.
⑭ They need permission to receive visitors.
⑮ They believe time and tide heal all things.
⑯ They can't send e-mail without permission.
⑰ They are compelled to believe in a religion.
⑱ They are often dumped by their loved ones.
⑲ They can't complain about being mistreated.
⑳ They are sometimes abused sexually by others of the same sex.

[해설] 1underprivileged [ʌ̀ndərprívəlidʒd]: poor; impoverished 가난한, 혜택 받지 못한: underprivileged children 혜택을 받지 못하는 아이들

죄수와 군인

① 제복을 입어야 한다.
② 일련의 번호가 있다.
③ 점호를 받아야 한다.
④ 24시간 감시된다.
⑤ 날을 지워나간다.
⑥ 가끔 맞아 죽는다.
⑦ 언론의 자유가 없다.
⑧ 대다수 비특권층이다.
⑨ 외출하려면 외출증이 필요하다.
⑩ 단체기합을 종종 받는다.
⑪ 내무검사를 정기적으로 받는다.
⑫ 일정한 장소에 구속되어야 한다.
⑬ 술을 마시고 싶을 때 못 마신다.
⑭ 면회할 때 허락을 받아야 한다.
⑮ 세월이 약이라 믿는다.
⑯ 허락 없이 이메일을 보낼 수 없다.
⑰ 하나의 종교를 갖으라고 강요된다.
⑱ 사랑하는 사람들로부터 종종 차인다.
⑲ 억울해도 불평하지 못한다.
⑳ 동성에 의해 가끔 성추행을 당한다.

● After 3 years of military life,

① I became a mother-in-law after giving lectures.
② I became a robber after going on errands for seniors.
③ I became a male prostitute after serving seniors.
④ I became like a blackman after lying in a muddy trench[1].
⑤ I became a stunt-man[2] after receiving ranger training.
⑥ I became a sniper[3] after doing **PRI** (preliminary rifle instruction)[4].
⑦ I became an A frame coolie[5] after marching in full combat gear[6].
⑧ I became a walker after marching.
⑨ I became an owl after doing sentry duty at night.
⑩ I became a gutsy[7] man after receiving disciplinary punishment.
⑪ I became a barber after cutting other's hair.
⑫ I became a shoe polisher after shining shoes.
⑬ I became a kitchen maid after working as a kitchen orderly[8].
⑭ I became a cleaner after sweeping the streets.
⑮ I became a writer after writing love letters to my lover.
⑯ I became a heavy smoker after smoking one or two cigarettes.
⑰ I became a heavy drinker after drinking one or two glasses of alcohol.
⑱ I became a singer after singing military songs.
⑲ I became a soccer player after playing soccer.
⑳ I became a Confucius[9] after enduring hardship.
㉑ I became a sick chicken after nodding off in a lecture.
㉒ I became a dramatic actor after serving in the military.

[해설] [1]muddy trench (긴) 참호. [2]stunt-man: a person who does dangerous acts in a movie 스턴트맨. [3]sniper[snaipər]: a person who shoots at people from a hidden position 저격수. [4]PRI (preliminary rifle instruction) 사격예비훈련으로 **P**나고 **R**베이고 **I**(이) 갈린다는 훈련. [5]A-frame coolie 지게꾼. [6]full combat gear(FCG); full battle dress 완전군장. [7]gusty [gʌsti]: courageous 용기/담력 있는. [8]kitchen orderly: a worker who cleans and does chores in a kitchen 식당 청소부. 군대 식당에서 취사병은 kitchen police라고 한다. (미군에서 police는 "to clean" or "to restore to order" 청소 또는 정리하다"뜻으로 사용되기도 한다). [9]Confucius [kənfjuːəs] 공자 (a Chinese thinker and social philosopher, whose teachings and philosophy have deeply influenced Chinese, Korean, Japanese, and Vietnamese thought and life)

🔶 군생활 3년 후에

① 잔소리 하다 보니 시어머니 되었고
② 고참들 심부름하다 보니 깡패 되었고
③ 고참들 시중들다 보니 창남 되었고
④ 매복훈련 하다 보니 깜둥이 되었고
⑤ 유격훈련 받다보니 스턴트맨 되었고
⑥ 사격예비훈련 하다 보니 저격수 되었고
⑦ 완전군장하고 행군하다 보니 지게꾼 되었고
⑧ 행군 하다 보니 경보선수 되었고
⑨ 야간 경계 서다 보니 올빼미 되었고
⑩ 기합 받다보니 깡다구 생겼고
⑪ 다른 사람 머리 깎다보니 깎쇠 되었고
⑫ 군화 닦다 보니 딱쇠 되었고
⑬ 식기당번 하다 보니 식순이 되었
⑭ 거리 청소하다 보니 청소부 되었고
⑮ 애인에게 편지 쓰다 보니 작가 되었고
⑯ 한 대 두 대 피우다 보니 골초 되었고
⑰ 한 잔 두 잔 하다 보니 술고래 되었고
⑱ 군가 부르다 보니 가수 되었고
⑲ 축구 하다 보니 축구 선수 되었고
⑳ 역경을 참다보니 공자 되었고
㉑ 교육시간에 고개 끄덕이다 보니 병든 닭 되었고
㉒ 군생활 하다 보니 연극배우 되었다.

Unauthorized damage to government property

A cadet at ○○ Academy was circumcised[1] during his winter vacation without prior official permission from the superior authority. He came back to the barracks before he was fully recovered, so he couldn't jog after morning roll call. His company commander noticed this. Sad to say, the cadet was punished for being in breach of the regulations, "misconduct II" which is "unauthorized damage to government property."

[해설] [1]circumcise [sə́ːrkəmsaiz]: to cut off the skin at the end of the penis 포경수술하다.

허가되지 않은 관물 파손

○○ 사관학교 한 생도가 동계 휴가 기간 중 상부의 허락 없이 포경수술을 했다. 그는 완치가 덜 된 채로 복귀하여 일조점호 후 구보에 참석할 수 없었다. 그의 중대장이 이 사실을 알아차렸다. 슬프게도 그 생도는 "허가되지 않은 관물파손"이란 죄목(罪目)으로 "II급 비행"을 받았다.

처 벌 공 고

소 속	성 명	비행사유	벌칙내용	본인확인
2중대 3소대	최오규	허가되지 않은 관물파손	벌칙구보 3시간(2회) 잡초제거 3시간(2회)	*최오규*

상기자는 1981년 1월 30일부로 ○○사관학교 규정에 의거
위와 같이 처벌함을 공고 함.
벌칙권자 : 대위 유 양 원 *유 양 원*

🔸 A frog mark on my cap

My discharge day came at last.
I attached a frog mark to my cap, which is the discharge symbol. I am very proud of myself. This is like receiving a military medal in reward for 3 years of devotion.

🔸 모자에 개구리 마크

드디어 제대하는 날 아침이 밝았습니다.
모자에는 전역을 상징하는 개구리마크를 박았습니다.
제 자신 스스로가 너무도 대견스럽습니다.
3년간의 대가로 훈장을 탄 느낌입니다.

🔸 The last word at the discharging party

[First Sgt.: Sgt. Kim]

FS: Sgt. Kim, thanks for your hard work in the military for 26 months. Say something now.

SK: I feel like I joined the army a few days ago, but it has already been 26 months. I give my thanks to our platoon leader and platoon sergeant. You treated me as if I were your real brother. To repay your great favor, I will live ardently for our country as well as myself. If a war breaks out[1], I will immediately join up with you. Let me propose a toast to the good health of our platoon leader, our platoon sergeant, and all of us. Cheers!

[해설] [1]break out: start suddenly(a fire, war, disease, etc) (화재, 전쟁, 질병이) 갑자기 시작되다: This morning a big fire broke out in the 14th Street warehouse. 오늘 아침 14번가 창고에서 큰 불이 났다.

🔸 전역 회식에서 마지막 한마디

선임부사관: 김병장, 26개월 동안 수고했다. 이제 한마디 해라.

김 병 장: 제가 입대한 지가 엊그제 같은데 벌써 26개월이 흘렀습니다. 그 동안 저를 친동생처럼 따뜻하게 지도해주신 소대장님, 소대 선임부사관님께 진심으로 감사드립니다. 그 은혜에 보답한다는 의미에서, 저 자신을 위해서, 또한 우리나라 발전을 위해서 열심히 생활하겠습니다. 혹시라도 전쟁이 나면 즉각 응소하겠습니다. 제가 소대장님, 선임하사님과 우리 모두의 건승을 위하여 "축배"를 제의하겠습니다. 위하여!

🔸 On the night before the discharge day

Tomorrow I will be discharged.
This boring smelly khaki blanket,
these boring smelly boots,
this boring view of my barracks and
I have to say "adieu forever" to everything I'm familiar with.

It's funny, isn't it?
Leaving here now, I'm feeling lingering affection, regret and a sense of loss.
I never imagined this feeling even in my dreams.

전역 전날 밤에

내일이면 제대랍니다.
이 지긋지긋한 국방색 모포 냄새,
지긋지긋한 군화 냄새,
따분한 내무반 풍경도,
이젠 모두 "영원히 안녕"입니다.

참 우습지 않아요?
막상 떠나려니 착잡함, 후회, 상실감.
이런 기분 꿈에서도 상상 못했어요.

Reporting for discharge

Reporting as ordered, sir.
Sgt. Kim Kil-dong,
ordered to be discharged from military service
as of March 31, 2002.
Reporting as ordered!

전역신고

신고합니다. 병장 김길동은
2002년 3월 31일부로
전역을 명 받았습니다.
이에 신고합니다!

◯ Advice from senior boots

PVT (Trainee)	While you are at basic training, you want to see her more than ever. So when you write a letter to her, you may make promises that you later realize you cannot keep. Don't try to gain sympathy from her by telling her about your tough situation, but you'd better care for her.
PVT	To think of your sweetheart? That's a perfect luxury! You don't have time to even sleep. You may not receive a letter as frequently as you did when you were in boot camp. Make a good plan so that you can captivate her on your 100th-day's leave.
PFC	You may worry that she is left alone. But if you worry about her like an 'old woman' and try to control her life, it may drive her away. Tell her when it is possible for her to visit you, but don't beg her to come and see you.
CPL	Now you are so adapted to the military environment that you know the ropes and can get things done. This sometimes brings out the worst in you. Long separation makes you feel awkward and that it will be awkward to see her. When you write a letter to her, you can't find any new idea as to how to begin a letter. It takes longer and longer to finish a letter!
SGT	Although a ray of hope begins to light on your lengthy military life, you'll have mixed feelings about the following: going back to college, your course of life and HER. Do you think she will be supportive enough for you to accomplish your dream? Do you think both of you are compatible? Weren't the tears she shed on your enlistment day crocodile tears?

고참 군화의 충고

훈련병	네가 훈련 중일 때 애인이 가장 보고 싶을 거다. 그래서 너는 그녀에게 보내는 편지에서 나중에 책임지지도 못할 약속을 할 지 모른다. 너의 힘든 처지를 그녀에게 알려 동정을 구하지 말고 오히려 혼자 남아 있는 그녀를 생각해줘라.
이병	애인 생각? 그것은 완전히 사치다! 너는 잠잘 시간조차도 없다. 네가 훈련소에 있을 때만큼 편지를 자주 받지 못할 것이다. 휴가 계획을 잘 짜서 100일 휴가 때 그녀를 사로잡을 수 있도록 해라.
일병	너는 혼자 남겨둔 그녀가 자꾸만 걱정될지 모른다. 하지만 "노파심"에서 그녀를 통제하는 것은 오히려 그녀를 달아나게 한다. 너의 면회 가능한 날짜를 알려주되 너무 강요하지는 마라.
상병	이제 너는 군생활에 적응도 되었고 일하는 요령도 안다. 그래서 이것이 너의 본성을 가끔 드러낸다. 애인과 오래 떨어져 있으니 그녀를 만나는 것도 어색하다. 편지를 쓰는데 어떻게 시작해야 하는지 착상이 떠오르지 않는다. 편지 한 통 쓰는데 시간이 점점 더 걸린다.
병장	비록 지루한 군생활에 서광이 오기 시작했지만 복학, 진로, 그녀로 착잡해진다. 너는 그녀가 너의 인생을 성취하는데 충분히 도움을 줄 것이라고 생각이 되나? 둘이 궁합은 맞아? 네 입대 일에 그녀가 흘린 눈물은 악어의 눈물이 아니었을까?

군대생활의 고뇌 추억 지혜
군대영어 Military English!

Serving as Officers or NCOs
(장교 · 부사관)

- ☐ 임관선서**
- ☐ 장교의 책무*
- ☐ 부사관의 임무*
- ☐ 장교는 시인 같아야**
- ☐ 장교의 존재이유는?
- ☐ 부사관은 군대의 척추*
- ☐ 장교의 4가지 등급*
- ☐ 부하의 4가지 분류*
- ☐ 능력있는 장군 밑에*
- ☐ 장교의 칠거지악***
- ☐ 움직이지 못하는 상어
- ☐ 야생으로 키우기
- ☐ 개인소개**
- ☐ 영외거주
- ☐ 잠자러 출근해?
- ☐ 꽃밭에 물주기
- ☐ 네 부하는 이렇지 않니?
- ☐ 초병이 총을 분실**
- ☐ 무장 탈영***
- ☐ 두 병사가 탈영
- ☐ 바람 잘날 없구먼!
- ☐ 중위가 초병을 패다**
- ☐ 우리 "군차렷" 걸렸어***

- ☐ 구타 및 가혹 행위 근절 서약*
- ☐ 통화 중이면 1234로
- ☐ 장교 바꿔*
- ☐ 7사단 근무해봤어?
- ☐ 전속신고*
- ☐ 대대장님을 떠나기 전에
- ☐ 대대장님과 같은 리더가 되겠습니다!*
- ☐ 얘기 들었습니다
- ☐ 전입신고
- ☐ 보직신고
- ☐ 너는 운 좋다
- ☐ 너 행운이다!
- ☐ 그분은 FM이래**
- ☐ 미군 벨트
- ☐ 교육, 훈련, 잔소리**
- ☐ 상사와 시어머니**
- ☐ 모기 회식
- ☐ 불쌍한 리더십**
- ☐ 라면으로 때우다**
- ☐ 젊은 장교들을 개××라고 부르지 마
- ☐ 김대위님께 경례하지 말자

- ☐ 전투호 2개 파라
- ☐ 0-2기가 비행기냐?*
- ☐ 내일부터 검열이다
- ☐ 너 소설을 썼구나
- ☐ 얼음을 다리미로 녹여**
- ☐ 가서 좀 자라
- ☐ 군대 말뚝 박아라**
- ☐ 너 왜 경례 안 해?
- ☐ "충성!" 해봐!**
- ☐ "님"자 빼지 마라***
- ☐ 부사관은 항상 중요하다**
- ☐ 너 군대 한 번 더 가라
- ☐ 보안평가**
- ☐ 비인가 디스켓
- ☐ 검열 준비해야 돼
- ☐ 비인가 전열기
- ☐ 화재예방 표어
- ☐ 담배 빈대
- ☐ 불만 있어
- ☐ 금연결의문**
- ☐ 비흡연자의 신음소리***
- ☐ 골프와 영어 배우기**
- ☐ 내기 골프 금지*

Military English

Serving as Officers or NCOs
(장교 · 부사관)

- 20번 홀까지 가다!***
- 저는 더 이상 골프 안 쳐요*
- 너 없이 검열을 받을 수 있나?
- 토요일 오후에 테니스*
- 테니스 코트에서
- 아부 테니스 게임**
- 나는 그와 한편 하기 싫어
- 삼겹살에 소주**
- 삼겹살
- 마음의 잔*
- 첫 잔은 마셔라**
- 코리안 비아그라***
- 내일은 휴일이나 다름없어
- 이번에는 뭐 내기?***
- 오늘 저녁 회식이야
- 회식 취소
- 어떻게 회식에 안갈 수 있나?
- 10일전에 날 잡았어요
- 너 식사만 해
- 벌주***
- 계급주***
- 우턴하겠습니다*
- 왼쪽으로 두 클릭**

- 이상한 "건배"*
- 음주운전은 살인행위***
- 모두 커피?
- 음주운전
- 음주운전 금지 서약**
- 윤잔과 윤간***
- 퇴근 못해
- 잦은 회식은***
- 느닷없는 "건배"***
- 진급심사
- 위로주***
- 그의 진급은 끝났군!
- 누군가의 큰 짐
- 진급이 모든 것은 아니다*
- 찬물을 끼얹다
- 그는 장군감이 아니다
- 지는 별*
- 장군 될 비전
- 선거와 진급***
- 시체가 일어날지도 몰라**
- 모든 군인은 불평불만 자
- 군인들의 군살
- 청춘을 불살랐다

- 사고보고***
- 이라크 파병 지원***
- 네 얼굴이 분화구 같아
- 나는 찌들었소
- 제대타령**
- 내년에 제대해야지
- 면세양주 한 병 줘
- 중대장님, 저 언제 오프합니까?
- 지휘관의 책무**
- 지휘관의 근무 십계명**
- 지휘관의 의도**
- 지휘관은 결코 잊지 않는다
- 너의 상관은 크고 살찐 늙은 말이다
- 세 가지 보고
- 중대장님 지시사항***
- "예, 알겠습니다!" 라고 대답해라
- 미군에서 준수사항***
- 현역에 짐이 되지 말자**
- 늙은 군인의 노래
- 영어의 전략적 능력*

🟡 Oath of Office

I, 2nd Lt., Hong Kil-dong,
having been appointed a second lieutenant
in the Republic of Korea Air Force, do solemnly[1] swear[2] that
I will render[3] devoted service to our country and people, and
I will observe our constitution[4] and laws, and
I will complete[5] the missions that are entrusted[6] to me.
April 1, 2000, Air Force 2nd Lt., Hong Kil-dong!

[해설] [1]solemn [sáləm]: very serious 엄숙한, 진지한: His face grew solemn. 그의 표정이 엄숙해졌다. [2]swear[swɛər]: to promise that you will do sth 맹세하다: Do you swear to tell the truth? 당신은 진실을 말할 것을 맹세하는가? [3]render [réndə:] : provide service/help (본분·의무를) 행하다. [4]constitution: a set of laws governing a country 헌법. [5]complete: to finish doing or making sth 완성하다: The book took three years to complete. 그 책을 완성하는데 3년이 걸렸다. [6]entrust [entrʌst]: to give sb sth to be responsible for 위임하다: I was entrusted with the task of organizing the party. 나는 그 파티를 조직하는 임무를 위임받았다.

🟡 임관선서

소위 홍길동은
대한민국 공군장교로서,
국가와 민족을 위하여 충성을 다하고,
헌법과 법규를 준수하며,
부여된 직책과 임무를 성실히 수행할 것을
엄숙히 선서합니다.
2000년 4월 1일 공군소위 홍길동!

🔘 An officer's duty   장교의 책무

An officer is the mainstay[1] of the army. So he/she should be conscious of his/her responsibility and learn professional knowledge and skills. He/she has to exert himself/herself[2] to build up his/her character, body, and mind. Also, he/she should enact proper procedures, observe the law, and take the initiative[3] in everything so that he/she has insight and authority to make right decisions and take proper measures[4] under any adversity.

[해설] [1]mainstay [méinstèi]: a key person or element 핵심적인 사람·물건. [2]exert oneself: to work very hard 열심히 일하다. [3]take the initiative 주도권을 쥐다, 솔선하다: The squad leader must take the initiative to keep his squad alert. 분대장은 자기 분대가 정신을 바짝 차리도록 주도권을 쥐어야 한다. [4]take measures: to perform a specific action 조치를 취하다: We must take preventative measures to stop the spread of the disease. 우리는 질병 확산을 방지할 수 있는 예방책을 취해야 한다.

장교는 군대의 기간이다. 그러므로 장교는 그 책임의 중대함을 자각하여 직무수행에 필요한 전문지식과 기술을 습득하고 건전한 인격의 도야와 심신의 수련에 힘쓸 것이며 처사를 공명정대히 하고 법규를 준수하고 솔선수범함으로써 부하로부터 존경과 신뢰를 받아 역경에 처하여서도 올바른 판단과 조치를 할 수 있는 통찰력과 권위를 갖추어야 한다.

🔘 An NCO's duty   부사관의 임무

A non-commissioned officer is part of the managing staff for military troops. He/she should be familiar with his/her duties and take the lead in everything. He/she shall supervise enlisted soldiers, make sure that they observe the regulations, educate and train them, and lead their barracks lives. Also, he/she has to lead enlisted soldiers properly by understanding their personal problems, and make efforts to manage all equipments and supplies.

부사관은 군대의 간부이다. 그러므로 맡은 바 직무에 정통하고 모든 일에 솔선수범하며, 병의 법규 준수와 명령 이행을 감독하고 교육훈련과 내무생활을 지도하여야 한다. 또한 병의 신상을 파악하여 선도하고 각종 장비와 보급품 관리에 힘써야 한다.

🟠 An officer should be like a poet

An officer should be like a poet.
↳ He has some insight into the future.
An NCO should be like an essayist.
↳ He has lessons learned from his experience.
An enlisted man should be like a diarist.
↳ He has a responsibility to get things done.

🟠 장교는 시인 같아야

장교는 시인과 같아야 한다.
↳ 그는 미래에 대한 통찰력이 있어야 한다.
부사관은 수필가와 같아야 한다.
↳ 그는 경험으로부터 얻은 교훈이 있어야 한다.
사병은 일일 작가와 같아야 한다.
↳ 그는 업무완수를 위한 책임감이 있어야 한다.

🔸 Why officers exist?

Officers exist to make decisions.
NCOs exist to supervise soldiers.
Privates exist to carry out the mission.

- Learn from the skill and experience of NCOs.
- Intelligence recognizes what has happened.
- Genius recognizes what will happen.
- Officers should be able to foretell[1] what may happen in the future.
- NCOs should be able to remember what happened in the past.
- Private soldiers should be able to recognize what they should do today.

[해설] [1]foretell [fo:rtél]: to say/know what will happen in the future; to predict 예언・예고하다: Nobody can foretell what will happen tomorrow. 내일 무엇이 일어날지는 아무도 모른다.

🔸 장교의 존재이유는?

장교는 결정하기 위해서 존재한다.
부사관은 사병을 감독하기 위해 존재한다.
사병은 명령을 수행하기 위해 존재한다.

- 부사관들로부터 숙련과 경험을 배워라.
- 지식인은 지금까지 일어났던 일을 안다.
- 천재는 앞으로 일어날 것을 안다.
- 장교는 미래에 무엇이 일어날지 예견할 수 있어야 한다.
- 부사관은 지금까지 일어났던 일을 기억할 수 있어야 한다.
- 병사는 오늘 해야 할 일을 알 수 있어야 한다.

NCOs are the backbone

NCOs are the backbone[1] of the military forces.
Officers are the brains of the military forces.
Enlisted soldiers are the roots of the military forces.
Military wives are the backbone of the military home.
Military dogs are the guards of the military forces.

[해설] [1]backbone: the most important part of sth; mainstay 가장 소중한 부분: Manufacturing is the backbone of the economy. 제조업이 경제의 핵심이다.

부사관은 군대의 척추

부사관은 군대의 척추다
장교는 군대의 뇌다
병사는 군대의 뿌리다
군인 아내는 군인 가정의 척추다
군견은 군대의 수위다

Four classes of officers 장교의 4가지 등급

① The brilliant[1] and industrious.	총명하고 부지런한 장교
② The brilliant and lazy.	총명하고 게으른 장교
③ The stupid and lazy.	우매하고 게으른 장교
④ The stupid and industrious[2]	우매하고 부지런한 장교

[해설] [1]brilliant [bríljənt]: extremely intelligent 두뇌가 날카로운: He is a brilliant scientist. 그는 매우 총명한 과학자이다. [2]industrious[indʌstriəs]: tending to work hard 근면한, 부지런한: She is an industrious young woman. 그녀는 부지런한 젊은 여성이다.

● Four types of subordinates

① Working well and making his senior comfortable.
② Working well and making his senior uncomfortable.
③ Working badly and making his senior comfortable.
④ Working badly and making his senior uncomfortable.

● 부하의 4가지 분류

① 일도 잘하고 상관도 편안하게 하는 부하
② 일은 잘해도 상관을 불편하게 하는 부하
③ 일은 못해도 상관을 편안하게 하는 부하
④ 일도 못하고 상관을 불편하게 하는 부하

● Under competent general officers

Under competent general officers, competent field grade officers serve.
Under competent field grade officers, competent company grade officers serve.
Under competent company grade officers, competent NCOs serve.
Under competent NCOs, competent enlisted men serve.
Under competent enlisted men, competent military dogs serve.

● 능력 있는 장군 밑에

능력 있는 장군 장교 밑에 능력 있는 영관 장교가 복무하고
능력 있는 영관 장교 밑에 능력 있는 위관 장교가 복무하고
능력 있는 위관 장교 밑에 능력 있는 부사관이 복무하고
능력 있는 부사관 밑에 능력 있는 사병이 복무하고
능력 있는 사병 밑에 능력 있는 군견이 복무한다.

Officer's seven evils[1]

① He gives and takes bribes.
② He is ignorant[2].
③ He yells over nothing.
④ He doesn't read books.
⑤ He over-supervises his people.
⑥ He punishes men by the group over trivial matters.
⑦ He can't control his family.

[해설] [1]evil: actions and behavior that are morally wrong and cruel 악, 사악: the battle between good and evil 선과 악의 전투. [2]ignorant [íɡnərənt]: not knowing facts or information that you should know 마땅히 알아야 할 것을 모르는, 무식한

장교의 칠거지악

① 뇌물 수수자
② 무식한 자
③ 아무것도 아닌 것으로 호통 치는 자
④ 책을 읽지 않는 자
⑤ 부하를 지나치게 감독하는 자
⑥ 사소한 것으로 단체로 벌을 주는 자
⑦ 자기 가족도 통제 못하는 자

A motionless shark

The officer who has lost his moral authority is like a motionless shark in the sea. Nobody fears him.

움직이지 못하는 상어

도덕적 권위를 상실한 장교는 바다에서 움직이지 못하는 상어와 같다. 아무도 그를 겁내지 않는다.

◎ Cultivating wilderness

The lieutenant who has been over-supervised for decades becomes a timid, indecisive and incompetent commander. But the lieutenant who has been entrusted with responsibilities for decades becomes a firm, decisive and competent commander. The shortest way to make military officers incompetent is to over-supervise them.

Over-supervising your junior officers is not always the best choice. Sometimes, they must be sent out into the wilderness to act on their own initiative in unexpected situations. Though this is not easy for a commander, your officers have to make the best decision in accordance with varying war situation. No officer is ever a mere cog[1]!

[해설] [1]cog: 톱니바퀴의 이로서 조직에서 중요하지 않은 사람을 칭함(a cog in the machine/wheel: an unimportant worker in a large organization)

◎ 야생으로 키우기

십 수 년 동안 지나치게 감독되어 온 장교는 어리석고 우유부단하고 무능한 지휘관이 되었다. 하지만 십 수 년 동안 업무를 위임받아 온 장교는 확고하고 과단성 있는 유능한 지휘관이 되었다. 무능한 장교로 만드는 첩경은 지나치게 감독하는 것이다.

너의 부하 장교를 지나치게 감독하는 것이 항상 최선의 선택은 아니다. 때때로 그들은 예기치 않은 상황에서 주도적으로 행동할 수 있도록 황야로 보내져야 한다. 이것이 지휘관들에게는 쉽지 않지만 너의 부하장교들은 가변적인 전시 상황에서 최선의 결정을 해야 한다. 어떤 장교도 단순한 톱니바퀴의 이가 아니다!

● Self introduction

My name is Kim Ki-won.
I was born in Pochon in Gyeong-gi Province in 1968.
My hometown, Pochon, is well known as a military city which is near the DMZ. I spent my primary, middle and high school years there. After high school, I entered Kyung Hee University in Seoul. My major was business administration, but I was not very interested in it. During my college years, I wandered much like a colt released from captivity. My hobbies are swimming, horse-riding and traveling. I am very outgoing. I go to church every Sunday, but I am not very religious.

How I met my wife.
My wife was a daughter of the owners of my boarding house. At that time she was in the third grade at Duksung Girls' High School. I tutored her in English and math for 2 years. After she entered college, she became an attractive lady. One summer night in 1992, she asked me to go to a movie with her.
We married in 1998 when I was a captain. Now, she has become a half soldier. After my college education in 1992, I applied to be an officer candidate. I had 24 weeks of basic training at The 3rd Military Academy. After being commissioned as 2nd Lt., I took the Officer's Basic Course for 8 weeks at Gwangju. I wanted my branch to be the armored vehicle section but I got infantry.

My first assignment was as 3rd Platoon Leader, 2nd Company, 4th Battalion, 2nd Regiment, 7th Division. There I could finish up as a platoon leader with my company commander. He was very rational and lenient. And after taking the Officer's Advanced Course for 12 weeks at Gwangju, I was assigned to the 37th Division. Now as company commander, I feel that the new recruits have become hard to manage. They are self-centered and are not considerate to others. You know my motto? My Motto is "I will fulfill my duties as an officer." Thanks for listening to my details.

🔸 개인 소개

저의 이름은 김기원입니다.
저는 1968년 경기도 포천에서 태어났습니다.
저의 고향, 포천은 DMZ 인근 군사도시로 잘 알려져 있지요.
저는 거기서 초등학교에서 고등학교까지 마쳤습니다.
고교 졸업 후 서울에 있는 경희대학교에 들어갔습니다.
전공은 경영학이었지만, 그다지 관심이 없었습니다.
대학 재학 중에 고삐 풀린 망아지처럼 많이 방황을 했지요.
저의 취미는 수영, 승마, 여행입니다. 저는 매우 활달한 사람이지요.
저는 일요일마다 교회에 가지만, 아직 신앙심이 깊지는 않습니다.

저의 아내를 만난 것에 대해 말씀 드리면.
그녀는 제 하숙집의 딸이었습니다.
그 당시 그녀는 덕성여고 3학년 이었지요.
저는 그녀에게 영어와 수학을 2년 동안 가르쳤지요.
그녀가 대학을 들어가더니 매력적인 숙녀가 되더라구요.
1992년 어느 여름밤에 그녀가 영화 보러 같이 가자고 하더군요.
우리는 1998년, 제가 대위 때 결혼을 했습니다.
이제 그녀는 반 군인이 되었습니다.

제가 대학을 졸업하고 1992년 장교후보생으로 지원을 했습니다.
육군 3사관학교에서 24주간의 기초 군사훈련을 받았습니다.
소위로 임관하고 나서 광주에서 8주 동안의 장교기초과정교육을 받았습니다.
저는 기갑 특기를 원했지만 보병 특기를 받았습니다.

저의 첫 부임지는 7사단, 2연대, 4대대, 2중대, 3소대 소대장이었습니다. 거기서 중대장님의 도움으로 소대장 직위를 성공적으로 마칠 수 있었습니다. 그분은 합리적이고 인자하셨습니다. 그리고 광주에서 12주 동안의 장교고급군사교육을 마치고 37사단으로 배속 받았습니다. 지금 중대장으로서 요즘 들어오는 병사들을 다루기가 힘이 듭니다. 병사들은 자기중심적이고 다른 사람들을 배려할 줄 모르지요. 저의 신조가 뭔지 아십니까?
저의 신조는 "장교로서 직무에 충실하기"입니다.
저의 이런 소개를 들어주셔서 감사합니다.

Living outside of the barracks

[Staff Sgt. Kim : Staff Sgt. Park]

SP: Sgt. Kim, when will you begin living outside of the barracks?

SK: At the end of next month.

SP: Congratulations! I envy you.

SK: Well, it isn't as good as you think.

SP: You don't need to worry about barracks inspections, roll calls or anything else.

SK: But I have to rent a room.

Other guys say once we go out of the barracks, we will miss barracks life again. I think I'd rather live in the BNQ[1].

SP: Try to stay out of military accommodation.

You're going to stay in the military after your day is done? You are a born[2] soldier, aren't you?

[해설] [1]BNQ: Bachelor NCOs' Quarters 독신 부사관 숙소. [2]born: having a natural ability to do sth 타고난: a born leader/teacher 타고난 리더·교사. be born to do sth ~: ~을 하려고 태어나다: Jack was born to play baseball.

영외거주

박하사: 김하사, 너 언제 영외거주 나가니?

김하사: 다음 달 말.

박하사: 축하해. 부럽다.

김하사: 네가 생각하는 만큼 기쁘지 않아.

박하사: 점호, 내무검사 등을 신경 쓸 필요가 없잖아.

김하사: 하지만 방도 구해야 하고.

다른 애들이 그러는데 일단 나가면 영내 생활이 그립대.

그래서 BNQ에 살까 생각 중이야.

박하사: 영외에 살아라.

퇴근해서도 군대에 있겠다고?

너는 타고난 군인이지?

◯ You came to work just to sleep? 잠자러 출근해?

[Senior : Junior]

S: Hey, wake up!
J: Excuse me, sir.
S: What did you do last night?
J: I went to bed early, but I always feel tired.
S: You came to work just to sleep?
J: I'll be more careful, sir!
S: I've heard this excuse hundreds of times!

고참: 야, 일어나!
후참: 죄송합니다.
고참: 어제 저녁 뭐했어?
후참: 일찍 잤는데 매번 피곤합니다.
고참: 너 잠자러 출근했나?
후참: 더 주의하겠습니다.
고참: 그 변명 수백 번은 들었다!

◯ Watering flower beds 꽃밭에 물주기

You're always sleepy!
What are you doing every night?
I know you're busy watering flowerbeds[1] every night.
I also was busy watering flowerbeds when I was your age.
Don't enjoy it by yourself. Share it with me.

[해설] [1]flower는 속어로 여성의 거기(vagina)를 뜻하기도 한다. flowerbed: a place where beautiful women gather 미녀들이 모이는 곳. watering flowerbed 꽃밭에 물을 준다는 그런(?) 의미로 사용됨.

너는 만날 조는구나!
너는 밤마다 뭐하니?
너는 밤마다 꽃밭에 물 주느라 바쁜 거 안다.
나도 너 때는 꽃밭에 물 주느라 바빴다.
혼자 즐기지 마라. 같이 즐기자.

◯ Isn't your subordinate like this?

① He swears a lot.
② He smokes in the office.
③ He is a computer-blind.
④ He reads newspapers all day.
⑤ He isn't obedient to his seniors.
⑥ He is very unkind to the customers.
⑦ He hates to try new ways of working.
⑧ He comes to work just to read the Bible.
⑨ He blames his people for his mistakes.
⑩ He is often late for work, especially after lunch.
⑪ He is rude to anyone who is younger than himself.
⑫ He often forgets to report to his senior after leave.
⑬ He comes to work to study English rather than do his job.
⑭ He takes a nap in somebody else's office during duty hours.
⑮ He leaves his office too often to get his old lemon[1] repaired.

[해설] [1]lemon
① Yellow fruit containing high amounts of vitamin C.
비타민 C를 많이 함유한 노란 과일
② a defective product, esp. car (구어) 결함이 많은 물건 특히, 자동차
He's spent a fortune trying to that lemon to run right.
그는 그 똥차를 고치는데 엄청난 돈을 썼다.
③ a woman's breasts, especially if small (속어) 작은 유방
Lemon → Orange → Grapefruit → Melon (가슴을 뜻하는 과일: 小 → 大)
레몬(A)   오렌지(B)   자몽(C)   메론(D)
Alas, I found she had lemons where I wanted grapefruits.
슬픈 거사, 나는 그녀가 자몽쯤은 되는 줄 알았건만 레몬일세.

🔸 네 부하는 이렇지 않니?

① 그는 욕을 잘 한다.

② 그는 실내에서 담배를 피운다.

③ 그는 컴맹이다.

④ 그는 종일 신문을 본다.

⑤ 그는 상관에게 고분고분하지 않는다.

⑥ 그는 고객들에게 불친절하다.

⑦ 그는 새로운 방법으로 일하기를 싫어한다.

⑧ 그는 성경을 읽기 위해 출근한다.

⑨ 그는 자기 실수에 대해 부하들을 탓한다.

⑩ 그는 출근시간 특히, 점심시간 뒤에 늦는다.

⑪ 그는 자기보다 나이가 적은 사람에게는 무례하다.

⑫ 그는 휴가 후 상사에게 보고하는 것을 종종 까먹는다.

⑬ 그는 일보다는 영어 공부를 하려고 출근한다.

⑭ 그는 업무시간에 남의 사무실에 가서 낮잠을 잔다.

⑮ 그는 자기 똥차를 고치러 사무실을 너무 자주 이탈한다.

● A sentry lost his rifle

[Company commander : Platoon leader]

CC: Hello, 2nd Company commander, Capt. Kim. May I help you?

PL: Pilsung! This is 3rd Platoon Leader, 2nd Lt. Park.

CC: Anything new?

PL: I have something to report to you, sir.

CC: What's that? Go ahead.

PL: Do you remember Private Park in my platoon, sir?

CC: No, I don't. Who is he?

PL: He moved to my platoon last month.

And his father is a member of the National Assembly…

CC: You mean the guy wearing glasses?

PL: Yes, sir. That's right.

CC: Why do you ask? Did he have an accident?

PL: Yes, he lost his rifle while on guard duty.

CC: Is it possible for a sentry to lose his rifle?

And how come he lost his rifle?

PL: Maybe he fell asleep during guard duty.

CC: The sentry who loses his arms should kill himself.

How can he defend our country and citizens from the enemy? You make a report to me how you're going to punish him by tomorrow morning.

PL: Yes, sir.

(talking to himself) Anyway, he looked stupid from the beginning.

🔵 초병이 총을 분실

중대장: 여보세요. 2중대장, 김대위입니다. 무엇을 도와드릴까요?

소대장: 필승! 3소대장 박소위입니다.

중대장: 별일 없나?

소대장: 보고드릴 게 있습니다.

중대장: 뭐야? 이야기해 봐.

소대장: 저희 소대 박일병 기억나십니까?

중대장: 아니, 누구지?

소대장: 지난 달 전입한, 그의 아버지가 국회의원이고…

중대장: 아, 안경 쓴 그 친구?

소대장: 예, 그렇습니다.

중대장: 왜? 사고라도 쳤나?

소대장: 예, 그가 초병 근무 중 총을 분실했습니다.

중대장: 초병이 근무 중 총기를 잃어버렸다는 것이 가능한가?

　　　　도대체 어떻게 총을 잃어버렸나?

소대장: 아마도 잠들었던 것 같습니다.

중대장: 무기를 잃은 보초는 자살해야 한다.

　　　　어떻게 그가 우리나라와 국민을 지킬 수 있겠나?

　　　　어떻게 처벌할 건지 내일 아침까지 나한테 보고해라.

소대장: 예, 알겠습니다.

　　　　(혼자 말로) 그 자식은 어쩐지 처음부터 띨띨해 보이더라.

AWOL with arms

[Company commander : Platoon leader]

CC: Captain Kim, May I help you?

PL: Pilsung! This is Lt. Park, sir!
   One enlisted man went AWOL 10 minutes ago.

CC: What? AWOL with arms?

PL: No, just himself, sir!

CC: Without arms? That's the good side of this bad incident[1]!
   Did you report it to the Military Police Corps?

PL: Yes, sir!

[해설] [1]That's the good side of this bad incident! 나쁜 사고 중의 좋은 측면이다. → 불행 중 다행이다. → It's lucky it wasn't worse. 더 나쁘지 않아 다행이다.

무장 탈영

중대장: 김대위입니다. 무엇을 도와드릴까요?

소대장: 필승! 박중위입니다. 중대장님.

병사 하나가 10분전에 탈영했습니다.

중대장: 뭐? 무장탈영이냐?

소대장: 아닙니다. 그 자신만 탈영했습니다!

중대장: 무장 없이? 불행 중 다행이구나!
   헌병대로 보고했니?

소대장: 예, 그렇습니다.

Two privates went AWOL

[Company commander : Platoon leader]

PL: First Platoon Leader, Lt. Kim.

　　I have something to report to you, sir.

CC: What's that?

PL: Two of our privates went AWOL last night.

CC: What the hell are you saying?

　　Who was the duty officer last night?

PL: It was me, sir.

CC: You slept, didn't you?

PL: No, I didn't sir.

CC: Then how did this terrible thing happen?

두 병사가 탈영

소대장: 1소대장 김소위입니다.

　　　　중대장님 보고드릴 것이 있습니다.

중대장: 뭐야?

소대장: 어젯밤에 사병 2명이 탈영했습니다.

중대장: 도대체 무슨 말이야?

　　　　어제 밤 당직사관은 누구야?

소대장: 저입니다.

중대장: 너 잤지?

소대장: 아닙니다.

중대장: 그러면 왜 이런 끔찍한 일이 생기나?

🟠 The wind never stops blowing!

[Battalion commander : Company commander]

BC: What's up, Captain Kim?

CC: I'm sorry to report this, sir.

BC: Did something happen again?

CC: Yes, two enlisted men had a fight last night?

BC: Are they OK now?

CC: One guy is in the hospital.

BC: The wind never stops blowing in your unit!

🟠 바람 잘날 없구먼!

대대장: 무슨 일이야, 김 대위?

중대장: 이런 보고를 드려서 죄송합니다. 대대장님.

대대장: 또 무슨 일이라도 생겼니?

중대장: 예, 지난밤 두 병사가 싸웠습니다.

대대장: 지금 그들은 괜찮은가?

중대장: 한 병사는 입원했습니다.

대대장: 너의 중대는 바람 잘 날 없구먼!

🟠 A Lt. beat a sentry

[Lt. Park : Lt. Kim]

LK: Did you know Lt. Lee was in custody[1]?

LP: Why? Did he have an accident again?

LK: On his way back to his BOQ after drinking downtown, he beat a sentry.

LP: He beat a sentry?

LK: Yes, he beat a sentry.

LP: Now he's really screwed up[2] his military career!

[해설] [1]in or into custody [kʌstədi]: being kept in prison until going to court 구류되다: Two robbery suspects are being held/kept in custody. 두 명의 강도 용의자는 구금되었다. [2]screw up: to make a mistake 실수하다, 망치다: You really screwed up your life when you quit school. 너는 학교를 그만둬서 인생을 정말 망쳤다.

🟠 중위가 초병을 패다

김중위: 너, 이중위 구속 된 거 아니?

박중위: 왜? 또 사고라도 쳤나?

김중위: 시내에서 술 먹고 BOQ로 오는 길에 초병을 팼대.

박중위: 그가 초병을 팼다고?

김중위: 그래. 초병을 때렸데.

박중위: 그는 군생활 끝장났군!

● We got put on "military attention"

A: Let's go out and have a drink.

B: I'm sorry. I can't.

A: Why?

B: We got put on **military attention** as of today.

A: For what?

B: Staff Sgt. Park was arrested for drunk driving yesterday.

A: If a trivial thing happens, why does everybody have to be confined to barracks?

* **Military attention** is a kind of group punishment, which is often enforced in the case of a member of a certain unit causing an accident by drunk-driving, loose discipline or other kinds of carelessness. Once military attention is enforced, all members of the unit are confined to barracks or elsewhere in the garrison for a certain period of time.

● 우리 "군차렷" 걸렸어

A: 나가서 한잔 꺾자.

B: 미안해. 안 돼.

A: 왜?

B: 우리 금일 부로 군차렷이다.

A: 무슨 이유로?

B: 박하사가 음주운전으로 어제 구속 되었다.

A: 사소한 일만 생겨도 왜 모두가 영내 대기해야 돼?

* **군차렷**은 일종의 집단적으로 벌을 받는 것으로 음주운전, 군기강 해이 혹은 다른 부주의한 행동요인에 의해 사고가 날 경우에 시행된다. 일단 군차렷이 걸리면 그 소속 구성원 전원은 일정기간 동안 부대 내의 내무반, 또는 어떤 장소에 기거해야 한다.

🔸 Oath neither to assault nor abuse

First, I will never provoke[1] an assault[2].
Second, I will never assault nor align[3] myself with an assault.
Third, I will never conceal an assault which I witness.
Fourth, I will be impartial[4] in judging all cases of assault when a beating has occurred.

I'll solemnly pledge that I'll be punished under the military code if I violate any of the above.

September 3, 2002

Affiliation: Supply Sq.   Name: Hong Kil-dong   Signature: *Hong Kit Dong*

[해설] [1]provoke [prəvóuk]: to bring about; incite 유발시키다, 자극하다: His speech provoked criticism from the audience. 그의 연설은 청중으로부터 비난을 일으켰다. [2]assault [əsɔ́:lt]: the crime of attacking a person 폭행: He was charged with assault on a police officer. 그는 경찰관을 폭행해서 구속되었다. [3]align yourself with A: to support the opinions of A. A의 의견을 지지/동의하다. Many voters are not aligned with any party. 많은 유권자들이 어떤 당도 지지하지 않는다. [4]impartial [impá:ʃəl]: treating all sides fairly; objective 공평한, 편견이 없는 ↔ partial; biased 불공평한, 치우친

🔸 구타 및 가혹 행위 근절 서약

첫째, 나는 구타 유발 행위를 하지 않는다.
둘째, 나는 구타를 자행하거나 동조하지 않는다.
셋째, 나는 구타를 인지하면 은닉하지 않는다.
넷째, 나는 구타사고 발생시 정실(情實)처리 하지 않는다.

위 내용을 위반 시에는 법에 따라 어떠한 처벌도 감수할 것을 엄숙히 맹세합니다.

2002년 9월 3일
소속: 보급대대   성명: 홍 길 동   서명: 홍 길 동

🔸 If it's busy, dial 1234

[Lt. Kim : Capt. Park]

LK: Personnel section, Lt. Kim speaking. May I help you?

CP: This is Capt. Park at the Supply Squadron.

LK: Good morning, sir.

CP: Can I speak to Lt. Lee?

LK: We have two Lt. Lees. Which one?

CP: The guy with the Jella-do accent.

LK: Oh, he went to the visitors' center 10 minutes ago.

CP: Put me through to[1] the visitors' center.

LK: Yes, I'll do that, but if it's busy or disconnected, dial 1234.

CP: Thank you, Lt. Kim.

LK: You're welcome, sir.

[해설] [1]put A through to B: connect A with B A를 B에게 전화 연결시키다: Could you put me through to the personnel department? 인사부로 연결해주시겠어요?

🔸 통화 중이면 1234로

김중위: 인사과 김중위입니다. 무엇을 도와드릴까요?

박대위: 보급대대 박대위인데.

김중위: 굿모닝 써.

박대위: 이중위 좀 바꿔 줄래?

김중위: 이중위가 둘인데. 어떤 이중위 말입니까?

박대위: 전라도 억양이 있는 친구.

김중위: 그 친구 10분전에 면회실 갔습니다.

박대위: 면회실로 좀 돌려줘.

김중위: 네, 전화가 통화 중이거나 끊어지면 1234로 거십시오.

박대위: 김중위 고마워.

김중위: 아닙니다.

🟠 Get me an officer

[2nd Lt. Kim : Lt. Col.]

LK: Field Maintenance Squadron. Second Lt. Kim speaking. May I help you?

LC: Get me an officer!

LK: I'm sorry, but who is this calling?

LC: OK, This is Lt. Col. Park at the 122 SQ.

LK: Pilsung! I'm also an officer!

LC: This is an emergency. Get me an officer!

* Inexperienced new officers at a Field Maintenance Squadron, Air Wing were often ruled out in an emergency situation.

🟠 장교 바꿔

소위: 야전정비대대 김소위입니다.
　　　무엇을 도와 드릴까요?

중령: 장교 바꿔라!

소위: 실례지만 누구십니까?

중령: 122대대 박중령이다.

소위: 예, 필승. 저 장교입니다!

중령: 상황이 급해서 그래. 장교 바꿔!

* 비행단의 야전정비대대에서 신임 장교들은 비상 상황 하에서 업무에서 종종 배제되었다.

● Have you ever served in the 7th Division?

A: Have you ever served in the 7th Division?
B: Where is it located?
A: It's near ○○.
B: I worked there while I was a captain.
A: Who is the current division commander of the 7th Division?
B: I think it's General Park.

● 7사단 근무해봤어?

A: 7사단에 근무해봤니?
B: 7사단이 어디 있니?
A: ○○ 근처에 있지.
B: 내가 대위 때 거기서 근무했지.
A: 지금 7사단장이 누구지.
B: 박장군님인 것 같은데.

● Transferring report

Reporting as ordered, sir.
Captain Kim Kil-dong,
ordered to be transferred
to the 7th Division as of July 1, 2000.
Reporting as ordered!

● 전속신고

신고합니다. 대위 김길동은
2000년 7월 1일부로
7사단으로 전속을 명 받았습니다.
이에 신고합니다!

● Before saying "good-bye" to the commander

[Lt. Col.: Capt. Kim]

CK: With your help I have worked here without any problems.

LC: No, I should say, "thank you."

I was able to carry out my mission successfully with your positive support. I don't know who can take your place.

CK: Although I am going to move to the next station, please watch over me, sir!

LC: Yes, I will if I can. Let's keep in touch from time to time.

● 대대장님을 떠나기 전에

대 위: 대대장님의 배려로 문제없이 잘 근무할 수 있었습니다.

대대장: 아니야, 내가 고맙다고 해야 돼.

나는 너의 적극적인 도움으로 나의 임무를 성공적으로 수행할 수 있었다. 누가 너의 자리를 대신할지 모르겠구나.

대 위: 비록 다음 부대로 가더라도 잘 봐 주십시오.

대대장: 내가 도와 줄 수 있다면 그러지. 가끔 서로 연락하자.

◎ I am going to be a leader like you, sir!

[Lt. Col.: Capt. Kim]

LC: Capt. Kim, did you have any inconveniences or difficulties working with me?

CK: No, sir. I wish I could work with you forever.

LC: What makes you say so?

CK: You did not ask us to do unrealistic or unreasonable things. A more important thing is that you didn't ask me to have dinner with you after work so I was free to do what I wanted. I mean you're no burden at all after work. I am going to be a leader like you, sir!

◎ 대대장님과 같은 리더가 되겠습니다!

대대장: 김대위, 나와 일하면서 불편하거나 힘든 일 없었나?

김대위: 없었습니다. 대대장님과 평생 같이 일하고 싶습니다.

대대장: 그 이유가 뭔가?

김대위: 대대장님은 비현실적이거나 불합리한 것을 시키지 않습니다.
더욱 중요한 것은 우리에게 저녁식사를 같이하자고 안 하시니까
우리가 원하는 것을 마음대로 할 수 있어서 좋습니다.
대대장님은 일과 후에는 우리에게 부담이 되지 않습니다.
대대장님과 같은 리더가 되겠습니다.

I've heard of it

[Maj. Kim : Lt. Col. Park]

MK: Major Kim, Operation Section, 7th Division. May I help you?

CP: This is Lt. Col. Park, 8th Division.

MK: Pilsung!

CP: A Capt. Kim in my office is being transferred to your division as of next Monday.

MK: Yes, I've heard about it, sir.

CP: He is an honest, sincere, and dedicated officer.

MK: I'll take good care of him, sir.
I'll reserve a condo this summer.
Come and have a drink of soju[1] with me, sir.

CP: Oh, I see. Thank you, Major Kim.

[해설] 1soju: Korean traditional distilled liquor 소주. Its taste is comparable to vodka. 그것의 맛은 보드카와 유사하다.

얘기 들었습니다

김소령: 7사단 작전과 김소령입니다. 무엇을 도와드릴까요?

박중령: 그래, 8사단 박중령인데.

김소령: 필승!

박중령: 내 사무실에 있는 김대위가 다음 주 월요일부로 너의 사단으로 전속 간다.

김소령: 예, 얘기 들었습니다.

박중령: 그는 정직하며 성실하고 헌신적인 장교야.

김소령: 예, 잘 보살펴 주겠습니다.
이번 여름에 여기 콘도 하나 예약해 놓겠습니다.
저와 소주 한 잔 하시죠.

박중령: 알았다. 고마워, 김소령.

Move-in Report

Reporting as ordered, sir.
Captain Kim Kil-dong,
ordered to move into the 7th Division
as of July 1, 2003.
Reporting as ordered!

전입신고

신고합니다. 대위 김길동은
2003년 7월 1일부로
7사단으로 전입을 명 받았습니다.
이에 신고합니다!

Position Report

Reporting as ordered, sir.
Captain Kim Kil-dong,
ordered to be assigned as the Operations Officer in the 7th Division
as of July 1, 2003.
Reporting as ordered!

보직신고

신고합니다. 대위 김길동은
2003년 7월 1일부로 7사단 작전장교로
보직을 명 받았습니다.
이에 신고합니다!

You're fortunate

You're fortunate to work under me. You have to have pride in yourself to work under me. Maybe you haven't worked for a person like me. I think I am honest, sincere, educated, rational and considerate. I will not ask you to do anything that is for my private business.

너는 운 좋다

너는 내 밑에서 근무해서 운이 좋다. 너는 내 밑에서 근무하는 것을 자랑스럽게 여겨야 한다. 너는 나 같은 사람 밑에서 근무해본 적이 없을 거다. 나는 정직하고, 성실하고, 배웠고, 합리적이고 또한 남을 배려할 줄 안다. 나는 내 개인적인 어떤 일도 너에게 시키지 않겠다.

🟠 You're lucky!

A: Buy me a drink tonight, Lt. Kim.

B: Why?

A: Because you're lucky!

B: Why do you say that?

A: Your new commander is gentle, nice, and considerate to his people.

B: Who is he?

A: Captain Kim at the 3rd Battalion.

　　I worked for him when I was a Lt.

　　He is a really wonderful commander.

B: I have had a hard time with my present commander.

🟠 너 행운이다!

A: 김중위, 너 오늘 저녁 나한테 한잔 사라.

B: 뭣 때문에?

A: 너 행운이다!

B: 왜 그런 소리를?

A: 새로 오시는 너의 중대장님은 점잖고 부하를 배려할 줄 아는 사람이야.

B: 누군데?

A: 3대대 김대위님.

　　내가 소위 때 모셨지.

　　그분은 정말 훌륭한 지휘관이셔.

B: 나는 지금 중대장님과는 힘든 시간이었어.

He is an FM

A: Do you know anything about our new commander?

B: I heard he is an **FM**.

A: "Better the devil you know than the devil you don't know.[1]"

B: I heard that he changed his driver five times last year.

A: Be well prepared for the commander's first inspection tour.

* **FM** is a Field Manual, meaning a rule oriented, strict person.

[해설] [1]구관이 명관을 "You don't know what you've got until it's gone."라고도 한다.

그분은 FM이래

A: 새로 오시는 대대장님에 대해서 좀 아니?

B: 그분은 FM이래.

A: "구관이 명관이지."

B: 그는 지난해 운전병을 5번이나 바꿨대.

A: 초도순시에 대비해서 준비 잘 해놔.

* **FM** 이란 야전 교범으로 규칙에 철저한 엄격한 사람을 의미한다.

🔸 A US soldier's belt

[Captain : Lieutenant]

C: Hey, Lt. Kim! Your belt looks different today.

L: I bought this when I was in the United States last year.

C: But you have to use our military supplies.

L: Yes, but this US made one is elastic.

   It's more convenient.

C: I know, but regulations are regulations.

🔸 미군 벨트

대 위: 야, 김중위 오늘 너의 벨트는 다르다.

중 위: 작년 미국에 있을 때 하나 샀습니다.

대 위: 하지만 우리 지급품을 사용해야지.

중 위: 알겠습니다, 하지만 미제 벨트는 신축성이 있습니다.

   그래서 더욱 편합니다.

대 위: 나도 안다, 하지만 규정은 규정이다.

Education, training, and nagging

A: What is Captain John like?

B: He is nice, but too talkative.

A: Isn't he an officer commissioned from the ranks?

B: Yes, he is. He is like a mother-in-law.

A: He can't tell the difference between education, training, nagging, and brainwashing.

B: Could you define each of them?

A: Sure, why not. Listen!

* Education is to give people information about something so that they understand it better. Education as a whole should be a continuous process of "aha."
* Training is to teach someone how to do something, usually a skill that is needed for a job.
* Nagging is to keep criticizing or giving advice to someone in an annoying way.
* Brainwashing is to make someone believe something by telling them that it is true many times.

교육, 훈련, 잔소리

A: 존대위는 어떠니?

B: 그는 좋지만 말이 너무 많아.

A: 그는 사병에서 장교가 된 사람 아닌가?

B: 맞아. 그는 시어머니 같아.

A: 그는 교육, 훈련, 잔소리, 그리고 세뇌의 차이를 몰라.

B: 그들의 정의를 각각 내려줄래?

A: 그래. 들어봐!

* 교육은 사람들이 어떤 것을 더 잘 이해할 수 있도록 정보를 주는 것. 교육은 전체적으로 "아하"의 계속적인 과정이어야 한다.
* 훈련은 무엇을 할 수 있도록 가르치는 것으로 보통 직업의 기능과 관련되는 것이다.
* 잔소리는 계속 비난하거나 어떤 사람을 짜증나는 방법으로 충고를 주는 것이다.
* 세뇌란 어떤 사람에게 어떤 것을 진실이라고 여러 번 이야기해서 믿도록 하는 것이다.

🔵 Bosses and mothers-in-law

① They are sulky[1].

② They are stingy[2].

③ They are greedy.

④ They give lectures[3].

⑤ They are wise, though.

⑥ They are old-fashioned[4].

⑦ They worry over nothing.

⑧ They give unwanted advice.

⑨ They are good targets for gossip.

⑩ They want to be served faithfully.

[해설] [1]sulky [sʌ́lki]: to act as if hurt and angry by being silent 삐진, 시무룩한: When her bf will not see her, she sulks for days. 그녀의 남친이 그녀를 보지 않는다면 그녀는 며칠 삐질 것이다. [2]stingy [stíndʒi]: unwilling to share or spend 인색한: Don't be stingy; give me a bite of your sandwich. 아끼지 말고 너의 샌드위치 조금만 줘라. [3]lecture: (to give) a long, serious talk with a warning (긴) 훈계, 훈계하다: The boy's mother lectured him on bicycle safety. 어머니는 아들에게 자전거의 안전에 대해 훈계했다. [4]old-fashioned: not considered to be modern 구식의

🔵 상사와 시어머니

① 잘 삐친다.

② 인색하다.

③ 요구가 많다.

④ 훈계를 한다.

⑤ 지혜는 있다.

⑥ 구식이다.

⑦ 쓸데없는 걱정을 한다.

⑧ 원치 않는 충고를 한다.

⑨ 험담의 훌륭한 대상이다.

⑩ 극진히 섬겨주길 바란다.

Bleeding to death from mosquito bites

[Company commander : Lieutenant]

CC: Hey, Lt. Kim! What are you doing now?

LT: I'm educating my enlisted men.

CC: Why do you have them standing here in swarms of mosquitoes?

LT: It has only been 3 minutes so far.

CC: Did you happen to get some bribes from the mosquitoes?

LT: What are you talking about, sir?

CC: I think you're giving mosquitoes an opportunity to suck blood from your men. Dismiss[1] your soldiers right now! Your men have the right to receive effective instruction.

LT: Yes, sir!

[해설] [1]dismiss: to give sb official permission to leave 해산하다: The bell rang and the teacher dismissed the class. 벨이 울리자 교사는 학생들을 해산했다.

모기 회식

중대장: 야, 김중위, 지금 뭐하고 있나?

중 위: 병사들 교육 좀 시키고 있습니다.

중대장: 모기가 우글거리는데 병사들을 왜 여기 세워두고 있나?

중 위: 3분밖에 안 지났습니다.

중대장: 모기한테 뇌물이라도 받은 거 아니야?

중 위: 무슨 말씀입니까?

중대장: 모기들에게 너의 병사들의 피를 빨아 먹을 기회를 주고 있구나. 당장 해산시켜라! 네 부하들은 효과적으로 교육 받을 권리가 있다.

중 위: 예, 알겠습니다.

◎ Poor leadership

[Company commander: Platoon leader]

CC: Hey, Lt. Kim? What're you doing now?

PL: I'm disciplining the troops.

CC: For what?

PL: One of the them was late returning to the barracks.

CC: But why are you punishing the whole group?

PL: Isn't esprit de corps important in the military?

CC: Never punish your troops in a group because of someone's trivial mistakes. Group punishment is poor leadership according to *The Marine Officer's Guide.*

PL: Yes, I'll keep that in mind, sir.

CC: Dismiss your troops now.

PL: Yes, sir!

* "Nothing makes an innocent person more infuriated than being unfairly included in a group punishment." Where and how can he get compensation for this injustice? Never make someone an innocent victim!

* It is better that ten guilty persons escape than one innocent suffer.
  – Sir William Blackstone, a lawyer in England (1723-1780) –

🔸 불쌍한 리더십

중대장: 야, 김중위? 너 지금 뭐하고 있어?

소대장: 병사들 군기 좀 잡고 있습니다.

중대장: 무엇 때문에?

소대장: 병사 한 명이 귀영시간에 늦었습니다.

중대장: 그렇다고 왜 단체기합을 주지?

소대장: 군대는 단체정신이 중요하지 않습니까?

중대장: 사소한 개인의 잘못으로 절대 단체기합 주지 마라.

　　　　미 해병대 가이드에 의하면 단체기합은 불쌍한 리더십이다.

소대장: 명심하겠습니다.

중대장: 당장 해산시켜라.

소대장: 알겠습니다.

＊ 죄 없는 사람이 단체기합에 억울하게 포함되는 것보다 그를 더 분하게 하는 것은 없다. 그가 어디서 어떻게 그의 억울함을 보상받을 수 있겠나? 절대 생사람 잡지 마라.

＊ 한 사람의 죄 없는 사람이 처벌받기보다는 10명의 죄인이 도망가는 편이 낫다.

－ 블랙스턴, 영국의 법학자(1723-1780) －

🟠 I'll satisfy hunger with ramyon

A: Let's go have lunch.

B: No, I won't.

A: Did you bring a box lunch?

B: No. I didn't. I'll satisfy my hunger[1] with ramyon.

A: And why? Instant noodles are not good.
　　Let's go to the officer's dining facility.

B: I'm not going there because the military discipline officer is watching in front of the dining facility!

A: Then, I won't go, either.

B: Isn't it mean to enforce[2] military discipline in front of the mess hall[3]? This kind of military discipline is not enforced in the US armed forces.

[해설] [1]satisfy sb's hunger/appetite/thirst 허기/식욕/갈증을 해소하다: There's nothing like a cold beer to satisfy your thirst. 갈증해소에 시원한 맥주만 한 게 없다. [2]enforce [enfɔːrs]: to make people obey a rule or law (법을) 집행하다: The speed limit is strictly enforced. 속도 제한이 엄격히 시행된다. [3]mess hall: a cafeteria in a US military installation (미군 기지의) 식당으로 **chow hall**이라 하기도 하며, 정식명칭은 **dining facility** (**DFAC** [diːfæk] 디팩)이다.

🟠 라면으로 때우다

A: 점심 먹으러 가자.

B: 나 안 갈래.

A: 너 도시락 싸왔어?

B: 아니야. 라면으로 때워야겠어.

A: 왜 라면으로 때워? 인스턴트는 안 좋아.
　　장교 식당으로 같이 가자.

B: 나 안 갈래. 군기 순찰 장교가 식당 앞에 감시하고 있어!

A: 그럼 나도 안 갈래.

B: 식당 앞에서 군기를 잡는 것은 비열하지 않는가?
　　이렇게 군기를 잡는 것은 미군에서도 시행되지 않는다.

🟤 Don't call younger Lts. SOBs

[Major : Captain]

M: Captain Cho, could you come here?

C: Yes. sir.

M: Don't call younger Lts. SOBs or fucking guys.

C: I'm very sorry, sir. I was very angry at that moment.

M: Officers should control their tempers.

If you get a promotion to a higher position, you might hurl[1] ashtrays at your subordinates.

[해설] [1]hurl: to throw sth with great force (세게) 던지다: Protesters hurled rocks at the police. 항의자들은 경찰에 돌을 던졌다. 전치사 at은 목표물을 향한 "의도성"을, to는 "방향"을 나타낸다.

🟤 젊은 장교들을 개××라고 부르지 마

소령: 조대위, 이리 좀 와 줄래?

대위: 왜 그러십니까?

소령: 신참 중위들을 부를 때 개××나 18놈이라고 부르지 마라.

대위: 죄송합니다. 그때 너무 화가 나서.

소령: 장교로서 감정을 통제하도록 해.

넌 더 높은 자리에 오르면 부하들에게 재떨이를 던질지 모르겠다.

Let's not salute Captain Kim

A: Let's not salute Captain Kim anymore.
B: Why?
A: He never returns my salute.
B: When he receives a salute, he just nods.
A: I salute his rank, not him.

김대위님께 경례하지 말자

A: 김대위님에게 더 이상 경례하지 말자.
B: 왜?
A: 그분은 답례를 안 해.
B: 그가 경례를 받으면 고개만 끄덕이더라.
A: 나는 그의 계급에 경례할 뿐이야.

Dig two foxholes

[Company commander : Platoon leader]

CC: Lt. Kim, dig two foxholes[1] by next Saturday.
PL: I'm sorry, sir. We have lots of things to do besides that.
CC: So, you can't?
PL: Just give us another week, sir.
CC: If I were you, I could do it in three days.
　　When I was a Lt., I used to dig 3 foxholes in a week.
PL: You're still living in the Old Stone Age, sir!

[해설] [1]foxhole: a hole dug in the ground where soldiers stay for protection against enemy gunfire 참호: It is necessary for a foxhole to be deep so it can protect a soldier. 참호는 군인을 보호할 수 있도록 깊어야 한다.

🔸 전투호 2개 파라

중대장: 김중위, 다음 주말까지 전투호 2개 파라.

소대장: 죄송합니다. 그것 말고도 할 일이 많습니다.

중대장: 그래서 못하겠다고?

소대장: 일주일만 더 주십시오.

중대장: 내가 너라면 3일 만에 하겠다.

　　　　내가 중위 때는 일주일에 전투호 3개를 파곤 했다.

소대장: 중대장님은 아직도 구석기 시대에 살고 계십니다!

🔸 Is an O-2 an airplane?

A: What type of plane does he fly?

B: An O-2.

A: Is an O-2 an airplane?

B: Yes, it is still in operation.

A: If an O-2 is an airplane, a dung fly is a bird.

🔸 O-2기가 비행기냐?

A: 그의 기종이 뭐냐?

B: O-2기.

A: O-2기가 비행기냐?

B: 그럼, 아직도 운용중인데.

A: O-2기가 비행기라면 똥파리도 새다.

🔸 O-2 aircraft (O-2 전술항공통제기)

　　전투기는 고속으로 비행하기 때문에 작전지역에서 이동하는 차량과 소규모 병력 등 작은 표적은 관찰하기 어렵다. 이에 비해 O-2기는 상대적으로 저속으로 비행하여 작전지역의 정보를 관찰해서 전투기에게 정보를 주는 역할을 한다.

　　한국에는 1974년 한국에 도입되어 2007년 퇴역하고 국산 KO1기로 대체되고 있다. O-2 항공기의 가격 및 O-2기 조종사에 대한 대우가 전투기의 그것에 미치지 못하기 때문에 여기서 폄하되고 있다.

🔸 Our inspection begins tomorrow

[Battalion commander : Lieutenant Kim]

BC: Our inspection begins tomorrow, right[1]?

LK: Yes, it does.

BC: Did you make a reservation for rooms for the inspection team?

LK: Yes, I did. I reserved 3 VIP rooms at the BOQ.

BC: Try to get to know what they like and dislike.

LK: I heard that they don't like to get special treatment anymore.

[해설] [1]부가 의문문에서 aren't you?는 현재 대화를 나누는 상대에게 사용하고, right는 제3자의 입장에서 어떤 정보를 확인할 때 사용한다. You're from South Korea, aren't you? (미국에서 교관이 당신에게), The movie starts at nine, right? 영화가 9시에 시작하는 거 맞죠?

🔸 내일부터 검열이다

대대장: 내일부터 검열이 시작되지?

김중위: 예, 그렇습니다.

대대장: 검열관들 숙소는 예약했니?

김중위: 예, BOQ에 VIP룸 3개를 예약했습니다.

대대장: 그들이 좋아하는 것과 싫어하는 것도 파악해라.

김중위: 요즘 그들은 특별 대접받기를 좋아하지 않는다고 합니다.

🔸 You wrote a novel

[Major : Lieutenant]

M: Lt. Kim, did you finish the report?

L: Yes, sir. Here you go.

M: You wrote a novel rather than a military report!
Brand new Lts. tend to write reports like novels.
In the military the report should be brief.
Preview, contents, and conclusion.

🔸 너 소설을 썼구나

소 령: 김중위, 너 그 보고서 끝냈니?

소 위: 예, 여기 있습니다.

소 령: 너는 군대 보고서라기보다는 소설을 썼구나!
신임 장교들은 소설 같은 보고서를 쓰는 경향이 많아.
군대 보고서는 간단해야 한다.
서론, 본론, 결론으로 말이다.

🔸 Thaw the ice with an electric iron

A VIP will visit tomorrow.

Clean indoors and outdoors thoroughly.

First impressions are very important.

Be sure to crack the ice on the entrance to the porch with a hammer and a chisel[1].

Then, thaw[2] the ice on the porch with an electric iron.

After that, spread boiling water over the ice and mop it up.

[해설] [1]chisel [tʃízəl]: a metal tool used to cut wood or stone 끌. [2]thaw [θɔː]: of (snow/ice) turns into water (눈/얼음이) 녹다: The snow was beginning to thaw. 눈이 녹기 시작했다. mop ~ up: to clean liquid off a surface using a mop 밀대질 하다: The waitress mopped up the mess. 웨이트리스가 어지른 것을 치웠다.

🔸 얼음을 다리미로 녹여

내일 중요한 분이 방문한다.

실내외 청소를 철저히 하라.

첫 인상은 매우 중요하다.

현관 입구의 얼음은 망치와 끌로 깨라.

그리고 현관의 얼음은 전기다리미로 녹여라.

그 다음 끓는 물을 얼음에 붓고 밀대질 해라.

🟠 Go and get some sleep

[Platoon leader : Company commander]

PL: Sir, may I have the rest of the day off?

CC: Oh, you were on duty[1] last night.

PL: Yes, I was.

CC: You look very tired. Go and get some sleep.

PL: Yes, take care. sir!

[해설] [1]be on/off duty: to be working or not working at a particular time 근무/비번인: Which nurse was on duty last night? 어젯밤 근무는 어느 간호사였나?

🟠 가서 좀 자라

소대장: 중대장님, 그만 퇴근해도 되겠습니까?

중대장: 너 어제 당직 섰구나.

소대장: 예, 그렇습니다.

중대장: 피곤해 보이는구나. 가서 좀 자라.

소대장: 예, 알겠습니다. 수고하십시오.

🟡 Pound a stake in the military

[Captain : Lieutenant]

C: Hey, Lt. Kim. You'd better **pound a stake in the military**.
L: What do you mean, sir?
C: I think you are more of[1] a military kind of guy.
L: Am I? I don't think so.
C: I think you're a typical military guy.
   You drink well, sing well, and you are good at[2] all sports!
L: I'm sorry, sir. If I pound stakes in the military, I'll **cook my finger**.
C: But you will regret it soon after you leave the military.
L: Never, sir!

* **Pound a stake in the military** is a slang expression in Korea, which is often used among the soldiers when "a short-period soldier applies to be a long-term soldier." **cook one's finger** means "to eat one's hat" in Korea.
* **말뚝을 박다**라는 말은 한국에서 속으로 "단기복무 군인이 장기복무 지원을 하다"는 말로 종종 사용된다. **손으로 장을 지지다**는 "전혀 가능성이 없음"을 의미한다.

[해설] [1]more of an A: A에 더 가까운 → 체질인: He isn't really officer material. 그는 장교 체질이 아니다. [2]be good at: talented, skillful 익숙한, 잘하는: She is good/talented/skillful at playing the piano. 그녀는 피아노를 잘 친다.

🟡 군대 말뚝 박아라

대위: 김중위, 너 군대 말뚝 박아라.
중위: 예, 무슨 말씀이십니까? 중대장님.
대위: 너는 군대 체질이다.
중위: 제가요? 저는 그렇지 않다고 생각하는데.
대위: 너는 전형적인 군인이다.
     술 잘해, 노래 잘해, 운동 잘하지.
중위: 죄송합니다. 제가 말뚝 박으면 손가락에 장을 지지겠습니다.
대위: 그래도 제대하면 후회할걸.
중위: 절대 아닙니다.

Why didn't you salute me?

[Lieutenant : Staff Sgt]

L: Hey, Sergeant! Stop right there.

S: Excuse me, sir?

L: Why didn't you salute me?

S: I'm sorry. I didn't notice you.

L: You didn't see me? Does that make sense?

S: I forgot to put on my glasses this morning.

L: Put on your glasses if you can't see people properly.

* A hand salute is the principal symbol of military courtesy and it must always be rendered solemnly and decently. When giving a hand salute, unauthorized catchwords such as "take care", "good morning" and "have you eaten?" must not be addressed. "Military courtesy is a prerequisite to military discipline."

너 왜 경례 안 해?

중위: 이봐, 하사 거기 서 봐.

하사: 왜 그러시죠?

중위: 너 왜 경례 안 하니?

하사: 죄송합니다. 못 봤습니다.

중위: 날 못 봤다고? 그게 말이 돼?

하사: 오늘 아침 안경 쓰는 것을 잊었습니다.

중위: 사람을 몰라보면 안경을 쓰라.

* 거수경례는 엄정한 군기를 상징하는 군대예절의 기본이므로 항상 엄숙 단 정하게 실시되어야 한다. 경례를 하면서 "수고 하십니다", "안녕 하십니까", "식사하셨습니까?"와 같은 비인가 구호를 절대로 사용해서는 안 된다. "군대예절은 군기 이전의 문제다."

◉ Say "Chungsung!"

[Sgt. Park : Capt. Kim]

SP: Master Sgt. Park at the Supply Squadron. May I help you?

CK: Capt. Kim speaking at the Personnel Dept.

SP: What's the purpose of your call?

CK: Sgt., don't you know the correct military telephone manner? Say "Chungsung!"

SP: Chungsung!

CK: If you receive a telephone call from a senior, say "Chungsung" before you state your business.

SP: I'm so sorry, sir! I didn't hear you properly.

* While you may not be reprimanded on the spot for the omission of "Chungsung," that omission is quickly noted and usually remembered. The exchange of military salutes between officers and enlisted men should not be overlooked. Its omission indicates poor discipline.

◉ "충성" 해 봐!

박중사: 보급대 박중사입니다. 무엇을 도와드릴까요?

김대위: 인사처 김대위입니다.

박중사: 어떻게 전화하셨습니까?

김대위: 이봐, 당신은 군대 전화 매너도 모르나?
"충성!"이라고 해봐.

박중사: 충성!

김대위: 상관으로부터 전화 받으면 업무를 얘기하기 전에 충성이라고 해야지.

박중사: 정말 죄송합니다! 잘못 알아들었습니다.

* 당신이 "충성"이라고 하지 않았다고 해서 현장에서 꾸중 받지 않을지 모르지만 "충성"을 빼먹은 것은 대번에 인지되고 항상 기억된다. 장교와 사병 간에 경례를 주고받는 것은 간과되어서는 안 된다. 경례를 안 하는 것은 군기가 빠진 것을 의미한다.

Never forget "sir"

Never forget that "sir" or "ma'am" are important words in communication with anyone senior. While you may not be reprimanded on the spot for the omission of "sir" or "ma'am," that omission is quickly noted and usually remembered.

"님"자 빼지 마라

상관과의 대화에서도 "님"자가 중요한 말임을 절대로 잊지 마라. 당신이 "님"자를 붙이지 않았다고 해서 현장에서 꾸중을 듣지 않을지도 모르지만, 상관은 "님"자를 뺀 것을 대번에 알아차리고 그것을 항상 기억한다.

NCOs have always been important

NCOs have always been important. Respect the skill and experience of your NCOs. Learn from the wisdom of NCOs, but never let them snow[1] you. Do everything in your power to enhance the skill, prestige[2], and authority of NCOs, except at the expense of[3] your own prestige and authority.

[해설] [1] snow: to persuade sb to do sth by flattering or deceiving sb 아첨/감언으로 설득하다: I'd been a fool letting him snow me with his big ideas. 나는 그가 거창한 아이디어로 나를 속이도록 내버려둔 바보였다. [2] prestige [prestíːdʒ]: having a high reputation 명성, 위신: Our company has gained international prestige. 우리 회사는 국제적인 명성을 얻었다. [3] at the expense of ~: ~의 비용으로

부사관은 항상 중요하다

부사관은 항상 중요하다. 부사관의 경험과 기술을 존경하라. 부사관으로부터 지혜를 배우되 그들이 너를 감언이설로 압도하도록 내버려두지 마라. 너 자신의 위신과 권위를 희생하지 않는 범위 내에서 모든 것을 네가 장악하고 부사관의 직무기술, 명성과 권위를 높여라.

🔸 You go into the military again

A: A man can be a real man after serving in the military.
B: I was exempted from the military.
   Then I can't be a man among men.
   You can go into the military again.
   And you can be a man again.
A: I already became a man among men.

🔸 Although he served in the Air Force for over 10 years, he didn't become a human being. I don't know what the Air Force has done to him. 그는 공군에서 10년 넘게 근무했지만 인간이 되지 않았다. 공군이 그에게 뭘 가르쳤는지 모르겠다.

🔸 너 군대 한 번 더 가라

A: 남자는 군대 갔다 와야 사람 된다.
B: 나는 군대 면제 받았는데.
   나는 사나이 될 수 없네.
   너는 군대 한 번 더 가라.
   그러면 너는 사람 한 번 더 되겠다.
A: 나는 이미 사나이가 되었는데.

🔸 Security test

A: Let's go for a drink after work.

B: I'm sorry. I have a test tomorrow.

A: What sort of test?

B: A test on security.

A: Never mind. It's an open book test. Let's go.

B: But an open book test is more difficult.

A: Haven't you taken tests once or twice before in the military?

B: I see, but if we score under 70 percent, we won't get a pass tomorrow.

🔸 보안 평가

A: 퇴근 후에 술 한잔하러 가자.

B: 안 돼. 내일 시험 있어.

A: 무슨 시험?

B: 보안평가.

A: 신경 꺼. 오픈 북이야. 가자.

B: 그래? 오픈 북이 더 어려워.

A: 군대시험 한두 번 보나?

B: 알았어, 하지만 70점미만의 점수를 받으면 우리 외출증 못 받아.

Unauthorized disk

A: Do you have a blank floppy disk?

B: Use the one on my desk.

A: Isn't this an unauthorized disk?

B: Yes, it is.

A: You'd better not use an unauthorized disk.

B: Do you know we have an inspection next week?

A: Then let's register it now.

비인가 디스켓

A: 빈 플로피 디스켓 한 장 있나?

B: 내 책상 위에 있는 거 하나 써.

A: 이거 비인가 디스켓 아냐?

B: 맞아.

A: 비인가 디스켓 안 쓰는 게 좋아.

B: 다음 주에 검열 있는 거 알아?

A: 그러면 지금 등록하자.

🔘 I have to prepare for the inspection

[Lt. Kim : Lt. Park]

LK: Hello, This is Lt. Kim of Personnel Section. May I help you?

LP: This is Lt. Park. Come on over to the tennis court.

LK: I'm sorry. I have to prepare for the inspection.

LP: You can do it tonight. Our commander is here.

LK: I'm really sorry, Lt. Park.

LP: We need one more player for tennis.

LK: Oh, I see!

🔘 검열 준비해야 돼

김중위: 인사처 김중위 입니다. 무엇을 도와 드릴까요?

박중위: 박중위야. 테니스 코트로 나와라.

김중위: 미안해. 검열 준비해야 돼.

박중위: 오늘밤에 해도 되잖아. 대대장님 여기 계셔.

김중위: 박중위 미안해.

박중위: 한 명이 부족해.

김중위: 그래 알았어!

◯ An unauthorized electric heater

[Fire inspector : User of an unauthorized heater]

F: Isn't this an unauthorized electric heater?

U: Yes, it is, sir.

F: Why are you using this?

U: Sorry, but it's freezing[1] here.

F: Only you are cold?

U: I'll never use it again, sir.

F: I am confiscating[2] this.

[해설] [1]freezing: very cold 매우 추운: Hurry up! I'm freezing! 서둘러! 추워죽겠어! [2]confiscate [kánfiskèit]: to take sth away from sb; to seize 몰수・압류하다: The police confiscated the criminal's pistol. 경찰은 범죄자의 권총을 압수했다.

◯ 비인가 전열기

검열관: 이거 비인가 전열기 아니야?

사용자: 예, 맞습니다.

검열관: 왜 이것을 사용하나?

사용자: 죄송합니다. 여기 너무 추워서.

검열관: 너만 춥냐?

사용자: 다시는 사용하지 않겠습니다.

검열관: 이거 압수한다.

◯ Slogans for fire prevention   화재예방 표어

Fire Prevention Week	화재예방 주간
Re-check Extinguished Fire	꺼진불도 다시보자
Fire Prevention Asleep or Awake	자나깨나 불조심

◎ Cigarette bummer

A: Got a cigarette?

B: Buy and smoke your own. Cigarettes don't grow on trees!

A: Just one, please.

B: For you, bumming[1] a cigarette is just a greeting.
   You're a habitual cigarette bummer.

[해설] [1]bum: to borrow without expectation of returning 갚을 뜻이 없이 무엇을 요청하다: He's always bumming cigarettes from me. 그는 항상 담배를 달라고 한다.

◎ 담배 빈대

A: 담배 있어?

B: 사서 피워. 담배가 나무에서 그저 자라는 줄 알아!

A: 하나만 줘.

B: 너는 담배 구걸이 인사구먼.
   너는 담배를 구걸하는 상습 빈대다.

◎ Only a lighter

A: Can I bum a cigarette?

B: Yes, but do you have a lighter?

A: Yes, I do. I'm a guy who carries only a lighter.

◎ 불만 있어

A: 담배 한 개비 빌릴까?

B: 그래, 너 불 있니?

A: 그래 있지. 나는 불만 있는 놈이야.

🟠 Oath not to smoke

- I swear not to smoke to protect my health.
- I swear not to smoke to protect my loving family and colleagues' health.
- I swear not to smoke to maintain my physical strength and fighting strength.
- I swear not to smoke in any environment and under any circumstances.

February 22, 2003.

Captain   Kim Gol Cho   *Kim Gol Cho*

🟠 금연결의문

- 나는 나 자신의 건강을 위해서 금연을 결의한다.
- 나는 사랑하는 가족과 동료들의 건강을 위해 금연을 결의한다.
- 나는 체력 향상과 전투력 보존을 위해 금연을 결의한다.
- 나는 어떠한 환경과 여건에도 굴하지 않고 금연을 결의한다.

2003년 2월 22일

대위   김 골 초   *김 골 초*

🟠 Non-smoker's complaints

Smokers' love for smoke	Nonsmokers' suffocating
Smokers' love for smoke	Nonsmokers' groaning
Smokers' love for smoke	The harelipped increasing
Puffing smoke as a dessert	Nonsmokers' suffocating
Puffing smoke as a dessert	Indirect damage increasing
Puffing smoke as a dessert	Neighbors' damage increasing
Increasing smoking	Decreased kissing
Increasing smoking	Decreasing fertility
Increasing smoking	Decreasing sexuality
Puffing cigarettes to kill time	Withering human cells
Puffing cigarettes to kill time	Blackening youthful lives
Puffing cigarettes to kill time	Youth smoke addiction

* Smoking was prohibited in public buildings in 1995 in the Republic of Korea. But some rude smokers still smoke in the presence of non-smokers, especially in the presence of subordinates who have no power to protect themselves.

🔸 비흡연자의 신음소리

애연가의 연기사랑   숨막히는 비흡연자
애연가의 연기사랑   신음하는 비흡연자
애연가의 연기사랑   늘어나는 언청이들

디저트로 뿜은연기   질식되는 비흡연자
디저트로 뿜은연기   늘어나는 간접피해
디저트로 뿜은연기   피해보는 이웃사촌

늘어나는 흡연횟수   줄어드는 키스횟수
늘어나는 흡연횟수   줄어드는 남녀씨앗
늘어나는 흡연횟수   줄어드는 섹스횟수

심심풀이 빠끔담배   말라가는 인간세포
심심풀이 빠끔담배   그을리는 푸른청춘
심심풀이 빠끔담배   중독되는 젊은청춘

* 대한민국에서는 1995년 공공건물 내에서 흡연이 금지되었다. 하지만 일부 몰지각한 사람들은 비흡연자들, 특히 자신을 보호할 힘이 없는 부하들 앞에서 여전히 담배를 피운다.

🔵 Learning golf and English

① They need motivation.

② They can be addictive.

③ They need a good coach.

④ They broaden one's view of life.

⑤ They are widespread these days.

⑥ They need much time and money.

⑦ The equipment sometimes needs upgrading.

⑧ They need equipment which is tailored to the individual.

⑨ They are enormously helpful to achieve success in Korea.

⑩ They can't be completely mastered although you practice endlessly.

🔵 골프와 영어 배우기

① 동기부여가 필요하다.

② 중독성이 있다.

③ 훌륭한 코치가 필요하다.

④ 인생의 시야를 넓혀준다.

⑤ 요즘은 보편화되고 있다.

⑥ 많은 시간과 돈이 필요하다.

⑦ 도구를 때때로 업그레이드해야 한다.

⑧ 자기에 맞는 용품이 필요하다.

⑨ 한국에서는 출세에 무진장 도움이 된다.

⑩ 끝없는 노력에도 마스터할 수 없다.

Never bet on golf games

Never bet[1] on playing golf.

Today's golf is ten thousand won per stroke.

Let's make it five thousand won per stroke today.

We played golf for ten thousand won per stroke last sunday.

I don't play golf because I hate to bet money.

How many times have I told you not to bet on golf games?

[해설] [1]bet: to risk an amount of money on the result of a race, game, competition, etc. 내기하다: He bet all his money on a horse that came in last. 그는 마지막에 들어온 말에 그의 돈을 모두 걸었다.

내기 골프 금지

내기 골프 하지 마라.

오늘의 골프는 타당 만원이다.

오늘은 타당 오천 원짜리다.

우리는 지난주 타당 만 원짜리 골프 쳤다.

나는 돈내기하기 싫어서 골프 안친다.

내가 내기 골프 치지 말라고 몇 번을 얘기했나?

🔸 Wound up at the 20th hole

A: What did you shoot yesterday?

B: Two over par[1].

A: Did you have a drink at the **19th hole**?

B: Yes, I did. And I wound up[2] at the **20th hole**.

* 19th hole means the bar in a clubhouse.
* 20th hole is a caddy's hole meaning to have a sexual relationship with a female caddy.

[해설] [1]par: an average or normal standard score (골프) 기준 타수: After nine holes of golf, my score was three strokes below par. 나인 홀까지 골프를 친 후에 나는 기준보다 3타 적었다. [2]wind up: to finally be somewhere or do sth, especially without having planned it 예측하지 않게 어디에 처하다, 무엇을 하다: Most of them wound up in prison. 그들 중 대부분이 수감되었다.

🔸 20번 홀까지 가다

A: 어제 얼마 쳤니?

B: 투 오버 파.

A: 19번 홀에서 한잔했어?

B: 그럼. 20번 홀까지 갔지.

* 19번 홀이란 클럽하우스의 술집을 의미한다.
* 20번 홀이란 캐디의 구멍이란 뜻으로 여자 캐디와 성관계를 한다는 것을 의미한다.

🔵 I don't play golf anymore

Recently I gave up playing golf.
Playing golf is very pleasant,
but why do people hang around[1] bars after dinner together?
That's really disgusting to me.
I won't play golf until I emigrate[2] to a western country!

[해설] [1]hang around: to spend time doing nothing; to loiter 노닥거리다, 쓸데없이 배회하다: He hangs around the street corner every evening. 그는 매일 저녁에 거리를 배회한다. [2]emigrate [émǝgrèit]: to leave one's country to live in another 타국으로 이주하다. ↔ immigrate [ímǝgrèit]: to come to a country to live in permanently (타국에서) 이주해 오다.

🔵 저는 더 이상 골프 안 쳐요

최근에 나는 골프를 접었습니다.
골프 치는 것은 매우 즐거운데,
왜 사람들은 식사 후에 2차, 3차를 가지?
그것이 정말 나를 신물 나게 합니다.
나는 서양의 어떤 나라로 이민 가기 전에는 골프 안칠 겁니다.

How can we take ATT without you?

[Company commander : Battalion commander]

CC: Sir, may I go on leave from next Monday.

BC: What? At the busiest time?

CC: My wife is due to[1] give birth next Monday.

BC: Are you giving birth yourself?

CC: I'm sorry, but I have no relatives here in Gangwon-do.

BC: Hey, I couldn't even attend my own father's funeral.

CC: But according to regulations we can go on paternity leave[2] for 7days when one's wife is expecting.

BC: I know that, but how can we take the ATT (Army Training Test) without you?

[해설] [1]be due to: to be expected to happen ~할 예정인. [2]paternity/maternity leave 남성의/여성의 출산휴가: It is rare for us to find a father who is brave enough to take paternity leave. 출산휴가를 나갈 만큼 용기 있는 아버지를 찾기란 드물다. Why should men go on paternity leave for? 왜 남자들이 출산휴가를 나가야 해?

너 없이 검열을 받을 수 있나?

중대장: 대대장님, 저 다음주 월요일부터 휴가 좀 나갔으면 합니다.

대대장: 뭐? 한참 바쁜 시간에?

중대장: 저의 아내가 다음주 출산 예정입니다.

대대장: 네가 애를 직접 낳기라도 하나?

중대장: 죄송합니다. 하지만 강원도에는 친척이 아무도 없어서.

대대장: 야, 나는 아버님 장례식도 참석 못했어.

중대장: 하지만 규정에 따라 아내가 출산할 때 7일간의 출산휴가를 나갈 수 있습니다.

대대장: 나도 알지만, 너 없이 어떻게 ATT(육군훈련시험)을 받을 수 있겠나?

◎ Playing tennis on Saturday afternoon

A: We have a tennis game this afternoon with our commander.
B: I have to go to my cousin's wedding.
A: I wish I could have some time with my family on weekends.
B: Our commander doesn't care what we want.
　　What we want is free time on weekends!

◎ 토요일 오후에 테니스

A: 우리 오늘 오후에 대대장님과 테니스 게임 있다.
B: 나는 조카 결혼식에 가야 하는데.
A: 주말에는 개인 시간을 좀 가졌으면 좋겠어.
B: 우리 대대장님은 우리가 무엇을 원하는지 상관 안 해.
　　우리가 원하는 것은 주말에 개인 시간을 갖는 거라고!

At the tennis court

[General : Adjutant]

G: Stay there!

A: Yes, sir!

G: Move nearer to the net.

A: Yes, sir!

G: One step, left.

A: Yes, sir!

G: Don't you understand what I mean?

A: I won't be on your team anymore.

테니스 코트에서

장군: 거기 있어!

부관: 예!

장군: 네트로 더 가란 말이야.

부관: 예!

장군: 왼쪽으로 1보.

부관: 예!

장군: 내가 무슨 말 하는지 모르겠어?

부관: 저 이제 사단장님과 한편 안 하겠습니다.

🎾 Play a flattering tennis game

A: I don't play tennis with General Lee.
B: Why?
A: His attitude is so bad.
B: Have you ever played tennis with him?
A: He instructs me during the game.
B: He is not a good player, though.
A: I usually lose the game because of his bossy attitude.
B: It is directly against the spirit of the sport.
A: That's why all my coworkers flatter him when we play tennis with him.
B: Last week I had a hard time losing the tennis game against my new boss without being too obvious.

* Playing a flattering tennis game is often called, "kisaeng tennis" in Korea

🎾 아부 테니스게임

A: 나는 이장군님과 테니스 안칠 거야.
B: 왜?
A: 그의 태도가 매우 나빠.
B: 너 그분과 테니스 쳐봤어?
A: 게임 중에도 얼마나 훈시가 많은지.
B: 그 분은 잘 치지도 못하는 주제에.
A: 그 분의 허세 때문에 게임에서 늘 지지.
B: 그건 스포츠 정신에 정면으로 위배야.
A: 그래서 내 동료들이 그 분과 테니스 칠 때 아부해.
B: 지난주 새로 오신 사장님과 테니스 게임에서 교묘히 져주느라고 애먹었어.

* 한국에서 아부 테니스를 친다는 것은 종종 "기생 테니스"로 불린다.

🟠 I don't like to be his teammate

A: Park, you should join up with Mr. Kim.
B: No. I don't like to be his teammate.
A: Why? He is a good player.
B: He nags his partner a lot, even though he isn't a good tennis player.

🟠 나는 그와 한편 하기 싫어

A: 박, 너 김과 한편 해.
B: 안 해. 나는 그와 한편하기 싫어.
A: 왜? 그는 실력 있는데.
B: 그도 잘 치지도 못하는 주제에 자기 파트너에게 잔소리가 많아.

🟠 Sliced pork belly and soju

A: What are most frequently eaten and drunk at gatherings in the military?
B: That would be sliced pork belly and soju.

🟠 삼겹살에 소주

A: 군대 회식에서 무엇을 가장 많이 먹고 마시지?
B: 그야 삼겹살에 소주지.

◯ Sliced pork belly

A: What shall we give our **old man** as a treat?

B: How about sliced pork belly?

A: He is allergic[1] to pork.

B: Then let's have dog.

C: I can't eat dog.

A: Then you eat chicken instead.

C: Let's eat beef.

B: Try to eat dog meat. It's good for men!

* Old man is a <u>commanding officer</u>, but its use is not recommended.
  ↳ the officer in command of a military unit 지휘관
* Military personnel must be able to eat all kinds of food, even dog meat, in order to be prepare themselves for wartime and to relieve their juniors of meal costs.

[해설] [1]allergic: very sensitive to something ~: ~에 알레르기가 있는, 민감한: She is allergic to tomatoes. 그녀는 토마토에 알레르기가 있다.

◯ 삼겹살

A: 영감님 뭘로 대접하지?

B: 삼겹살 어때?

A: 그는 돼지고기에 알레르기가 있어.

B: 그러면 개고기 먹자.

C: 나는 개고기는 못 먹어.

A: 그러면 넌 닭고기 먹어라.

C: 소고기 먹자.

B: 개고기 먹어보자. 남자에게 좋다구!

* 영감이란 지휘관을 뜻하나 권장할만한 표현은 아니다.
* 군인들은 전시에 대비해서 뿐만 아니라 부하들의 식사비 부담을 줄이기 위해서라도 모든 종류의 음식, 심지어 개고기도 먹을 수 있어야 한다.

🔘 A glass from my heart

[Captain : Lt. Kim]

C: Have a glass of soju, Lt. Kim.

L: I'm sorry. I can't drink a drop of soju[1].

C: Hey, this is my first offer of a drink.

　　This is a glass from my heart.

L: Oh, how can I refuse a glass from your heart?

[해설] [1]술은 입에도 안 대: I don't drink at all. I don't touch any alcoholic stuff. ↔ 그 사람 술고래야: He's a drunkard. He drinks like a fish.

🔘 마음의 잔

대위: 김중위, 소주 한잔 해.

중위: 실례합니다. 저는 소주 한 방울도 못합니다.

대위: 이거 처음 권하는 거야.

　　　이것은 내 마음의 잔이다.

중위: 예, 제가 대위님의 마음의 잔을 어떻게 거부하겠습니까?

◯ Be sure to drink the first glass

If you refuse the first glass of alcohol, the offerer gets embarrassed. The first glass of alcohol isn't considered to be just alcoholic beverage, but it's a mixture of friendship, affection, faithfulness and everything in Korea. Alcohol is like blood or electricity which runs from the offerer and the receiver. Every culture is unique and it should be cherished. Once you're in Korea, follow the general rules. Don't complain about the culture.

◯ 첫 잔은 꼭 마셔라

만약에 당신이 첫 잔을 거절한다면, 술을 권하는 사람은 당혹함을 느낀다. 한국에서 첫 잔은 술 자체가 아니라 우정, 관심, 충절 그리고 모든 것들의 혼합물이다. 술은 술을 권하는 사람과 받는 사람 사이에 흐르는 피나 전기와도 같다. 모든 문화는 독특하며 그것은 소중히 간직 되어야 한다. 당신이 한국에 왔다면 일반 규칙을 따르라. 그 문화에 대해서 불평하지 말라.

🔸 Korean Viagra

[Captain : Lieutenant]

C: Where shall we have a going away dinner for our departing commander?

L: How about having dog meat as it's summer?

C: Is there anyone among us who can't eat dog meat?

L: Not, as far as I know.

C: What's your favorite restaurant?

L: There is one near the rear gate.

C: Doesn't the signboard say, "Korean Viagra[1]?"

L: That's right, sir. It opened last month. And even the hostess is beautiful!

C: Oh, that's icing on the cake! Then, let's go there.

L: Then I'll make a reservation for this evening.

[해설] [1]Viagra: A registered trademark of Pfizer. This pill helps men get an erection. 비아그라; 미국의 제약회사 '파이저'사가 만든 남성의 발기 부전 치료제.

🔸 코리안 비아그라

대위: 이번 대대장님 전속회식 어디서 할까?

중위: 여름인데 개고기 한번 드시죠?

대위: 우리 중에 개고기 못 먹는 사람 있나?

중위: 예, 제가 알기로는 없습니다.

대위: 너 어디 좋아하는 식당 있나?

중위: 후문근처에 있습니다.

대위: 간판이 "Korean Viagra" 아냐?

중위: 예, 맞습니다. 지난달 오픈 했습니다. 그리고 아줌마도 예쁘고!

대위: 와, 금상첨화로군! 그럼 거기로 가자.

중위: 그럼 제가 오늘 저녁으로 예약해 놓겠습니다.

🔸 Tomorrow is like a holiday

A: Let's get back to the BOQ now.

B: Oh, no. Let's drink all night.

A: You won't be able to get up tomorrow morning.

B: Tomorrow is like a holiday.

A: Why do you say that?

B: Our boss will go on a business trip to New York.

A: Oh, I see.

B: Miss Kim, bring another bottle of Windsor 17, here!

A: Don't you know that when **zero one** (01) is away, **zero two** (02) plays more? "When the cat's away, the mice will play." We should do better while 01 is away.

* **Zero one** (01) is the highest ranking person in a unit; **zero two** (02) is the second highest ranking person in a unit.

🔸 내일은 휴일이나 다름없어

A: 이제 BOQ로 돌아가자.

B: 싫어. 밤새도록 마시자.

A: 너, 내일 아침 못 일어나.

B: 내일은 휴일이나 다름없어.

A: 무슨 말이야?

B: 대대장님이 내일 뉴욕으로 출장 가거든.

A: 알겠어.

B: 미스 김, 여기 윈저 17 한 병 더 가져 와!

A: **제로 원** (01)이 없으면 **제로 투** (02)가 더 설치는 거 몰라? 고양이가 없으면 생쥐가 설친 다구. 우린 제로 원 (01)이 없을 때 더 잘해야 돼.

* **제로 원** (01) 은 단위 부대에서 가장 계급이 높은 사람이며, **제로 투** (02)는 두 번째로 계급이 높은 사람이다.

What shall we bet on this game?

A: What shall we bet on this game?

B: Five bottles of beer and a fried chicken.

A: It isn't enough. Let's bet something more.

B: How about girls at a singing room?

A: Good. A girl for one hour.

B: Roger[1]. But how much is it for one hour per girl?

A: Thirty thousand won.

B: I prefer middle aged women or widowed women.

A: I don't understand the songs young girls sing.

[해설] [1]roger [rɑ́dʒəːr]: used in radio communications to mean that a message has been received and understood 통신상의 교신에서 메시지를 받았으며 이해했다는 말:"You are clear to land." "Roger, I'm coming in to land now." "당신은 착륙해도 된다." "알았다. 지금 착륙하겠다."

이번에는 뭐 내기?

A: 이번엔 뭐 내기할래?

B: 맥주 다섯 병에 통닭 한 마리.

A: 그것 가지고 되겠어. 뭐 좀 더 걸자.

B: 노래방에서 여자 내기 어때?

A: 좋지. 한 시간에 여자 한 명은 얼마지?

B: 알았다. 한 시간에 여자 한 명 부르는데 얼마지?

A: 3만원.

B: 나는 중년 여성이나 과부를 더 좋아해.

A: 나도 젊은 여자 애들이 부르는 노래는 하나도 모르겠어.

◯ I have a social gathering tonight

[Husband : Wife]

H: Hello, It's me, dear.
W: When are you coming home?
H: I'm sorry. I have a social gathering tonight.
W: You know today is our first wedding anniversary?
H: I know, but⋯.
W: Then, I'll have cold boiled rice by myself.
H: Honey, I'm really sorry.
W: I know you're going to the party to support us.

◯ 오늘 저녁 회식이야

남편: 여보세요, 나야 자기야.

아내: 집에 언제와?

남편: 미안해, 오늘 저녁 회식이야.

아내: 오늘 우리 첫 번째 결혼기념일인 거 알아?

남편: 알아, 하지만⋯

아내: 그러면 혼자 찬밥 먹어야겠다.

남편: 여보, 정말 미안해.

아내: 회식에 참석하는 것도 우리 먹여 살리려고 가는 거 알아요.

The get-together was cancelled

[Husband : Wife]

H: The get-together[1] was cancelled.

W: Oh, dear! I haven't prepared any dinner.
   What do you want to eat?

H: Something delicious.

W: How can I fix dinner now.
   Why didn't you call me up earlier.

[해설] [1]get-together: an informal meeting for fun 비공식 모임, 친목회: After work, some of us had a get-together at Sgt. Kim's house. 퇴근 후에 우리들 중 몇 명은 김하사 집에서 모임을 가졌다.

회식 취소

남편: 회식이 취소됐어.

아내: 오, 이런! 저녁 준비 하나도 안 했는데.
   뭐 먹고 싶어?

남편: 아무거나 맛있는 거.

아내: 지금 저녁을 어떻게 해.
   좀 더 일찍 전화해주지 않고.

How can I avoid the social gatherings

[Husband : Wife]

W: Honey, do you know how much you spent on your social gatherings last month?

H: I think it came to about 300,000 won.

W: More than that. Almost 400,000 won.

H: I had five social gatherings last month.

W: You know I've used only sample cosmetics for the whole year?

H: But how can I not join the social gatherings unless I quit my job tomorrow?

W: Anyway don't you think it's too much?
　　You spend 30% of your month's pay on gatherings.

어떻게 회식에 안갈 수 있나?

아내: 여보, 당신 지난달 회식비 얼만지 아세요?

남편: 한 30만원 될 걸.

아내: 그보다 많아. 거의 40만원.

남편: 지난달 회식을 다섯 번 했지.

아내: 당신은 내가 올해 화장품 견본만 사용해 온 거 아세요?

남편: 하지만 내일 그만두지 않는 한 어떻게 회식에 빠질 수 있나?

아내: 어쨌든 회식비가 너무 많다고 생각하지 않아요?
　　　당신은 월급의 30%를 회식비에 쓰고 있다 구요.

● I fixed it 10 days ago

A: Kil-dong, we have a get-together at 18:30 today.

B: I'm sorry. I have a previous engagement, sir.

A: Are there any guys who don't have a previous engagement?

B: I'm really sorry. I arranged it 10 days ago.

A: Hey, joining social gatherings is one of your major missions.

B: Oh, I see. I won't miss any gatherings from now on.

● 10일전에 날 잡았어요

A: 길동, 오늘 18시30분에 회식이다.

B: 죄송합니다만, 선약이 있습니다.

A: 선약 없는 사람 어디 있나?

B: 정말 죄송합니다. 10일 전에 날을 잡았습니다.

A: 이봐, 회식 참석도 중요한 임무 중의 하나다.

B: 알겠습니다. 지금부터 어떤 회식도 다 참석하겠습니다.

🔸 You just eat the meal

A: We have to go out to dinner this evening.

B: Oh, damn! I hate[1] to start drinking on Mondays.

A: You just eat the meal, then.

B: How can we control the mood of the gatherings.

A: Not to drink at social gatherings is more difficult than to become a president.

B: Can I pay a fine[2] instead of going to the dinner party?

A: Don't you know that we are living in very feudalistic[3] society?

[해설] [1]hate: to dislike sb or sth very much 매우 싫어하다. [2]fine: money paid as punishment for wrongdoing 벌금: I paid a fine for parking illegally. 나는 불법 주차로 벌금을 물었다. [3]feudalistic [fju:dəlístik] 봉건적인〈 feudal: related to the feudal era or system 봉건시대의, feudalism 봉건제도

🔸 Koreans have a group psychology for everything and especially drinking, you have to drink when you're with other people *if you don't want to be excluded*.

🔸 너 식사만 해

A: 야 오늘 저녁 식사 있다.

B: 제기랄! 월요일부터 술 마시기 싫은데.

A: 저녁 식사만 하면 되지 뭐.

B: 그게 마음대로 되나?

A: 회식 장소에 가서 술 안 마시기가 대통령 되기 보다 더 힘들어.

B: 벌금이라도 내고 안 가면 안 될까?

A: 넌 우리가 아주 봉건적인 사회에 살고 있다는 것을 모르냐?

🔸 한국 사람들은 모든 것에 대해서 특히, 술을 마실 때는 집단 심리가 작용한다. 당신은 다른 사람들과 있을 때 **따돌림을 당하지 않으려면** 술을 마셔야 한다.

🔸 Penalty cup

[Captain : Lieutenant]

C: Why didn't you empty[1] your cup?

L: I'm sorry. I can't drink at all, sir.

C: Is there anybody who likes to drink? You have to drink a "penalty cup."

L: What's a "penalty cup," sir?

C: I said "bottoms up" and you had to drink up.
    But you violated my offering, though it's not an order.

L: Do I have to drink up at "Cheers!"

C: No, you don't have to. Just drink the amount you want.
    If you don't like to drink, just touch your cup.

L: Oh, I see. Now I know what "Bottoms up" and "Cheers" mean.

C: No pain, no gain!

[해설] [1]empty: 1) without contents; vacant 빈, 비어 있는, 2) to remove the contents of 비우다: I emptied the drawer by taking my clothes out of it.

🔸 벌주

대위: 너 왜 다 안 마셨니?

소위: 죄송합니다만, 저는 술을 전혀 못합니다.

대위: 누구는 술을 좋아한다냐? 너는 "벌주"를 마셔야겠다.

소위: "벌주"가 뭡니까?

대위: 내가 "건배"라고 했으니까 네가 술을 다 마셔야 했다.
     그런데 넌 나의 제안을 위반했다. 비록 그것이 명령은 아니지만.

소위: "축배"에서도 다 마셔야 됩니까?

대위: 아니다. 그럴 필요는 없다. 네가 원하는 만큼만 마셔.
     네가 술을 못하면 그냥 잔에 입만 대라.

소위: 알겠습니다. 저는 이제 "건배"와 "축배"의 의미를 알겠습니다.

대위: 고통 없이는 배울 수 없는 법!

🟠 Gyeogeubju

[Captain : General]

C: Sir, may I offer you a glass of soju?

G: Okay, but before you offer me a soju, you have to drink 5 glasses of soju first. Have you ever heard of "gyeogeubju"?

C: No, sir!

G: A captain has to drink 5 glasses to offer one glass to a two star general because there are five gaps between the ranks of captain and two-star general. You see what I am saying? Can you drink five glasses of soju?

C: I'm sorry. I can't, sir!

G: Then, go back to your seat!

🟠 계급주

대위: 장군님, 제가 소주 한잔 권해도 되겠습니까?

장군: 좋아, 네가 나에게 소주 한잔을 권하기 전에 먼저 다섯 잔을 마셔야 한다. 계급주라고 들어봤어?

대위: 아닙니다.

장군: 좋아. 대위는 소장에게 한 잔의 소주를 권하기 위해서는 소주 다섯 잔을 마셔야 한다. 왜냐하면 대위와 소장 사이에는 다섯 간격이 있기 때문이다. 무슨 말인지 알겠어? 소주 다섯 잔을 마실 수 있겠나?

대위: 죄송하지만 마실 수 없습니다.

소장: 그러면 너의 자리로 돌아가!

● Pass the cup to your right

Congratulations on Major Kim's promotion and transfer to a higher position, Commander of the 3rd Battalion, and we all wish you good luck and happiness in the military. For all this I propose "Bottoms up," and after drinking up, pass the cup to your right.

When I say, "to the sky" and you respond "to space[1]."   (Air Force)
　　　　　　"to the sea"　　　　　　　"to the world."　(Navy)
　　　　　　"to Seoul"　　　　　　　　"to Pyongyang." (Army)
　　　　　　"to Mt. Pakdu"　　　　　　"to Mt. Halla."　(Army)

[해설] [1]space는 끝없는 공간, 우주를 뜻하는 불가산 명사이므로 정관사 the를 붙이지 않는다. (space: the area beyond the Earth where the stars and planets are.)

● 우턴 하겠습니다

김 소령의 중령 진급을 축하하며 3대대장으로 영전한 김소령의 앞날에 무궁한 건승과 행운이 함께 하길 기원합니다. 이 모든 것을 위해서 "건배"를 제의합니다. 잔을 비운 후에는 우턴 하겠습니다.

제가 "하늘로" 라고 하면, 여러분은 "우주로" 라고 해 주세요. (공군)
　　　"바다로"　　　　　　　"세계로"　　　　　　(해군)
　　　"서울로"　　　　　　　"평양으로"　　　　　(육군)
　　　"백두산으로"　　　　　"한라산으로"　　　　(육군)

◎ Two clicks to your left

For all this I propose "Bottoms up," and after drinking up,
- pass the cup to your right.
- offer a drink to the person you admire.
- offer a drink to the person in front of you.
- two **clicks** to your left.

* **click** is a scale on a rifle, if the toaster says "two clicks to your left" you should pass your cup to the next person to your left.

◎ 왼쪽으로 두 클릭

이 모든 것을 위해서 건배를 제의합니다. 마시고 난 후 잔은
- 우로 돌립니다.
- 자기가 존경하는 사람에게 한잔 권합니다.
- 자기 앞에 있는 사람에게 한잔 권합니다.
- 자기 왼쪽으로 두 **클릭** 합니다.

* **클릭**이란 소총에 있는 눈금이며, 축배나 건배를 제안하는 사람이 "왼쪽으로 두 클릭" 하면 당신의 왼쪽에 있는 사람의 다음 사람에게 잔을 건네야 한다.

◎ Strange "bottoms up"

I'll offer "bottoms up" for our parting commander's health and for our successful sex tonight. If you don't empty your glass, I'll consider you aren't faithful to our parting commander. Anyway, drink as much as you admire him.

◎ 이상한 "건배"

떠나는 사령관님의 건강과 오늘밤 우리들의 성공적인 섹스를 위하여, 제가 "건배"를 제의하겠습니다. 여러분이 다 마시지 않는다면 사령관님에게 충성심이 없는 것으로 간주하겠습니다. 어쨌든, 여러분 사령관님을 존경하는 만큼만 드십시오.

◎ Drunk driving is an act of murder

Now drunk-driving will end your military career.
Drunk-driving is like an act of murder.
It can take other's lives away as well as yours.
Therefore it must be stopped.
Are there guys who still drink and drive in our unit?

◎ 음주운전은 살인행위

이제 음주운전 하면 군생활 끝장이다.
음주운전은 살인행위나 다름없다.
음주운전은 본인은 물론 타인의 생명까지 앗아갈 수 있다.
그러므로 반드시 근절되어야 한다.
우리 부대에 음주운전 하는 사람이 아직도 있다는 말이냐?

🔸 Coffees for everybody?

[Waitress : Senior : Junior]

W: What shall I get you for dessert?

S: All you guys, want coffee?

Here, five coffees!

J: I'm sorry, sir.

I'll have green tea.

S: It's already ordered. You're always complaining!

Soldiers shouldn't complain about anything seniors do, you see? You have to drink whatever I choose, even if it's a poisonous drink.

That is also a way of being faithful to me.

🔸 모두 커피?

웨터: 주문하시겠습니까?

고참: 모두 커피 마실래?

웨이터, 커피 다섯 잔.

후참: 죄송합니다.

저는 녹차 마시겠습니다.

고참: 이미 주문 끝났다. 너는 항상 불평이구나!

군인은 상관이 무엇을 하든 불평하면 안 돼, 알겠나?

넌 내가 마시는 뭐든 따라 마셔야 한다. 설사 그것이 독약이라도.

그것 또한 나에게 충성심을 표현하는 방법이다.

🔸 Drunk driver

A staff sergeant at ○○ unit, who lives out of the barracks, drank with his girlfriend in downtown Seoul at around 00:05, Monday, May 27, 2003. While he was driving with his girlfriend to a motel, he got caught by a police officer. (His blood alcohol level had reached 0.164)

* His pass to the unit was withdrawn and all 154 personnel of his unit were put on military attention from Thursday, May 28 to Sunday, May 31, 2003.

🔸 음주운전

○○부대 하사가 '03. 5. 27(월) 00:05분경 서울 시내에서 여자친구와 음주한 후 자신의 승용차를 운전하여 여자 친구와 여관으로 가다가 경찰에 적발됨. (혈중알콜농도 0.164%)

* 그의 부대 출입증은 회수되었으며, '03. 5. 28(목) ~ 5. 31(일) 소속대 154명 전원을 대상으로 군차렷을 실시하였음.

🔸 Oath not to drink and drive

① I will never drink and drive under any circumstances, keeping in mind that drunk driving is an act of murder.
② I will use public transportation to social gatherings as much as possible.
③ I will never offer even one glass of alcohol to the drivers.
④ I will never get into a drunk-driver's car, and I will certainly make him stop driving if he is drunk.

I solemnly pledge that I will accept my rightful punishment in case of violation of the above.

Affiliation: HQ. company   Rank: 1st Lt.   Name: Hong Kil Dong

Hong Kil Dong

🔸 음주운전 금지 서약

① 나는 음주운전이 살인 행위임을 명심하고 어떠한 경우에도 음주운전을 하지 않는다.
② 나는 각종 모임 시 대중교통수단을 최대한 이용한다.
③ 나는 차량 운전자에 대하여 한 잔의 술도 권하지 않는다.
④ 나는 음주운전 차량에 동승하지 않으며 음주운전 목격 시 기필코 운전을 중지시킨다.

상기 내용 위반 시는 어떠한 처벌도 감수할 것을 엄숙히 선서합니다.

소속: 본부중대   계급: 중위   성명: 홍 길 동

홍 길 동

Pass around a glass and a woman

[Lt. Col.: Capt. Kim]

LC: Capt. Kim, I know you like alcohol. But why do you pass around a boilermaker[1] at every gathering?

CK: Only to boost our spirits quickly, sir.

LC: I think nondrinkers have a hard time with you.

CK: But I've never forced anyone to drink, sir!

LC: But if you pour soju for a private, how can he refuse it? Can you refuse the glass offered by generals?

CK: I'm sorry, sir. Whenever I got drunk, I couldn't control myself.

LC: Passing around a boilermaker is also a violation of the guideline for "healthy social gathering culture."

CK: I'll be more careful next time, sir.

LC: To pass round the glass is nothing but raping a woman in turn!

[해설] [1]boilermaker: a beer with whiskey 폭탄주: We drink boilermakers at every gathering. 우리는 회식 때마다 폭탄주를 마신다. Keep in mind that a 'boilermaker' could become a 'spoiler maker,' or even a 'disaster maker,'" 폭탄주는 '(파티를) 망치는 것' 또는 '재난을 유발하는 것'이 될 수도 있음 명심해라.

윤잔과 윤간

중 령: 김대위, 너 술 좋아하는 거 안다. 하지만 회식 때마다 왜 폭탄주를 돌리나?

김대위: 빨리 분위기를 좀 띄우려고 그랬습니다.

중 령: 술 못하는 사람들은 너와 같이 있는 거 힘들겠군.

김대위: 하지만 저는 누구에게도 술을 강권하지 않았습니다.

중 령: 네가 어떤 사병에게 술을 권하면 그가 어떻게 거절할 수 있겠나? 너는 장군에게 받은 잔을 거절할 수 있겠어?

김대위: 죄송합니다. 술에 취하면 주체를 못해서.

중 령: 폭탄주를 돌리는 것은 "건전한 회식문화"에도 위배된다.

김대위: 다음엔 더 주의하겠습니다.

중 령: 윤잔은 윤간과 다를 바가 없다고!

I can't go home

[Husband : Wife]

H: Hello, Master Sgt. Kim speaking. May I help you?
W: It's me, honey.
H: What's up?
W: When are you coming home?
H; I'm sorry. I can't go home until this Saturday.
W: What's the reason this time?
H: One of my colleagues was arrested on charges of drunk driving.
W: Whew! How can I celebrate Chel-ho's birthday party?
H: I'm sorry. You're a poor soldier's wife!
W: Oh, I forgot the fate of a soldier's wife again! You waste your life confined[1] to the garrison[2] by the drinkers, though you don't drink a drop of alcohol. How miserable you are!

[해설] [1]confine [kənfáin]: to keep sb in a place 제한하다, 감금하다. [2]garrison [gǽrəsən]: the place where such troops are stationed 주둔지, 부대: Yongsan Garrison (미군) 용산 부대

퇴근 못해

남편: 여보세요. 김상사입니다. 무엇을 도와드릴까요?
아내: 나야.
남편: 무슨 일 있어?
아내: 집에 언제와?
남편: 미안해. 이번 주 토요일까지 퇴근 못해.
아내: 이번엔 왜 또?
남편: 동료 중에 한 명이 음주운전으로 구속되었거든.
아내: 어휴, 철호의 생일파티를 어떻게 해?
남편: 미안해. 당신은 가엾은 군인의 아내로군!
아내: 오, 내가 군인 아내의 숙명을 또 잊었군! 당신은 술 한 방울도 못 마시면서도 음주자들 때문에 부대에 갇혀서 인생을 낭비하고 있군. 당신 참 딱하군!

● Frequent drinking parties are 잦은 회식은

① a major cause of wasting time.	시간낭비의 주범이다.
② a major cause of ruining homes.	가정파괴의 주범이다.
③ a major cause of drunk driving.	음주운전의 주범이다.
④ a major cause of chronic[1] fatigue.	만성피로의 주범이다.
⑤ a major cause of wives' nagging.	아내잔소리 주범이다.
⑥ a major cause of careless accidents.	안전사고의 주범이다.
⑦ a major cause of stomach cancer.	위암발생의 주범이다.
⑧ a major cause of leftover cold rice.	남는찬밥의 주범이다.
⑨ a major cause of alcohol addiction.	알콜중독의 주범이다.
⑩ a major cause of extramarital[2] affairs.	혼외정사의 주범이다.
⑪ a major cause of losing credit cards.	카드분실의 주범이다.
⑫ a major cause of the culture of flattery.	아부문화의 주범이다.
⑬ a major cause of squandering[3] fortunes.	가산탕진의 주범이다.
⑭ a major cause of waning[4] sexual vigor.	정력약화의 주범이다.
⑮ a major cause of violence in the family.	가정폭력의 주범이다.
⑯ a major cause of the destruction of cohesion.	단결저해의 주범이다.
⑰ a major cause of hindering self-development.	발전저해의 주범이다.
⑱ a major cause of indifference to one's siblings.	자식불찰의 주범이다.
⑲ a major cause of the transmission of Confucianism[5].	유교세습의 주범이다.
⑳ a major cause of quarrels between husbands and wives.	부부싸움의 주범이다.

[해설] [1]chronic [kránik]: lasting for a long time; persistent (병) 만성적인, 고질의: chronic back pain. [2]extramarital [èkstrəmǽrətəl]: outside of marriage 혼외의: She had an extramarital affair with a man she met at work. 그녀는 직장에서 만난 남자와 간통을 했다. [3]squander[skwάndə:r]: to use or spend sth wastefully 낭비하다: They've squandered two thousand dollars on the old car. 그들은 고물차를 고치는데 2천 달러를 쏟아 부었다. [4]wane [wein]: to weaken, get smaller 약해지다, 작아지다. [5]Confucianism 유교

Unexpected "bottoms ups"

Unexpected gatherings	Increasing cold boiled rice
Unexpected gatherings	Devastating married life
Continued gatherings	Decreasing fortune
Continued gatherings	Skipping family occasions
Exchanging glasses	Increasing hepatitis[1]
Exchanging glasses	Increasing blood pressure
Unexpected bottoms ups	Uncomfortable non-drinkers
Unexpected husband's gatherings	Increasing wives eating alone

[해설] [1]hepatitis [hèpətáitis]: (pl) -titides (의학) 간염

느닷없는 "건배"

예고없는 회식속에	늘어나는 식은찬밥
느닷없는 회식속에	황폐되는 결혼생활
계속되는 회식속에	줄어드는 가계살림
계속되는 회식속에	못챙기는 기념일들
주고받는 술잔속에	늘어나는 간염환자
주고받는 술잔속에	높아지는 혈압수치
느닷없는 건배속에	걱정되는 비음주자
느닷없는 남편회식	늘어나는 孤妻取食

◯ At promotion board

A: Tom should be promoted this year.
B: Why do you support him?
A: He has been doing his job successfully.
B: Are there any guys who haven't been doing their job successfully?
A: Doing one's work is basic.
   Not everybody can get a promotion.

◯ 진급 심사

A: 탐은 금년에 진급해야 돼.
B: 너 왜 그를 지지하니?
A: 그는 그의 일을 성공적으로 해왔어.
B: 자기일 성공적으로 안 한 사람이 어디 있어?
A: 자기 일은 기본이야.
   진급 아무나 하는 거 아니야.

◯ A calming drink

A: Promotion will be announced tomorrow.
   Aren't you nervous?
B: No, I am not, sir.
A: Did you give up on promotion?
B: Last year was the last chance.
   This year I'll be acting as a foil[1] for junior officers.
A: I'll buy you a drink tonight to calm your nerves.

[해설] [1]foil: a person or an object used to show contrast (주인공을) 돋보이게 하기 위해 대조하는데 사용되는 사람/물건: The princess kept an ugly servant woman as a foil to emphasize her own beauty. 그 공주는 자신의 아름다움을 강조하기 위해 하녀를 들러리로 옆에 세워두었다.

◎ 위로주

A: 진급 결과가 내일 발표될거다.

　　초조하지 않니?

B: 아닙니다.

A: 진급 포기했니?

B: 지난해가 마지막 기회였습니다.

　　올해는 후배 장교들 들러리나 설 겁니다.

A: 오늘 저녁에 위로주 한 잔 살게.

◎ He'll never get promoted now!

A: I can't find Major Kim on the list.

B: Why wasn't he selected?

C: He had an accident.

A: What sort of accident?

C: Drunk driving.

A: He'll never get promoted now!

◎ 그의 진급은 끝났군!

A: 김소령이 진급자 명단에 없다.

B: 왜 그가 선발이 안 됐지?

C: 그는 사고가 있었습니다.

A: 도대체 무슨 사고?

C: 음주운전

A: 이제 그의 진급은 끝났군!

◎ Big burden to someone else

A: Let's me see the promotion list.

B: Here you are, sir.

A: Major Park got a promotion. It's very unexpected.

　He should not have been promoted.

　He will be a big burden[1] to someone else.

[해설] [1]burden: (fig.) responsibility, worry, trouble (비유적) 책임, 걱정, 고민: I don't want to be a burden on my parents anymore. 부모님께 더 이상 짐이 되고 싶지 않다.

◎ 누군가의 큰 짐

A: 진급자 명단 좀 보자.

B: 여기 있습니다.

A: 박소령 진급했네. 정말 뜻밖이다.

　그는 진급되지 말았어야 했는데.

　그는 누군가의 큰 짐이 될 거야.

◎ Promotion is not everything

[Lt. Col.: Capt. Kim]

LC: Captain Kim, don't take it too hard.

CK: I'm sorry, sir. You've supported me a lot.

LC: I know how you feel now. As you know I got promoted to Lt. Col. on my third attempt[1].

CK: It's OK now, sir. I'll work harder next year.

LC: Try to console[2] your wife.

CK: Yes, sir.

LC: Promotion is not everything. Acknowledge it, but don't dwell on[3] it.

CK: Thank you for your advice.

[해설] [1] on my third attempt 세 번째 시도에서. [2] console [kənsóul]: to make sb who is sad feel better 위로하다: I tried to console her but she just kept crying. 나는 그녀를 위로하려고 했지만 그녀는 계속 울었다. [3] dwell on: to continue thinking or speaking about ~: ~에 대해서 계속 생각/말하다: The teacher dwelt on the topic too long. 그 교사는 그 주제에 대해 너무 오래 얘기했다.

◎ 진급이 모든 것은 아니다

중　령: 김대위 너무 상심 마라.

김대위: 죄송합니다. 저를 많이 도와 주셨는데.

중　령: 너의 기분 내가 안다. 너도 알다시피, 나도 3차로 중령 진급했잖니.

김대위: 이제 괜찮습니다. 내년에 더 열심히 하겠습니다.

중　령: 너의 집사람 위로 해줘라.

김대위: 알겠습니다.

중　령: 진급이 인생의 모든 것은 아니다. 그것을 인정하되 너무 연연해하지 마라.

김대위: 충고해주셔서 감사합니다.

Throw cold water on

[Platoon leader : Company commander]

PL: Sir, I'm here to report an accident.

CC: What is it this time?

PL: One corporal in my platoon didn't come back after his annual leave.

CC: Your platoon is throwing cold water[1] on our commander's promotion. You know the selection board is meeting next week?

PL: I'm sorry, sir!

[해설] [1]throw cold water는 진행되는 일을 방해해서 제동을 걸거나 빛을 못 보게 한다는 뜻의 비유적인 말이다. throw 대신 pour를 쓰기도 한다: He constantly throws cold water on everything I do. 그는 내가 하는 일마다 찬물을 끼얹는다.

찬물을 끼얹다

소대장: 중대장님, 사고 보고하러 왔습니다.

중대장: 이번엔 또 무슨 사고야?

소대장: 저의 소대 병사 한 명이 정기휴가 나간 뒤 복귀하지 않았습니다.

중대장: 너의 소대가 대대장님 진급에 찬물을 끼얹는구나.
너, 대대장님의 진급심사위원회가 다음 주에 열리는 거 알아?

소대장: 죄송합니다.

🔵 He is not the right stuff for general

A: Let me see the promotion list.

B: Here you go, sir.

A: Wow, Thomas got promoted to general.

B: Yes, he did.

A: He doesn't have the right stuff[1] to be a general.

B: I don't know how he got a promotion to general.
 He is more like a sergeant than a general.

[해설] [1]stuff: qualities that are an important special part of sth 자질: I think Tom has the right stuff for the job. 나는 그 일에 탐이 적임자라고 생각한다.

🔵 그는 장군감이 아니다

A: 진급자 명단 좀 보자.

B: 여기 있습니다.

A: 와, 토마스가 장군 진급을 했어.

B: 예, 그렇습니다.

A: 그는 장군감이 아닌데.

B: 저도 그가 어떻게 장군 진급을 했는지 모르겠습니다.
 그는 장군이라기보다는 부사관 같습니다.

Setting star

A: I'm going to discuss this matter with General Brown.
B: You don't need to.
A: Why? He is very influential in this matter.
B: Yes, but he is a "setting star" now.
A: Then who is a "rising star"?
B: I think there is no one in our unit.

지는 별

A: 나는 이것을 브라운 장군과 상담해야겠다.
B: 너 그럴 필요 없다.
A: 왜? 그는 이 분야에 매우 영향력 있어.
B: 그래 하지만 그는 "지는 별"이야.
A: 그럼 "뜨는 별"은 누구냐?
B: 우리 부대에 뜨는 별은 아무도 없는 것 같아.

🔵 Possibility to become a general

A: Did you hear the news that our group commander will be transferred?
B: No, I didn't. He came only last year.
A: Where will he be transferred to?
B: To the Welfare Service Group as Chief.
A: Is that a general's position according to the TO (Table of Organization)?
B: Yes, it is.
A: It is still possible for him to become a general.
　Be nice to him.

🔵 장군 될 비전

A: 너는 우리 전대장님이 전속 간다는 소식 들었니?
B: 아니. 그분은 지난해 오셨는데.
A: 어디로 가는데?
B: 복지단 단장으로.
A: 그 TO가 장군이냐?
B: 그럼.
A: 그는 장군이 될 비전이 있어.
　그에게 잘 보여.

🟢 Election and promotion

① They're like total war.
② First you must be selected.
③ Connections are paramount[1].
④ They're nothing but a gamble.
⑤ You must grasp the right rope.
⑥ Rumors usually prove to be true.
⑦ One enemy offsets[2] ten friendly armies.
⑧ Your wife's assistance is also important.
⑨ They need more money than expectation.
⑩ You have to make the best use of religion.
⑪ One big shot[3] is worth 100 ordinary supporters.
⑫ You're obliged to make malicious[4] propaganda.
⑬ There are no eternal friends or eternal enemies.
⑭ Honesty and sincerity alone don't guarantee victory.
⑮ People often dispose of their property to raise funds[5].
⑯ Your home can be devastated when you aren't selected.
⑰ You should take good care of voters at Chusok and at Seol.
⑱ Important decisions are made at night or secretly in advance.
⑲ One of the common traits of winners is to be a jack-of-all-trades[6].
⑳ Everybody knows who's going to be selected except the candidate.

* **Chusok** is a word for Korean thanks giving day (August 15 by the lunar calendar); **Seol** for Lunar New Year's Day.

[해설] [1]paramount [pǽrəmàunt]: more important than anything else 가장 중요한. [2]offset: to balance; to compensate for 상쇄하다: His bad behavior is offset by his hard work. [3]big shot: an important person with power 거물급 사람. [4]malicious [məlíʃəs]: intended to harm or upset other people 악의에 찬: malicious gossip 악의에 찬 잡담. [5]fund: a sum of money for a specific purpose (특정 용도를 위한) 자금: I'm short of funds at the moment; I can't buy that new car. 난 지금 자금부족으로 차를 살 수 없다. [6]jack-of-all-trades: someone who can do many type of work 만물박사, 팔방미인

🔸 선거와 진급

① 총력전과 같다.
② 되고 봐야 한다.
③ 인맥이 매우 중요하다.
④ 노름이나 다름없다.
⑤ 옳은 밧줄을 잡아야 한다.
⑥ 대체로 소문이 맞다.
⑦ 1명의 적은 10명의 우군을 해친다.
⑧ 아내의 내조도 매우 중요하다.
⑨ 생각보다 돈이 많이 든다.
⑩ 종교를 최대한 이용해야 한다.
⑪ 한 거물은 보통 후원자 100명과 같다.
⑫ 흑색선전을 안 할 수 없다.
⑬ 영원한 친구도 적도 없다.
⑭ 정직과 성실만이 승리를 보장하지는 않는다.
⑮ 자금 조성을 위해 부동산을 종종 처분한다.
⑯ 선발되지 않으면 가정이 황폐화된다.
⑰ 추석과 설에 유권자를 잘 챙겨야 한다.
⑱ 중요한 결정은 밤이나 사전에 은밀히 결정된다.
⑲ 승자의 공통적 특징 중에 하나는 마당발 기질이다.
⑳ 누가 될지 다른 사람은 알지만 후보자 자신만 모른다.

* **추석**은 한국어로 한국의 추수감사절 (음력 8월 15일), **설**은 구정을 말한다.

🔸 Koreans spend a great deal of time, energy, and money creating and nurturing personal networks that are designed specifically to contribute to their goals. 한국인들은 자신들의 목적달성을 위하여 인맥을 형성하고 유지하는데 엄청난 시간, 에너지와 돈을 쓴다. (NTC's Dictionary of Korea's Business and Cultural Code Words)

The dead bodies might rise!

A: Why didn't Major Kim get a promotion this time?
B: Hey, don't talk about promotion near the National Cemetery.
A: Why can't we talk about promotion here?
B: The dead officers are still interested in their promotions.
   They might hear us and they might rise!

A: Aren't all dead soldiers cremated[1]?
B: Yes, most of them are cremated.
   But some generals are still buried.

[해설] [1]cremate [kríːmeit]: to burn a dead body to ashes for burial 화장하다: My father wants to be cremated after his death. 나의 아버지는 사후에 화장하기를 원한다.

시체가 일어날지도 몰라

A: 김소령은 이번에 왜 진급 못했지?
B: 이봐, 국립묘지 근처에서는 진급에 관해서 이야기하지 마.
A: 왜?
B: 고인이 된 장교들도 여전히 진급에 관해서 관심이 많거든.
   그들이 우리가 이야기하는 것을 듣고 일어날지도 몰라!
A: 모든 군인들은 화장되지 않아?
B: 그래, 대부분의 군인들은 화장되지.
   하지만 아직 일부 장군들은 매장되지.

🟠 All soldiers are complainers

All soldiers complain about not being promoted to the rank above.
Generals complain about not being selected to be the Minister of National Defense.
Colonels complain about not being promoted to General.
Lt. Colonels complain about not being promoted to Colonel.
Majors complain about not being promoted to Lt. Colonel.

🟠 모든 군인은 불평불만 자

군인들은 다음 계급으로 진급하지 못해서 불평한다.
대장은 국방부 장관으로 발탁되지 않아서.
대령은 장군 진급을 못해서.
중령은 대령 진급을 못해서.
소령은 중령 진급을 못해서.

Soldiers' surplus fat

What's surplus[1] fat to soldiers?
It's a burden to the heart,
it's the source of all kinds of disease,
it can give a negative image to the people,
it's a crucial[2] factor in weakening fighting strength[3],
it's unnecessary flesh to get rid of[4] as soon as possible.

[해설] [1]surplus [səːrplʌs]: more than is needed 여분의, 너무 많은: Lose those surplus pounds with new diet plan. 새 다이어트 계획으로 살 좀 빼라. [2]crucial [krúːʃəl]: very important 매우 중요한: This election is crucial to Israel's future. 이 선거는 이스라엘 미래에 매우 중요하다. [3]fighting/combat strength 전투력. [4]get rid of: to dispose of; to eliminate 제거하다: She got rid of her old clothes by giving them to the poor. 그녀는 낡은 옷을 가난한 사람들에게 줘서 없앴다.

군인들의 군살

군인에게 있어서 군살이란?
심장에 짐이며,
만병의 근원이며,
국민에게 부정적인 이미지를 주며,
전투력 약화의 결정적 요인이므로,
가장 빠른 시간 내에 제거해야 하는 불필요한 살점이다.

I burned up my whole youth

A: How long have you been in the military?

B: Twenty five years.

A: Wow, 25 years in the military?

B: Yeah, I burned up 25 years of my youth in the military.

A: Didn't you get paid?

청춘을 불살랐다

A: 군대생활 얼마나 했나?

B: 25년

A: 와, 군대생활 25년을?

B: 그래, 내 청춘 25년을 불살랐다.

A: 봉급은 안 받았어?

🔸 Accident reports

① Smoke from the warehouse!

② A sentry lost his rifle on duty.

③ One corporal hanged himself.

④ We captured 20 insurgents[1] in this battle.

⑤ A U.S. helicopter crashed near Tikrit.

⑥ Two of our soldiers drowned in the river.

⑦ I heard a big blast[2] near sentry post No. 7.

⑧ A soldier went AWOL with live grenades[3].

⑨ Some smoke from the ammo store house.

⑩ An ambulance to the hospital was attacked.

⑪ An NCO eloped[4] with an Iraqi woman last week.

⑫ A female corporal was captured by Iraqi troops.

⑬ Two service men didn't come back after leave.

⑭ A truck flipped[5] over on the highway to Baghdad.

⑮ One corporal stepped on an anti-personnel mine[6].

⑯ A group of Iraqi insurgents broke into the rear gate.

⑰ Two female officers were taken hostage[7] by insurgents.

[해설] [1]insurgent [insə́:rdʒənt]: one of a group of people fighting against the government of their own country. 폭도, 반란자. [2]blast [blæst]: an explosion 폭발: The blast was heard two miles away. 폭발음이 2마일 떨어진 곳에서도 들렸다. [3]grenade [grənéid]: a hand-sized, small bomb 수류탄: A soldier threw a grenade into a building. 한 군인이 수류탄 하나를 건물 속에 던졌다. [4]elope [ilóup]: to go away secretly with someone to get married 몰래 결혼하려고 눈이 맞아 도망치다. [5]flip: to turn over suddenly 전복되다: A truck flipped over on its side on the icy road. 트럭 한 대가 얼음판이 된 도로 옆에 전복되었다. [6]anti-personnel mine 대인지뢰. [7]hostage[hástidʒ]: someone who is kept as a prisoner by an enemy 인질: Three nurses were taken/held hostage by the rebels. 3명의 간호사들이 반군들에 의해 인질로 잡혔다.

🔸 사고보고

① 창고에서 연기!

② 한 초병이 근무 중 소총을 분실했습니다.

③ 한 상병이 목메어 자살 했습니다.

④ 우리는 이번 전투에서 반군 20명을 체포했습니다.

⑤ 미군헬기 한 대가 티크리트 부근에 추락 했습니다.

⑥ 병사 두 명이 강에서 익사했습니다.

⑦ 7초소 근처에서 큰 폭발음이 났습니다.

⑧ 한 병사가 수류탄을 가지고 탈영했습니다.

⑨ 무기고에서 연기가 납니다.

⑩ 병원으로 가던 구급차가 습격당했습니다.

⑪ 지난주 한 부사관은 이라크 여성과 눈이 맞아 도망갔다.

⑫ 한 여군 상병이 이라크 군에 포로로 잡혔습니다.

⑬ 두 명의 사병이 휴가 후 복귀하지 않았습니다.

⑭ 바그다드로 가는 고속도로에서 트럭 한 대가 전복되었습니다.

⑮ 상병 하나가 대인 지뢰를 밟았습니다.

⑯ 일당의 이라크 반군이 후문으로 난입했습니다.

⑰ 두 명의 여군 장교가 반군에 인질로 잡혔습니다.

🟡 Apply for Iraq

W: Honey, why don't you apply for Iraq?

H: What?

W: I heard that if you go there, your salary is doubled.

H: Now this woman has gone crazy about money!

W: Other people apply, though.

H: In Iraq, the situation is insecure[1] and it's still dangerous.

W: Oh, what a chicken[2] soldier.

H: And my service record is not good enough for me to be selected.

W: Gee, what have you been doing for the past 10 years?
   I've always done my best as a military wife to support you.

[해설] [1]insecure [insikjúər]: not safe or not protected 불안정/불안전한, 위험에 처한: Many of our staff are worried because their jobs are insecure. 우리 직원들 중 많은 사람들은 직업이 안정되지 않아서 걱정한다. [2]chicken: (informal) someone who lacks courage 용기 없는 사람: Don't be such a chicken! 겁쟁이가 되지 마!

🟡 이라크 파병 지원

아내: 여보, 당신도 이라크에 지원 좀 하지?

남편: 뭘?

아내: 동티모르에 가면 월급도 두 배로 받는다며.

남편: 이 여자 돈에 환장을 했구먼.

아내: 그래도 남들은 지원하더라.

남편: 이라크는 전황이 불확실하고 위험해.

아내: 이런 겁쟁이 군인 아저씨.

남편: 내 근무성적으로는 곤란해.

아내: 당신은 지난 10년 동안 뭐했어요?
   나는 군인의 아내로서 당신을 지원하는데 항상 최선을 다했는데.

🔸 Your face looks like a crater

A: Your face looks like a crater[1].
   What has became of your face?
B: Sunburned after 20 years of infantry training.
A: I think it is because of your excessive drinking.

[해설] [1]crater [kréitər]: a large hole in the ground 구멍, 분화구: the crater of a volcano 화산의 분화구

🔸 네 얼굴이 분화구 같아

A: 네 얼굴은 완전 분화구다.
   네 얼굴이 왜 그렇게 되었니?
B: 훈련받는다고 20년 그을리고 나니.
A: 과음해서 그렇지 뭐.

🔸 I got worn out   나는 찌들었소

① First, I got worn out[1] by work.　　　첫째, 업무에 찌들었고
② Second, I got worn out by inspections.　둘째, 검열에 찌들었고
③ Third, I got worn out by reports.　　　셋째, 보고에 찌들었고
④ Fourth, I got worn out by drinking.　　넷째, 술에 찌들었고
⑤ Fifth, I got worn out by smoking.　　　다섯째, 담배에 찌들었고
⑥ Sixth, I got worn out by my seniors.　 여섯째, 상사에 찌들었고
⑦ Seventh, I got worn out by my juniors. 일곱째, 부하에 찌들었고
⑧ Eighth, I got worn out by my wife.　　 여덟째, 마누라에 찌들었고
⑨ Ninth, I got worn out by conferences.　아홉째, 회의에 찌들었고
⑩ Tenth, I got worn out by moving home.　열번째, 이사에 찌들었다.

[해설] [1]wear sb/sth ~ out: to feel extremely tired 매우 피곤하게/지치게 하다: You look really worn out. 너 정말 피곤해 보인다.

🔵 I want a discharge!

A: Damn, I want a discharge!

B: You say that all the time[1].

A: It drives me crazy.

B: Do you need an application form for retirement?

A: That's okay.

B: Never say that again. I really hate the way that sounds!

[해설] [1] say sth all the time 항상 얘기하다, 타령하다: My wife always says money. 아내는 늘 돈타령이다.

🔵 제대해야겠어!

A: 빌어먹을, 제대해야겠어!

B: 너는 항상 제대 타령이군.

A: 미치겠어.

B: 전역 지원서 갖다 줄까?

A: 그냥 나둬 봐.

B: 제대 소리 그만해, 듣기 거북하다!

◎ I'm going to retire next year

A: How long do you think you'll be in the military?

B: I'm going to be discharged next year.

A: How much pension[1] will you get if you retire next year?

B: I haven't figured it out, but it'll be about one million and five hundred thousand won a month.

A: How can you survive on that amount?

B: I'll be a janitor of an apartment building if I can't find a better job.

A: Do you think that anybody can be a janitor?

[해설] [1] pension[pénʃən]: a regular payment to a retired person 연금

◎ 내년에 제대해야지

A: 너 군생활 얼마나 할 것 같니?

B: 내년에 제대할 거야.

A: 내년에 전역하면 연금이 얼마나 되니?

B: 아직 계산 안 해봤는데 월 150만원 정도될 거야.

A: 그 돈으로 어떻게 사니?

B: 할 게 없으면 아파트 수위라도 해야지.

A: 아파트 수위는 아무나 하는 줄 아나?

Give me a tax-free whiskey

[Soldier : Civilian]

C: Could you get me a tax-free whiskey?

S: Why do you need that?

C: I'd like to take part in my boss' housewarming party[1].

S: What kind of liquor do you want?

C: Something special or Passport.

S: I'm sorry, civilians should not drink tax-free whisky.

C: Are you kidding?

S: I'll get you a bottle of Passport.

C: Buy me a box of tax free Passport. I'll pay for that.

S: We can buy only four tax-free liquors in a year, you know?

C: I thought you could buy as much as you want.

[해설] [1]housewarming party: a party to celebrate moving into a new house 집들이

면세양주 한 병 줘

민간인: 면세양주 한 병 갖다 줄 수 있겠어?

군 인: 양주는 왜?

민간인: 우리 사장님 집들이 가려고.

군 인: 어떤 술을 원하지?

민간인: 썸씽스페셜이나 패스포트.

군 인: 미안해. 민간인들은 면세주 마시면 안 돼.

민간인: 날 놀리나?

군 인: 내가 패스포트 한 병 갖다 줄게.

민간인: 패스포트 한 박스 사줘라. 내가 돈 줄게.

군 인: 우리는 1년에 면세주 4병밖에 못 사는 거 알아?

민간인: 나는 얼마든지 살 수 있는 줄 알았지.

🟠 When am I off, sir?

[Lt. Kim : Company commander]

LK: When am I off, sir?

CC: What do you mean by "**off**"?

LK: All of my colleagues in other units are already exempted from work.

CC: You still have one month left until your discharge day! Use your annual leave, then.

LK: I'm sorry. I have already used all my annual leave.

CC: Once you have used your entire annual leave, that's all you get.

LK: But I can't concentrate on my work, sir.

CC: I don't have authority to exempt you one month earlier. Don't negotiate with me to get additional leave. I want you to perform your duties well right up to the last day.

∗ Off often means unauthorized additional leave before discharge day.

🟠 중대장님, 저 언제 오프합니까?

김중위: 중대장님, 저 언제 오프합니까?

중대장: "오프"가 무슨 말이야?

김중위: 다른 부대 제 동기들은 다 열외 했습니다.

중대장: 너 제대까지는 한 달이나 더 남았어! 그러면 연가(年暇)써라.

김중위: 죄송합니다. 연가를 다 써버렸습니다.

중대장: 연가 다 썼으면 그만이다.

김중위: 하지만, 일에 집중이 안 됩니다.

중대장: 나는 너를 한 달 더 일찍 오프시켜줄 권한이 없다. 휴가를 더 얻으려고 나에게 협상하지 마라. 끝까지 근무 잘해라.

∗ Off는 제대 전에 공인되지 않은 부가적인 휴가를 의미한다.

🟡 A commander's duty

A commander is the core of military troops. He/she commands, manages, and trains military troops, taking responsibility for command and accomplishing his/her duties by coordinating all the capacity of the unit. He/she has to keep in mind that strict military discipline, high morale, and the spirit of unity of the corps are up to a commander, so he/she should lead and control his/her subordinates exercising the right to command strictly, and make every effort for welfare improvement and effective management of resources.

🟡 지휘관의 책무

지휘관은 부대의 핵심으로 부대를 지휘, 관리 및 훈련하며 부대의 성패에 대하여 책임을 진다. 그러므로 지휘관은 부대의 모든 역량을 통합하여 부여된 임무를 완수하여야 한다. 부대의 엄정한 군기와 왕성한 사기 그리고 굳은 단결은 지휘관에 달려 있음을 명심하여 지휘권을 엄정하게 행사하고 부하를 지도, 감독하며 부하의 복지향상과 자원의 효율적 관리에 힘써야 한다.

🔸 A Commander's Ten Commandments

① A commander should always remember that he is like a goldfish in a goldfish bowl.
② A commander should have his men recognize that he loves them truly.
③ A commander should recognize and respect NCOs' honor and authority.
④ A commander should command his men based on principle and flexibility.
⑤ Decisions should be made carefully, actions should be based on importance and urgency.
⑥ A commander should command his men and his unit with absolute authority.
⑦ A commander should adopt the "whole person approach" in education.
⑧ A commander should strictly differentiate[1] public from private and reward from punishment.
⑨ A commander should be especially transparent[2] regarding money.
⑩ A commander should try to ensure his men have positive memories of the military.

[해설] [1]differentiate [dìfərénʃièit]: to notice how two things or people are different from each other 구별 짓다: He can't differentiate between blue and green. [2]transparent [trænspέərənt]: easy to notice and not deceiving anyone; obvious 투명한

🔸 지휘관의 근무 십계명

① 지휘관은 어항 속의 금붕어임을 항상 명심해야 한다.
② 부하를 진심으로 사랑하고 있다는 것을 인식시켜야 한다.
③ 부사관의 체면과 권위를 인정해 주어야 한다.
④ 원리원칙과 융통성을 구분하여 지휘해야 한다.
⑤ 결심은 심사숙고하고 실천은 경중완급을 가려해야 한다.
⑥ 지휘관은 하늘과 같이 부하와 부대를 지휘해야 한다.
⑦ 지휘관은 모든 교육을 전인교육으로 승화시켜야 한다.
⑧ 공과 사, 신상필벌을 엄히 구분해야 한다.
⑨ 지휘관은 특히 금전 문제가 투명해야 한다.
⑩ 부하에게 건전한 추억을 만들어주어야 한다.

◯ Commander's wish

Though your commander says "I wish," it's still like a direct order you have to obey. Usually stupid guys take it as just his wish that they don't need to take any notice of.

◯ 지휘관의 의도

비록 당신의 지휘관이 "나는 바란다"라고 이야기하더라도 그것은 네가 반드시 따라야하는 명령과 같다. 보통 어리석은 사람들은 상관의 희망을 신경 쓰지 않아도 되는 것으로 받아들인다.

◯ Commanders never forget

Commanders never forget the instructions which they give to their subordinates. The instructions are like the commanders' seed or sperm that will make a baby. They supervise to make sure that they begin to sprout and are nurtured properly. You, his subordinates should value the instructions as if they were his children. For example, if your commander says to you, "the weeds in the parade ground are overgrown," that is NOT a declarative sentence, but implies that you should have weeded earlier!

◯ 지휘관은 결코 잊지 않는다

지휘관은 자신이 부하에게 지시한 것을 결코 잊지 않는다. 지시사항은 지휘관의 자식이 될 씨앗 혹은 정자와 같은 것이다. 지휘관들은 자신의 씨앗이 싹이 트기 시작하는지, 영양분이 적절히 공급되는지 은연중에 감독한다. 그의 부하인 당신은 그 지시사항들을 마치 지휘관의 자식처럼 소중히 여겨야 한다. 예를 들면 너의 상관이 너에게 "연병장에 잡초가 너무 자랐다"고 한다면 그것은 단순한 평서문이 아니라 네가 더 일찍 잡초제거를 했어야 함을 의미한다.

🟡 Your boss is like a big fat old horse

The best way to keep the boss out of your business is to prove you know what's going on and to keep him/her informed. Think of your boss as a big fat old horse in a stable[1] eating hay. If you feed him/her hay (info), they will be more inclined to stay out of your pasture.

[해설] [1]stable: a building where horses are kept 마구간, 가축우리

🟡 너의 상관은 크고 살찐 늙은 말과 같다

너의 상관이 너의 업무에 간섭하지 않도록 하는 가장 좋은 방법은 일이 어떻게 되어가고 있는지 당신이 알고 있음을 증명해 줌은 물론 그/녀에게 알려주는 것이다. 당신의 상사를 건초를 먹는 뚱뚱하고 늙은 말로 생각해라. 만약 당신이 그/녀에게 건초(정보)를 주면, 그들은 당신의 목초지에서 더 벗어나게 된다.

🟡 여기에서는 상관에게 시기적절한 보고의 중요성을 이야기하고 있다. 상관도 상황이 어떻게 돌아가는지 모르면 불안하게 되고 간섭이 늘어나게 됨을 시사한다. 미 공군 사관학교 홈페이지에 이런 내용이 있었다.

🟡 Three reports

A commander is often compared to a goldfish in a goldfish bowl. The fish is solely dependent on your feeding. That's why three reports (initial report, interim report, and final report) are important.

🟡 세 가지 보고

지휘관은 종종 어항속의 금붕어에 비유된다. 그 금붕어는 전적으로 당신의 먹이에 의존하여 살아가고 있다. 그것이 세 가지 보고(초도보고, 중간보고, 결과보고)가 중요한 이유다.

◯ Commander's instructions

① Never drink and drive.
② Never lie to cover up mistakes.
③ Never smoke in a non-smoking area.
④ Never omit giving and returning salutes.
⑤ Clean all areas to prepare for a VIP visit.
⑥ Prevent accidents at thawing season.
⑦ Never collect any unjust money from your men.
⑧ Maintain military discipline during holidays.
⑨ Never wear military uniform with civilian clothes.
⑩ Don't go out of the unit too often during office hours.
⑪ Never offer a boiler maker drink at social gatherings.
⑫ Don't go 2nd or 3rd bar hopping after gatherings.
⑬ Don't pass a cup around at social gatherings.
⑭ Abstain from having meaningless social gatherings.
⑮ Never join unauthorized social gatherings.
⑯ Never use government vehicles for private use.
⑰ Never offer and accept any bribe for promotion.
⑱ Never use an unauthorized electric heater.
⑲ Never punish and train in unauthorized ways.
⑳ Never take a leak in the street after drinking.
㉑ Never hang around amusement places in uniform.
㉒ Never wear boots which have zips instead of laces.
㉓ Never sing with a loud voice after work.
㉔ Don't toy with married women during the holiday making season.
㉕ Be sure to wear a rubber band when wearing combat boots.
㉖ Avoid assaults, harassment and verbally abusive behavior.
㉗ Refrain from unhealthy entertainment such as gostop and mahjong.
㉘ Don't smoke or chew gum in the street when you are in uniform.
㉙ When walking in uniform, keep your hands out of your pockets.
㉚ Never install unauthorized game programs on the computer.

🔸 중대장님 지시사항

① 음주운전 절대 금지
② 실수를 감추려고 거짓말 하지 말 것
③ 비흡연 구역에서 절대 금연
④ 경례 및 답례 철저
⑤ VIP 방문 대비 환경미화 철저
⑥ 해빙기 사고 방지
⑦ 사병으로부터 부당한 금전 갹출(醵出) 금지
⑧ 휴무군기 확립
⑨ 군복과 사복 혼착 금지
⑩ 일과 중 잦은 외출 금지
⑪ 회식에서 폭탄주 권주 금지
⑫ 회식에서 2차, 3차 안 가기
⑬ 회식에서 술잔 안 돌리기
⑭ 명목 없는 회식 삼가
⑮ 비인가 친목단체 가입 금지
⑯ 관용차의 사적 이용 금지
⑰ 진급 관련 뇌물수수 금지
⑱ 비인가 전열기 사용 금지
⑲ 비인가 벌칙훈련 금지
⑳ 취중 노상방뇨 금지
㉑ 군복 착용 후 유흥가 배회 금지
㉒ 지퍼 부착한 전투화 사용 금지
㉓ 일과 후 고성방가 금지
㉔ 행락철 부녀자 희롱 금지
㉕ 전투화 착용시 고무 밴드 착용
㉖ 구타, 가혹행위 및 욕설 금지
㉗ 고스톱 마작과 같은 불건전한 오락 삼가
㉘ 거리에서 제복입고 흡연 및 껌을 씹지 말 것
㉙ 제복입고 보행시 손을 호주머니에 넣지 말 것
㉚ 컴퓨터에 불법오락 게임 프로그램 설치 금지

🔸 Say "yes, sir!"

"Yes, sir!" is the most wonderful answer that soldiers can give to their seniors. Once you are being told to do something by your senior, do it exactly as you were told, though the order is somewhat unrealistic or unreasonable. You might not exactly understand his standpoint and what orders he received from his superior. Your senior may not have enough time to discuss details with you. Get things done first, and then ask him only if you are requested to do so. If the end result of his order goes wrong, he will assume the whole responsibility.

Never give him any advice unless requested. Who likes unwanted advice? Respect his decisions and follow him to the grave. Then you will definitely be rewarded.

🔸 "예, 알겠습니다!"라고 대답해라

"예, 알겠습니다!"라는 말은 군인이 상관에게 말할 수 있는 가장 훌륭한 대답이다. 당신이 당신 상관으로부터 무엇을 하라고 지시를 받으면, 비록 그 명령이 다소 비현실적이고 불합리하더라도 정확히 지시받은 대로 하라. 당신은 그의 입장과 또한 그가 그의 상관에게 어떻게 지시를 받았는지 정확히 이해할 수 없을지도 모른다. 일단 일을 완성하고 난 다음 그가 허락하는 경우에만 질문을 해라. 너의 상관은 사소한 것을 가지고 당신과 토론할 충분한 시간이 없을지도 모른다. 만약에 그의 명령에 대한 결과가 잘못되더라도 책임은 그가 진다.

절대로 상관이 물어보지도 않는데 충고하지 마라. 원치 않는 충고를 좋아하는 사람이 누가 있겠는가? 그의 결정을 존경하고 무덤까지 그를 따라라. 그러면 당신은 틀림없이 보상받을 것이다.

◯ Do's and don'ts in the U.S. military

① Don't offer excuses.
② Don't lean on a superior's desk.
③ Don't go over the heads of superiors.
④ Don't gamble with your subordinates.
⑤ Don't salute with anything in your hands and mouth.
⑥ Don't exploit your subordinates just for your own good.
⑦ Don't smoke or chew gum when on the street in uniform.
⑧ Don't criticize your subordinates in front of his or her troops.
⑨ Don't appear in uniform while under the influence of alcohol[1].
⑩ Don't turn and walk the other way to avoid giving the hand salute.
⑪ Don't run indoors to avoid standing at attention for Reveille[2] or Retreat[3].
⑫ Act upon the commander's "desire" or "suggestion" as if they were orders.
⑬ Don't sit on another soldier's bed or bunk in the barracks without permission.
⑭ Don't receive any gift from any person who receives a LESSER salary than you.
⑮ Don't criticize the Army, the Navy, the Marine Corps or the Air Force in front of civilians.
⑯ Don't "wear" a superior's rank by saying something like, "The colonel wants this done right away," when in fact the colonel has said no such thing.
⑰ With the exception of on-the-spot corrections[4], don't give orders to another's troop.
⑱ Refrain from criticizing unless you are able to provide a better solution.
⑲ Learn to accept criticism positively and with grace.
⑳ If you are a man, always show deference[5] to women and children.

[해설] [1]under the influence of alcohol 취중에. [2]reveille[révəli] 기상식. [3]retreat 하기식. [4]on-the-spot corrections 현장에서 교정하기. [5]deference[défərəns]: behavior that shows you respect someone 존경, 경의. 〈 defer 경의를 표하다.

미군에서 준수사항

① 변명하지 마라.
② 상관의 책상에 기대지 마라.
③ 최고 상관에게 곧장 달려가지 마라.(지휘계통을 무시하고)
④ 부하들과 노름하지 마라.
⑤ 손이나 입에 무엇이 있는 상태에서 경례하지 마라.
⑥ 너 자신의 이익을 위해서 너의 부하를 이용하지 마라.
⑦ 거리에서 제복을 입고 흡연하거나 껌을 씹지 마라.
⑧ 너의 부하를 그(그녀)의 부대원 앞에서 비난하지 마라.
⑨ 술에 취한 상태에서 제복을 입고 나타나지 마라.
⑩ 경례를 안 하려고 다른 길로 돌아가지 마라.
⑪ 게양식이나 하기식 때 차려 자세 하기 싫어서 실내로 뛰어들지 마라.
⑫ 지휘관의 "바람"이나 "제안"을 명령처럼 따라서 행동해라.
⑬ 내무반에서 허락 없이 다른 병사의 침대에 앉지 마라.
⑭ 너보다 봉급을 더 적게 받는 어떤 사람으로부터 선물을 받지 마라.
⑮ 민간인들 앞에서 육군, 해군, 해병대, 공군을 비난하지 마라.
⑯ 상관의 계급을 빌리지 마라. 대령은 그런 말을 한 적도 없는데도 "대령님은 이것이 즉시 되길 바랍니다."라고 말하지 마라.
⑰ 현장에서 지적하는 것은 예외로 하되, 다른 부대원에게 명령하지 마라.
⑱ 네가 더 좋은 해결책을 제시할 수 없으면 불평을 삼가라.
⑲ 질책을 긍정적으로, 품위 있게 받아들이도록 해라.
⑳ 당신이 남자라면 여성과 어린이를 항상 우선 배려하라.

🔸 Let's not be a burden to those on active duty

Douglas MacArthur said, "Old soldiers never die; they just fade away." And someone said,

"Old soldiers never die; they are just burdens on active duty[1]."

"Old soldiers never die; they just drain the national pension."

"Retired generals never die; they just take bribes from arm dealers."

✻ Although I get discharged, I won't visit the garrison where I worked and won't ask my old subordinates to buy certain insurance for my own good. I'll never be a burden to my old subordinates.

[해설] [1]active duty: a solider, pilot, etc, who is ready to take part in a battle 현역 (즉시 전투에 투입될 수 있는 군인, 조종사 등)

🔸 현역에 짐이 되지 말자

맥아더는 "노병은 죽지 않고 다만 사라질 뿐이다." 라고 했다.

또 누군가 말하기를,

"노병은 죽지 않고 현역에게 짐만 될 뿐이다."

"노병은 죽지 않고 국가 연금만 축낼 뿐이다."

"퇴역 장군은 죽지 않고 무기상으로부터 뇌물만 챙길 뿐이다."

✻ 비록 내가 전역하더라도 내 이익을 위해서 내가 근무했던 부대를 방문하여 나의 옛 부하들한테 어떤 보험을 들어달라고 부탁하지 않겠다. 나의 옛 부하들에게 짐이 되지 않겠다.

Ballade of an old soldier

(Written by Kim Min-Ki /Sung by Yang Hee-Eun)

I was born in this land, have become a soldier
Thirty years of blossoms and snows have glided along
What have I done and what have I longed for through my life
It'll be all done when they bury me in this land
Oh, gone is my youth, that will never be back again
The blossom of my youth was spent in all khakis

My sons and my daughters you don't be so sad
You are children of a proud soldier
You want some nice clothes, you want some good foods?
Though I love you so much, but no way, your daddy is a soldier
Oh, gone is my youth, that will never be back again
The blossom of my youth was spent in all khakis

What was it, you all know, my wish for life
I wanted to see Mt. Geomgang with my grandchildren
On one fine day, when all the mountain is in full blossom
I still keep waiting, though my life is nearly done
Oh, gone is my youth, that will never be back again
The blossom of my youth was spent in all khakis

The origin of this song

In 1976, an army master sergeant who was about to retire asked Kim Min-ki (the writer of this song) to write a song about the joys and sorrows of old soldiers. The sergeant bought the writer two mals(18 liters) of makgoli for writing a song. Before this song was released, it became widely known throughout the military. The surprised Minister of National Defense banned this song immediately. This was the first song banned by the Minister of National Defense in South Korea.

늙은 군인의 노래

(김민기 작사 / 노래 양희은)

나 태어난 이 강산에 군인이 되어
꽃 피고 눈 내리기 어언 삼십 년
무엇을 하였느냐 무엇을 바라느냐
나 죽어 이 흙 속에 묻히면 그만이지
아 다시 못 올 흘러간 내 청춘
푸른 옷에 실려 간 꽃다운 이 내 청춘

아들아 내 딸들아 서러워 마라
너희들은 자랑스런 군인의 자식이다.
좋은 옷 입고프냐 만난 것 먹고프냐
아서라 말아라 군인 아들 너로다
아 다시 못 올 흘러간 내 청춘
푸른 옷에 실려 간 꽃다운 이내 청춘

내 평생 소원이 무엇이더냐
우리 손주 손목잡고 금강산 구경일세
꽃 피어 만발하고 활짝 개인 그날을
기다리고 기다리다 이내 청춘 다 갔네
아 다시 못 올 흘러간 내 청춘
푸른 옷에 실려 간 꽃다운 이내 청춘

이 노래의 기원

1976년 퇴역을 앞둔 한 육군 상사가 김민기(이 노래의 작가)에게 노병의 애환과 설움을 담은 노래 하나를 지어 달라고 부탁했다. 그 상사는 노래를 짓는 대가로 김민기에게 막걸리 두 말을 사주었다. 노래가 발표되기도 전 군에 퍼지자 놀란 국방부 장관은 이 노래를 즉시 금지 시켰다. 이것은 한국 국방부장관에 의해 금지된 최초의 노래다.

Strategic Competence in the English Language

"The numbers of tanks and bullets don't always guarantee victory in war." The same principle applies when having conversation with native speakers of English. No matter how many English words you have memorized or how much you have studied grammar, it's all in vain if you cannot use these properly in a situation.

Now if you cannot remember a word, for example "eggplant", how can you convey its meaning to others? When you cannot remember a certain word, you should be able to substitute another word for it. That's one of the "strategic competences" in learning foreign languages. You should also be able to describe or define it in the following way: "It is a kind of vegetable and looks like a sausage or a banana. Its color is violet or purple. In Korea, it is said that widowed women love this vegetable instead of their husband and fortunate widowed women tend to stumble into eggplant plots!" Now let's try to foster a strategic competence in the English Language rather than studying English haphazardly!

영어의 전략적 능력

"탱크의 대수와 총알의 양이 전쟁에서 항상 승리를 보장해주는 것은 아니다." 그것은 모국인 화자와 영어로 대화하는 것과도 마찬가지다. 당신이 아무리 많은 단어를 암기했더라도 혹은 아무리 문법을 많이 공부했더라도, 어떤 상황에서 그것들을 적절히 사용하지 못하면 모두 헛일이다.

만약에 당신이 "가지"라는 단어가 생각나지 않을 때 다른 사람에게 그것을 어떻게 말하겠는가? 당신이 어떤 특정한 단어가 생각나지 않을 때, 당신은 그것을 적절한 단어로 대체할 수 있어야 한다. 그것이 영어에서 "전략적 능력" 중의 한가지이다. 당신은 그것을 다음과 같이 혹은 다른 방법으로 쉽게 설명할 수 있어야 한다. "그것은 소시지나 바나나같이 생겼다. 그것의 색은 자줏빛이다. 한국에서 과부들이 남편 대신에 좋아하고 운 좋은 과부들은 가지 밭에 넘어진다는 말이 있다." 이제 무모하게 영어 공부하지 말고 영어에서 전략적 능력을 함양하자!

Military English!

At a Female Boot Camp
[여군훈련소]

- 너 뭐 되고 싶어?
- 칠면조 점호
- 내무검사에서★★
- 군기가 빠진 김병장
- 너 머리 염색 했구나★
- 립스틱이 너무 진하다★★★
- 너의 브라는 지급품이 아니구나★★★
- 누가 또 면회 왔어?
- 면회 전
- 면회 후
- 저 커피타려고 군대 온 거…

What do you want to be?

[Teacher : Student]

T: What do you want to be?

S: A soldier.

T: What? Soldier? Are you serious?

S: What's wrong with becoming a female soldier?

T: After graduation get a job and try to lead a normal life[1].

S: Why can't I become a soldier?

T: To be a female soldier is not as easy as you think.

S: But I love people in uniform.

Recently the sons of powerful families won't go into the military. Don't you think we females have to go into the military instead?

[해설] [1]lead a normal/dull/healthy life: to have a normal/dull/healthy type of life 정상적인/따분한/건강한 삶을 유지하다: My husband and I are in our 60s, married 40 years. We have led an active sex life all through our marriage and enjoy sex three times a week. Is this healthy?

너 뭐 되고 싶어?

교사: 너 뭐가 되고 싶어?

학생: 군인입니다.

교사: 뭐? 군인? 정말이야?

학생: 여군 되는 게 뭐가 잘못되었어요?

교사: 졸업하고 취직해서 평범하게 살아라.

학생: 제가 군인 되는 게 어때서요?

교사: 여군 되는 것도 네 생각만큼 쉽지 않아.

학생: 하지만 저는 제복 입은 사람들이 좋더라구요.

최근에 빽있는 집안의 아들은 군대도 안 가려고 하는데.

그 대신 우리 여자들이라도 군대 가야 한다고 생각하지 않습니까?

🟠 A turkey roll call

Hey, you guys.
Have you ever tried turkey?
Tonight I'll take a turkey roll call.

Put on battle dress uniform blouse.
Put on your uniform skirt.
Put on pajama bottoms instead of stockings.
A shoe on your left foot,
a high-heeled shoe on your right foot, and
a helmet on your head.
Fall in[1] on the drill ground holding a needle within 3 minutes.
You got it?

[해설] [1]fall in: to take one's place in the ranks, as a soldier 정열하다, 집합하다. (자기 자리에 서다) ↔ fall out 해산, 해산하다

🟠 칠면조 점호

야, 너희들.
칠면조 먹어봤어?
오늘밤은 칠면조 점호를 취하겠다.

상의는 전투복.
하의는 정복치마.
스타킹 대신 잠옷바지.
왼쪽에 단화,
오른쪽엔 하이힐,
머리엔 철모 착용.
바늘 들고 3분 내에 연병장에 집합한다.
알겠냐?

🔵 At the barracks inspection

[Company commander : Cadet]

CC: Cadet number 22.

CA: Yes, number 22, Cadet Lee Susan.

CC: I think you are missing one piece of underwear!

CA: I'm sorry! I left it at home on my last leave.

CC: Don't forget to bring it next time. Open your beauty kit.

CA: Action!

CC: Let me see. Did you put on make-up recently?

CA: Yes, I did once. I'm so sorry, ma'am.

CC: What use is make-up to a cadet in boot camp?

　　Go into the corridor and drop!

* NCO cadets are given cosmetics at boot camp, but they are not allowed to put on make up before special occasions, such as commission day.

🔵 내무검사에서

중대장: 22번 후보생.

후보생: 네 22번, 이수잔 후보생.

중대장: 속옷이 하나 없구나.

후보생: 네! 지난 외출 때 집에 두고 왔습니다.

중대장: 다음 외출 때 꼭 가져와. 네 화장품 케이스 열어봐.

후보생: 실시!

중대장: 어디 보자. 너 요즘 화장한 적 있나?

후보생: 네, 지난주 한번 했습니다. 죄송합니다.

중대장: 후보생이 화장할 일이 뭐가 있어?

　　　　복도로 가서 엎드려!

* 훈련 중인 부사관 후보생들에게 화장품은 지급되지만 화장은 임관식과 같은 특별한 행사에만 가능하다.

🔸 Loosely disciplined Sgt. Kim

[Staff Sgt. Park : Sgt. Kim]

SP: Hey, Sgt. Kim!

SK: Yes, Ma'am, why did you call me?

SP: Why didn't you give me a salute?
   The badge of rank is not for appearance.

SK: Sorry, Sgt. Park. Do you know how much jjambab I've eaten?

SP: You don't know that rank is everything in the military.
   If you don't give me a salute once more, I'll send you to the disciplinary training unit.

🔸 군기가 빠진 김병장

박하사: 거기, 김병장!

김병장: 예, 김하사님. 저 왜 불렀어요?

박하사: 너 왜 경례 안 했어?
   계급장은 폼이 아니다.

김병장: 박 하사님, 죄송해요. 하지만 제가 짬밥을 얼마나 먹었는지 아세요?

박하사: 너는 군대가 계급인 줄 모르는구나.
   한 번만 더 경례 안하면 군기 교육대로 보낼 거다.

🔸 You had your hair dyed

[Platoon leader : Staff Sgt. Kim]

PL: Sgt. Kim, you had your hair dyed, didn't you?

SK: Yes, just a little bit.

PL: When?

SK: During last vacation.

PL: Is it okay if a soldier has her hair dyed?

SK: No, ma'am.

PL: Then, why did you have it dyed?

SK: I'm really sorry. I'll have it re-dyed black.

PL: I know that you are young, but don't attract[1] attention to yourself.

SK: Yes, ma'am.

[해설] [1]attract/arrest/draw 주의를 끌다(to)

🔸 너 머리 염색했구나

소대장: 김하사, 너 머리 염색했지?

김하사: 예, 좀 했습니다.

소대장: 언제 했니?

김하사: 지난 휴가 때요.

소대장: 군인이 머리 염색하면 되니?

김하사: 안됩니다.

소대장: 그런데 왜 했어?

김하사: 죄송합니다. 다시 검게 염색하겠습니다.

소대장: 네가 젊다는 것은 알지만, 주목 받지 마라.

김하사: 예, 알겠습니다.

Your lipstick is too dark

[Capt. Kim : Sgt. Park]

CK: Sgt. Park, your lipstick is too dark.
SP: I'm sorry!
CK: Your nail varnish is, too. When did you have it done?
SP: During the last vacation.
CK: OK. Well, how is it going with you?
SP: What are you saying, sir.
CK: You said you were introduced to a man by your parents last week.
SP: But his parents have some prejudices[1] against female soldiers.
CK: What? Female soldiers make the best brides.
　　Having served their seniors and dealt with subordinates, female soldiers will serve their parents-in-law well!

[해설] [1]prejudice [prédʒudis]: an unfair feeling of dislike against sb who is of a different race, sex, religion, etc. 편견, 치우친 생각

립스틱이 너무 진하다

김대위: 박하사, 너 립스틱이 너무 진하다.
박하사: 죄송합니다.
김대위: 손톱도 그렇고. 언제 그랬어?
박하사: 지난 휴가 때요.
김대위: 그건 그렇고, 그 일은 잘 돼가니?
박하사: 무슨 말씀입니까?
김대위: 지난주에 부모님의 소개로 선을 봤다며?
박하사: 하지만 그의 부모님은 여군에 대해서 편견이 있습니다.
김대위: 뭐라고? 여군만한 신붓감이 있을까.
　　　　군대에서 상관 모셔보고 부하도 다뤄봐서 시어른도 잘 모실 텐데!

Your bra isn't an issue item

[Company commander : Female cadet]

CC: Sgt. Kim, your bra isn't an issue item.

FC: No, it isn't.

CC: Where is the supplied bra, then?

FC: I lost it last week.

CC: Where?

FC: I couldn't find it after I hung it on the outdoor line in the area for drying clothes.

CC: You lost your belongings[1], it will cost you three demerits. Did you report it?

FC: No, not yet, ma'am.

CC: You will lose your rifle next!

[해설] [1]belongings: the things that you own, especially things that you are carrying with you 소지품. personal belongings 개인 소지품

너의 브라는 지급품이 아니구나

중대장: 김하사, 너의 브래지어는 지급품이 아니구나.

후보생: 예, 아닙니다.

중대장: 지급품은 어떻게 했어?

후보생: 분실했습니다.

중대장: 어디서?

후보생: 지난주 건조장에 널어뒀는데 없어졌습니다.

중대장: 소지품 분실, 감점 3점. 분실보고는 했니?

후보생: 아직 못했습니다!

중대장: 이제 너는 총도 잊어 먹겠구나!

You have a visitor again?

[Sgt. Kim : Sgt. Lee]

SK: Where are you going?
SL: To the visitor's center.
SK: You have a visitor again?
SL: The guy who came last Saturday.
SK: Oh, I envy you. I have to weed on the parade ground.
SL: I am bored by his frequent visits.
SK: As for me, I have no one to visit me during the year.
SL: Next time I'll ask him to bring one of his friends.
SK: I see. Have a good time!

announcement

It is overgrown with weeds after last weekend's rain. So soil has become soft and you can root out the weeds now. If you weed now, you can have an easy time this summer. On this Saturday, the battalion commander will be inspecting each area.

너 누가 또 면회 왔어?

김하사: 이하사, 어디 가니?

이하사: 면회실에.

김하사: 누가 또 면회 왔어?

이하사: 지난주 토요일 왔던 그 남자.

김하사: 부럽다. 우린 연병장 잡초사역 해야 하는데.

이하사: 자꾸 오니 귀찮아.

김하사: 난 일 년이 지나도록 면회 올 남자도 없으니!

이하사: 다음에 그이 친구 하나 데리고 오라 할 게.

김하사: 알았어. 좋은 시간 보내.

방송

지난 주말 비가 내려서 잡초가 많이 자랐습니다. 이제 흙이 부드러워져서 뿌리까지 뽑을 수 있습니다. 지금 잡초제거를 하시면 이번 여름을 편안히 보낼 수 있을 겁니다. 이번 주 토요일 대대장님께서 구역별로 점검하겠습니다.

🔵 Reporting before receiving visitors   면회 전

Cadet Lee	이 후보생
Dan-gyeol! Reporting as ordered, sir! NCO Cadet Lee Susan ordered to receive visitors from 10:20 to 16:00 June 20, 2003. Reporting as ordered. Dan-gyeol!	단결! 신고합니다. 부사관 후보생 이수잔은 2003년 6월20일 10:20부터 16:00까지 면회를 명 받았습니다. 이에 신고합니다. 단결!
Duty Officer 당직사관	
Have a good time, but make sure that military security is properly maintained. That's all! 좋은 시간 보내고 보안사항에 유의해라. 이상!	

🔵 Reporting after receiving visitors   면회 후

Cadet Lee	이 후보생
Dan-gyeol! Reporting as ordered, sir! NCO Cadet Lee Susan finished receiving visitors from 10:20 to 16:00 June 20, 2003 Reporting as ordered. Dan-gyeol!	단결! 신고합니다. 부사관 후보생 이수잔은 2003년 6월 20일10:20부터 16:00까지 면회를 마쳤습니다. 이에 신고합니다. 단결!
Duty Officer 당직사관	
Did you have a good time? ... Go back go your room and get some rest. Tomorrow will be a hard day!	좋은 시간 보냈니? ... 내무반에 가서 좀 쉬어라. 내일은 힘든 날 이잖니!

🟠 I'm not here to make coffee

[Master Sgt.: Staff Sgt.]

MS: Sgt. Kim, could you make a cup of coffee for me?
SS: I'm sorry. I'm not here to make coffee, sir.
MS: There's no one else here, you see?
SS: How do you like your coffee?
MS: Like it's from a vending machine. (after a few minutes)
SS: Here you are, sir.
MS: Thank you, Sgt. Kim.

🟠 저 커피 타려고 군대 온 거 …

상사: 김하사, 커피 좀 타 줄래?
하사: 죄송합니다. 저 커피나 타려고 군대 온 거 아닙니다.
상사: 야, 너도 알다시피 여기 사람이 아무도 없잖아.
하사: 어떻게 타 드릴까요?
상사: 자판기 커피 맛이 나게. (몇 분 후에)
하사: 여기 있습니다.
상사: 고마워, 김하사.

What is the meaning of the Rubber Shoes?

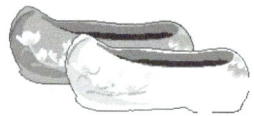

In South Korea,

a *rubber shoe* is a slang for

a girl whose boyfriend is serving

in the military; a *boot* is a slang for

a male soldier who is serving in the military.

Military English!

Voices from Rubber Shoes
(고무신 함성)

- 군바리 사랑*
- 제 남친이 곧 군대가는데**
- 상병은 여친을 차버리는가?
- 세상에서 가장 쉬운 일*
- 여자는 언제 우나?
- 세상에서 젤 나쁜 놈**
- 초보 고무신으로부터*
- 너의 소포 받았어**
- 오빠, 나야!*
- 군바리도 인간?***
- 원통엔 어떻게 가져?**
- 치마 입는 게 더 좋은가?**

- 서방님 보시와요~**
- 그의 손잡기도 쉽지 않았어
- 곰신님들~^^*
- 이미 임신 5개월***
- 수잔은 팬티를 잘 내려서**
- 아기가 아직 태어나지 않았어
- 고무신의 맹세***
- 고참 고무신의 맹세*
- 병장에게 보낸 소포*
- 그런 친구가 될게**
- 절교 편지**
- 고참 곰신의 충고***

🔸 Love of gunbaries

Dear all lonely women who don't have a loving mate!

The Army guys may die from crawling on land.
The Navy guys may die from drowning in the sea.
The Air Force guys may die from falling from the sky.
The Marine guys may be beaten to death.
The Combat Police guys may be stoned to death.
The Conscripted reserve guys may die from losing face[1].

Women, choose wisely!

[해설] [1]lose face: to lose status or the respect of others 체면을 잃다 ↔ save face 체면을 세우다: She is more interested in saving face than telling the truth. 그녀는 진실을 말하기 보다는 체면을 세우는데 더 관심이 많다.

🔸 군바리 사랑

짝 없는 모든 외로운 여인들이여!

육군은 땅에 기다 죽을지 모르고
해군은 물에 빠져 죽을지 모르고
공군은 하늘에서 떨어져 죽을지 모르고
해병은 맞아 죽을지 모르고
전경은 돌에 맞아 죽을지 모르고
방위는 쪽팔려 죽을지 모른다

여자들아, 현명한 선택을 하시라!

🟠 My bf is going into boot camp soon

I've been seeing my bf for 5 years.
He is going into boot camp soon.
I heard that most men change their minds by the time they become a corporal.
I am wondering very much whether my bf will do the same.
Should I get pregnant to trap him completely? (kidding^^)

Senior corporal:
You said soldiers change their minds when they are promoted to Corporal. That's totally groundless[1].
Now military life is much different from what it was 4 or 5 years ago.
We soldiers can't see girls except during our leave.
How can we fall in love with someone without seeing them!

[해설] [1]groundless: not based on facts or reason; baseless 근거 없는: I don't know who spread the rumor, but it was totally groundless. 누가 그 소문을 퍼뜨렸는지 모르지만 그것은 전혀 근거 없었다.

🟠 제 남친이 군대가는데

저는 남친과 사귄 지 5년 되었네여.
제 남친이 곧 군대를 갑니다.
대부분의 남자들은 상병 될 무렵 마음이 변한다고 하더라구여.
제 남친도 그렇지 않을까 정말 걱정입니다.
그를 꼭 붙잡기 위해서 임신이라도 해야 하는가? (농담^^)

말년 상병:
군인들이 상병 진급할 때 마음이 변한다고요.
전혀 근거 없는 소립니다.
요즘 군대 4~5년 전하고 많이 다릅니다.
우리 군인들은 휴가 때 아니면 여자 구경하기 힘듭니다.
님을 봐야 뽕을 따지 않겠소!

◯ Corporals dump their girlfriends?

By the time they become corporals, the guys in the military dump their girlfriends. Is that true?

I hope my boyfriend won't do that.

* Considering that, if a person sees someone of the opposite sex as a new date, he or she naturally secretes the "love hormones," but the average period of secretion is only for two years, so it is quite natural for a soldier to receive a "Dear John letter" by the time he becomes a corporal.

◯ 상병은 여친을 차버리는가?

보통 상병쯤 되면

여자 친구를 차버린다는데.

정말 그런가여?

울 앤은 안 그랬음 좋겠네여.

* 사람이 한 이성을 데이트의 상대자로 만나면 "사랑의 호르몬"이 자연스럽게 분비되는데 그 평균기간이 2년 밖에 되지 않는다는 점을 고려하면, 병사가 상병이 될 무렵 "절교 편지"를 받는 것은 매우 자연스러운 것이다.

◯ The easiest thing in the world

The easiest thing in the world is for a girl to make a pass at a gunbari. The most difficult thing in the world is for a gunbari to make a pass at a girl.

◯ 세상에서 가장 쉬운 일

세상에서 가장 쉬운 일은 여자가 군바리 꼬시기

세상에서 가장 어려운 일은 군바리가 여자 꼬시기

When does a woman cry?

① When her boyfriend is cheating on[1] her.
② When her husband is cheating on her.
③ When her son-in-law is cheating on her daughter.

[해설] [1]cheat on sb: to have a secret sexual relationship with someone who is not your usual sexual partner 일상적인 섹스 파트너가 아닌 사람과 성관계를 갖다: I think Jane is cheating on Tom again. 나는 제인이 탐을 속이고 다시 바람을 피운다고 생각한다.

여자는 언제 우나?

① 남자친구가 바람피울 때
② 남편이 바람피울 때
③ 사위가 바람피울 때

The worst guy in the world

A girl who jilts[1] her boyfriend after he joins the army is a really bad person. But the worst kind of person is a man who dumps his rubber shoes when she is waiting only for him.

[해설] [1]jilt [ʤilt]: to desert a friend or loved one without warning 애인을 차버리다: She jilted him for another man. 그녀는 그를 차버리고 딴 남자를 만난다.

세상에서 젤 나쁜 놈

정말 나쁜 사람은 군대 간 애인을 차버리는 여자구, 가장 나쁜 사람은 한 사람만 바라보고 기다리는 곰신 차버린 남자예요.

From a new rubber shoes

Today I've been to Nonsan to see my boyfriend off to boot camp.
It was a bitterly sad occasion.
Today, February 17th, he entered the military.
When does he leave the military?
Is it too early to talk about his discharge?
If I send a letter to him, can he get it?
Won't the assistant training instructors throw it in the waste basket?
I heard that his assignment to a new unit is influenced by his test scores as well as luck.
I would appreciate[1] it if someone makes an attachment to this.
From a new rubber shoes, Chungsung!

[해설] [1]appreciate [əprí:ʃièit]: to be grateful for sth 매우 고마워하다: My wife really appreciated the flowers I sent. 아내는 내가 보낸 꽃을 매우 고마워한다.

초보 고무신으로부터

오늘 남친 논산에 입대시키고 왔어여.
너무너무 슬푸더라구여.
오늘 2월17일 입대했는데.
언제쯤 제대하는지여?
제대 얘기하기 너무 이른가?
편지 보내면 남친이 받아볼 수 있나여?
거기 조교들이 쓰레기통에 버리진 않겠져?
자대배치 섬 잘치고 운도 따라야 된다던데.
리플 달아주시면 감사할게여.
초보 고무신으로부터, 충성!

🟢 I received your package

Myong-jun, I received your package today.
The clothes and shoes you wore on that day
are enclosed with your letter.
Unpacking the package walking to my house,
I flopped down[1] and burst into tears.
I can't believe you're in the military now.
Tears are flowing so hard that I'm going to die.
I really like "Endless Love" sung by Koyote.
This song expresses my feelings exactly.
I really want to see you on this starry night.
I really want to see you in my dreams!
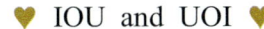
 ♥ IOU and UOI ♥

[해설] ¹flop [flap]: to fall or sit somewhere suddenly 떨어지다, 털썩 주저앉다: He flopped down on the sofa. 그는 소파에 털썩 주저앉았다. starry ['stari]: having many stars 별이 빛나는: The night before I joined the army, she and I are talked about our engagement under the starry sky. 입대 전야에 그녀와 나는 별이 비치는 하늘 아래서 우리의 약혼에 대해서 얘기했다.

🟢 너의 소포 받았어

명준아, 오늘 너의 소포를 받았어.
그 날 입고 갔던 네 옷, 신발
네 편지도 함께.
집에 들어가기도 전에 소포 뜯어보고서,
그 자리에서 주저앉아 울고 말았어.
네가 군대 간 거 정말 실감이 안나.
지금 눈물이 너무 나서 죽겠어.
코요테의 노래 "끝없는 사랑"이 너무 좋아.
이 노래가 정말 내 맘 같아.
별빛 비치는 이 밤 네가 너무 보고 싶어.
오늘밤 꿈에서라도 한번 봤으면 좋겠어!
 ♥ I Owe YOU and You Owe I ♥

Obba, it's me!

Obba, it's me!
Now, I feel that you are more of a lover than obba.
It was really devastating to send you off to the army.
I should have followed you to Nonsan.
Joining the army is a once in a life time event.

Once you're in the military, you will be a faithful soldier and
I will be an ardent[1] student and devote myself to studying.
After discharge, you should be a gentleman.
And I will be a fair lady to you.

You promised that you will take care of me after your discharge because you didn't care for me enough.
You have to keep that promise, right?

I wish you wouldn't put on your boots backwards.
I won't put on rubber shoes backwards, either.
I want our love to be eternal[2].
I love you with all my heart!

[해설] [1]ardent [á:rdənt]: enthusiastic or showing strong feelings 열렬한: He's an ardent supporter of the local football team. 그는 지방 풋볼팀의 열렬한 지지자이다. [2]eternal [itə́:rnəl]: lasting forever, timeless 영원한: People of many religions believe that God is eternal. 많은 종교인들은 God는 영원하다고 믿는다.

🔸 오빠, 나야!

오빠, 나야!
이제 오빠에서 애인으로 느끼기 시작했는데
군대 보내고 나니 하늘이 무너져 내리네
오빠 군대 가는 날 따라갔어야 했는데
일생에 한 번 가는 군댄데

오빠는 군대 간 이상 멋있는 군인이 되고
나는 학생으로 학업에 열중할게
오빠 제대하면 멋진 남자가 되겠지
나도 오빠에게 멋진 숙녀가 될게

군대 가기 전에 나한테 못한 거
제대하고 나서 잘 해준다고 약속했지?
꼭 지켜야 돼

군화 거꾸로 신지 말고
나도 고무신 절대 거꾸로 신지 않을게
우리 사랑 정말 영원했으면 좋겠어
당신을 정말 사랑해!

🔊 Is a gunbari a human being?

Before you joined the army,
I used to call soldiers gunbaries.
In fact, I didn't consider soldiers as human beings.

But once you went into the military,
I become furious[1] with the word gunbari.
Although we females in Korea don't go into the military
as they do in Israel or North Korea,
we should not call soldiers gunbaries anymore!

If some girls call soldiers gunbaries, I get angry.
Women of South Korea!
Let's not call our male soldiers gunbaries anymore!
They are doing sacred work-defending our country.

[해설] [1]furious [fjúəriəs]: very angry 매우 화난, 격노한: My boss was furious with me. 나의 상사는 내게 크게 화를 냈다. [화난 정도: annoyed (a little angry) 〈 irritated 〈 furious 〈 mad (very angry)]

군바리도 인간?

나는 네가 군대 가기 전에
군인을 군바리라 부르곤 했었지.
사실 나는 네가 군대 가기 전에 군인을 사람으로도 안 봤어.

하지만 네가 군대 가고 나서부터는
나는 군바리라는 말에 화가 치밀어.
우리나라 여성들은
이스라엘이나 북한 여성처럼 군대도 안가는 주제에
군인을 더 이상 군바리로 부르지 말아야 해.

누가 군인을 군바리라 부르면 나는 화가 난다.
대한민국 여성분들이여!
군인을 더 이상 군바리로 부르지 맙시다!
그들은 신성한 임무(나라를 지키는 일)를 하고 있습니다.

How to get to Wontong?

I'm a rubber shoes living in Mokpo,
the hometown of our former president.
My bf was assigned to ○○ unit in Wontong last week.
I am going to see him this coming Sunday.
Is there anyone who will help me get there?

Bosom[1]:
Oh, you poor rubber shoes!
First village under the sky, Wontong?
The roads are so narrow and winding that
a little snow often stops buses running.
It's very far from your place.
Try to be resolute!

Voluptuous[2]:
You may understand why your bf says this when he returns to his unit, "If I go now, when shall I come back? I will not survive the mistreatment."

Flat[3]:
The people there talk with a North Korean accent.
Try to adapt yourself to the North Korean accent.
Or you can listen to broadcasts from Pyongyang in advance.
Cheers!

[해설] [1]bosom [búzəm]: a woman's chest (女) 가슴. bosom buddy: a very close friend 절친한 친구. [2]voluptuous [vəlʌ́ptʃuəs]: (of a woman's body) having a large bosom and pleasing curves (女) 가슴이 크고 몸도 각선미가 있는 → 빵빵한. [3]flat. (of a woman) having small breasts; not well endowed; 'A' cup 가슴이 작은; 물려받은 게 없는; A컵 사이즈인: She uses falsies+ because she's flat. 그녀는 가슴이 없어 유방패드를 착용한다. falsies [fɔ́:lsiz]: pads worn inside a brassiere to make the breasts appear larger.(유방을 크게 보이기 위한) 유방 패드: Is she wearing falsies, or are those all hers? Only Buddha knows! 그녀의 가슴은 패드를 한 것이 아니면 모두 자신의 것인가? 부처님만 아셔!

🔸 원통엔 어떻게 가져?

저는 전직 대통령의 고향,
목포에 사는 고무신입니다.
지난주 저의 앤이 원통의 ○○부대로 배속 받았거든요.
이번 일요일 그의 면회를 갈려구요.
길 좀 갈쳐주실 분 없나여?

가슴:
오, 가여븐 곰신님!
하늘 아래 첫 동네, 원통?
길이 워낙 험악해서
눈이 조금만 와도 차가 안 다닐 때가 많아요.
거기에선 거리도 장난이 아녀요.
맘 단단히 먹어 세요!

빵빵女:
곰신님의 앤이 휴가 나와서 복귀할 때
이런 말을 왜 하는지 이해가 갈 거예요.
"이제가면 언제오나 원통해서 못살겠네."

절벽女:
거기 주민들은 북한 어투가 강해요.
북한 어투에 익숙해지세요.
미리 평양 방송을 들어보든지.
힘내세요!

Is it better to wear a skirt?

I'm going to see my bf in Gangwon-do next week.
Is it better to wear a skirt to go to see him?
People around me tell me to wear a skirt.
What should I wear?
Can anyone give me any advice?

Skirt:
Put on a skirt.
I put on a skirt and my bf was surprised at my skirt.
He said, "Oh, your skirt looks good on you!"
His eyes were fixed on my legs from top to bottom.

Girdle:
Show him how you've changed in the short time.
I advise you to wear a skirt, but be careful that your legs are not frozen.
The wind in Gangwon-do is like a knife.
It's still in the middle of January!

Nobra:
I think casual clothes are better as far as you and your bf are "friends."
What use is your sexy clothing in the military…
His colleagues or his seniors might follow your bf to see you.

🟡 치마 입는 게 더 좋은가?

다음 주 강원도 있는 남친에게 면회를 갑니다.

면회 갈 때 치마 입는 게 더 좋은가요?

주위 사람들이 다 치마를 입으라고 하거든요.

무엇을 입어야 할 지?

조언해 줄 사람 없나여?

스커트:

치마를 입으세요.

저두 치마를 입고 갔는데 남친이 깜짝 놀라더라구여.

"치마가 너한테 넘 잘 어울린다!"라고.

그가 내 다리에서 시선을 떼질 못하더라구여.

거들:

짧은 시간에 변화된 모습을 보여 주세요.

치마 입기를 권하지만, 다리가 얼지 않도록 하세요.

강원도 바람은 칼같이 살을 엡니다.

아직도 1월 중순이라!

노브라:

님과 님의 남친이 "친구"인 이상 캐주얼 복장이 좋을 듯해요.

군대에서 섹시한 옷이 무슨 소용이….

그의 동료나 고참들이 님을 보러 따라 올수도 있는데.

🔸 My dear fiance[1]~

Your lass' heart aches
sitting lonely in my room at night in darkness.
I am writing a sincere letter taking care over each word
missing you who was called up by our country.
The time I can see you is just around the corner[2].
Honey, I'm worried
that you might stay awake in bed thinking of your lass.
I wish you good health until you see me.
Goodbye until the day I see you ~~
November 11, 2003
Hyeo-young …★

[해설] [1] fiancé [fiá:nsei]: the man whom a woman is going to marry 여자가 결혼할 남자 ↔ fiancee: the woman whom a man is going to marry 남자가 결혼할 여자 [2] be just around the corner : to be going to happen very soon: 바로 근처에; 임박하여: Christmas is just round the corner. 이제는 곧 크리스마스이다.

🔸 서방님 보시와요~

서방님 오늘도 독수공방 홀로 어두운 밤을 지내려니
소녀 맘이 아픕니다.
나라의 부름을 받고 가신 서방님을 그리워하며
오늘두 한 자 한 자 정성스레 글을 올립니다.
서방님, 이제 얼굴 볼 날이 코앞에 닥쳤습니다.
서방님두 소녀 생각에 잠을 설칠까 걱정이옵니다.
얼굴 보는 그날까지 몸 건강히.
안녕히 계시옵소서~~~
2003년 11월 17일.
혜 영....★

🔸 It was not easy to hold his hands

My bf's mom, his sister and I went to see him with tasty[1] food.
When I arrived at the visitors' center, several of his colleagues came in with him.
My bf is the lowest ranking soldier,
and he sat in the corner, so it was not easy to hold his hands.
If I hold his hands, his seniors will get jealous of us.
I was with him from 10 a. m. through 4 p. m.
How fast the time goes when I am with my bf!
If only I could see him again next week.

[해설] [1]tasty: having a very good taste; flavorful 맛있는: We had a really tasty mushroom soup. 우리는 정말 맛있는 버섯 수프를 먹었다. [delicious 맛있는, sweet 단, disgusting/horrible/awful 맛없는, sour 신, salty 짠, hot/spicy 매운, bland: having little taste 맛이 거의 없는]

🔸 그의 손잡기도 쉽지 않았어

남친 엄마랑 언니랑 맛난 거 싸들고 갔죵.
면회실에 가니 남친 친구들 6-7명도 따라왔져.
울 남친은 말참이라,
구석에 앉아서 손잡기도 힘들었어요.
그의 손을 잡으면 고참들이 질투할 것 같았죠.
10시부터 4시까지 쭈욱 같이 있었죠.
울 남친과 같이 있으니 시간이 어찌나 빨리 갔는지!
다음 주에 또 봤으면 좋겠어요.

Dear rubber shoes

How are you all?

It's already 9 months since my bf went into the military.

Now I have become accustomed to the phrase "rubber shoes."

My bf said

He finished his ranger training several weeks ago.

His unit is notorious for marching.

He marched for a full 12 hours.

He barely managed to march for 8 hours.

But as time went by, he became dizzy.

Yesterday I went to see him.

He showed me the soles of his feet.

They were covered with burst blisters and he had athlete's foot.

I couldn't believe my eyes.

They must be very itchy and painful.

Dear rubber shoes…

It is hard to wait, isn't it?

But...

Who are we?

Aren't we rubber shoes, protectors of the sons of the Republic of Korea?

Let's motivate one another.

Until the legendary day, his discharge day, way to go!

Rush forward!

🔴 곰신님들

잘들 지내구 계시나용?

남친 군대 보낸 지 9개월이 훌쩍 지나버리고

어느새 "고무신"이란 말에도 익숙해졌네여

몇 주 전에 남친이 유격을 다녀왔어여

그 부대는 행군하기로 유명한 부대라

12시간을 꼬박 걸었대여

8시간까진 어떻게든 걸어 보겠는데

시간이 흐를수록 정신이 혼미해졌대여

엊그제 면회를 다녀왔거든 여

발바닥을 보여주는데

무좀과 물집이 뒤범벅이 되어 터졌고

아주 눈으로 보기가 힘들더라구여

매우 가렵고 아플 텐데

곰신님들…

기다리기 많이 힘드시져?

하지만…

우리가 누굽니까?

나라를 지키는 대한의 건아들을 지켜주는 곰신 아닙니까?

우리 다같이 힘냈음 해여

전설의 그날, 전역일까지 화이팅입니당!

돌격 앞으로!

🔸 I'm already five months pregnant

My boyfriend has been in the Air Force as an airman first class. I hurry to get married because I'm already five months pregnant. Is an airman first class given leave for his wedding?
Please, let me know ASAP.
From an Air Force wife-to-be

🔸 이미 임신 5개월

제 남자친구가 지금 일병으로 복무 중이구요.
저는 지금 임신5개월이라 빨리 결혼부터 해야 할 상황입니다.
공군 일병도 결혼 휴가를 받을 수 있나요?
가능한 빠른 답변 부탁드립니다.
공군의 예비 아내로부터

🔸 Susan lowered her underwear fortunately

Although Susan is a high school graduate, she became an Air Force officer's wife because she was clever enough to take her underwear off for her boyfriend. But her friend, Tina grabbed a ○○ because she unfortunately lowered⋯. "Women's lives are like the destiny of a gourd."

🔸 수잔은 팬티를 잘 내려서

비록 수잔은 고졸이지만 그녀의 남자친구에게 현명하게도 팬티를 내려서 공군 장교의 아내가 되었다. 하지만 그녀의 친구, 티나는 ⋯ 을 잘못 내려서 불행히도 ○○를 물었다. "여자 팔자는 뒤웅박 팔자다."

The baby hasn't been born yet

We all love and miss you deeply.
You are in our thoughts and prayers everyday.
We want you to know how very proud of you we are.
Things are lonely here without you,
and we can't wait until the day you return to us.
The baby hasn't been born yet.
I know you are sad
because you won't be here for the birth of our child.
But I want to you to know we are all fine.

- From your loving wife and daughter

아기가 아직 태어나지 않았어

우리 모두는 당신을 정말 사랑해요.
당신은 우리의 생각과 기도문 속에 있지요.
우리는 당신을 얼마나 자랑스러워하는지 알기 바라요.
당신 없는 여기는 모든 것이 외로워서,
우리는 당신이 돌아오는 날까지 기다릴 수 없어요.
아이는 아직 태어나지 않았어요.
당신은 슬프군요.
왜냐하면 당신은 우리 아이의 출산 때 여기 없을 테니까요.
그러나 나는 당신이 우리 모두 잘 있다는 것을 알았으면 합니다.

- 사랑하는 당신의 아내와 딸로부터

🔴 The rubber shoes' pledge

① I will hold a farewell party for him before he enlists.
② I will see him off to boot camp on his enlistment day.
③ I will write him a kiss-marked-letter once a week.
④ I will relieve his stress by giving him a call every Saturday.
⑤ I will spend time with him on his 100th-day's leave.
⑥ I will send him a box of chocolates on Valentine's Day.
⑦ I will go with his parents to see him on the first visiting day.
⑧ I will not send him a "Dear John" letter until he becomes a corporal.
⑨ I will not get him worried by being petty over little things.
⑩ I will not hang around computer chat rooms.
⑪ I will avoid seeing even his close friends if possible.
⑫ I will not console my loneliness with drinks at the year-end party.
⑬ I will not wear a wolf-skinned muffler however cold it is.
⑭ I will keep my chastity both, physically and mentally, until he is discharged.
⑮ I will try to make our friendship blossom into true love.

* A **wolf** is often compared to a sex-starved cunning male that steals a male's female friends. It is often believed that if a female wears a wolf-skinned muffler, she might fall victim to a wolf.

고무신의 맹세

① 입대 전에는 환송파티를 해주겠다.

② 입대 일에는 훈련소까지 바래다주겠다.

③ 일주일에 한번은 키스된 편지를 써주겠다.

④ 매주 토요일은 전화로 그의 스트레스를 풀어주겠다.

⑤ 100일 휴가 때는 그와 함께 지내겠다.

⑥ 밸런타인데이에는 초콜릿 한 상자를 보내겠다.

⑦ 첫 면회 때는 그의 부모님과 함께 가겠다.

⑧ 그가 상병이 될 때까지는 절교편지를 보내지 않겠다.

⑨ 사소한 일로 삐쳐서 그를 걱정시키지 않겠다.

⑩ 컴퓨터 채팅방을 배회하지 않겠다.

⑪ 가능한 한 그의 친한 친구들도 만나지 않겠다.

⑫ 연말 파티에서 외로움을 술로 달래지 않겠다.

⑬ 아무리 추워도 늑대 목도리를 하지 않겠다.

⑭ 그가 제대할 때까지 육체적, 정신적으로 순결하겠다.

⑮ 우리의 우정을 진정한 사랑으로 꽃 피우겠다.

* **늑대**는 종종 섹스에 굶주린 교활한 남자에 비유된다. 여자가 늑대목도리를 하면 그녀는 늑대의 먹이 감이 될지도 모른다는 말이 전해진다.

◎ The senior rubber shoes' pledge

I will be a better kisaeng than **Hwang Jin-i.**

I will be kinder than a Japanese woman

I will be more passionate than a French woman

I will be more active than an American woman

I will be sexually stronger than an English woman.

* **Hwang jin-i** was a celebrated singer, poet, and kisaeng in Korea in the sixteenth century. Young people in Korea often call her a "Korean Cleopatra." And it has been said that she did not give her favors to a man who couldn't appreciate wine, music, and poetry.

◎ 고참 고무신의 맹세

황진이보다 더 좋은 기생이 되며.

일본 여자보다 더 친절한 여자가 되며.

프랑스 여자보다 더 정열적인 여자가 되며.

미국 여자보다 생활력이 강한 여자가 되며.

영국 여자보다 정력이 센 여자가 되겠다.

* **황진이**는 16세기 한국에서 유명한 가수, 시인 겸 기생이다. 한국의 젊은이들은 그녀를 "한국의 클레오파트라"라고 종종 부른다. 하지만 그녀는 술, 음악, 시를 감상할 줄 모르는 남자에겐 정을 주지 않았다고 한다.

◯ A parcel sent to a sergeant

I don't know
but anyway I sent a big box of candy to my sergeant.
It came to 40,000 won.
But I heard that sending candy or cookies to a sergeant is a big mistake.
I wonder if he is embarrassed and will say,
"who sent this stuff to me?"
I heard that candy or cookies are usually for private soldiers.
What can I do about this?

◯ 병장에게 보낸 소포

제가 잘 몰라서
병장한테 디따 큰 박스에 과자를 보낸 거 있죠.
총 4만원 들었는데
근데 병장한텐 과자 보내는 거 아니라는데
그가 이것 받고 쪽팔려할까 걱정이에요.
"누가 이따위 보냈노?"라고.
과자는 이등병에게나 보내는 거라는데.
어쩌죠?

⬣ That's the kind of friend I'll be

When you don't say anything because you are tired
I won't ask you to give the reasons
but I'll wait for you for hours
That's the kind of friend I'll be

I won't stand on my dignity over trivia[1]
I'll speak to you frankly
but I won't damage your self-esteem[2]
That's the kind of friend I'll be

Although I am uneasy over trivia with you
I'll link arms with you in the street
when I run into your friends
That's the kind of friend I'll be

I'll value your interests
and I will try to share your hobbies
and can take you as you are now
That's the kind of friend I'll be

When I get introduced to your friends
I'll gladly put on a delightful smiling face
and will soon get along with them
That's the kind of friend I'll be

But someday, all at once
When I feel you don't love me anymore
I'll leave you and pray for your happiness
That's the kind of friend I'll be

[해설] [1] trivia [tríviə]: unimportant details, things 하찮은 일: He pays attention to trivia while he ignores important matters. 그는 중요한 일은 무시하고 하찮은 일에 신경을 쓴다.
[2] self-esteem: confidence in yourself 자존심: She suffers from low self-esteem.

그런 친구가 될게

네가 피곤해서 아무 말 하지 않을 때
무슨 일이 있었냐고 다그치기보다는
몇 시간이고 조용히 기다려주는
그런 친구가 될게

사소한 일에 자존심을 내세우지 않고
솔직한 말로 내 마음을 표현하되
네 자존심에 상처주지 않는
그런 친구가 될게

너와 사소한 언쟁으로 기분이 언짢아도
길거리에서 네 친구를 만나면
다정하게 팔짱을 해줄 줄 아는
그런 친구가 될게

너의 관심사에 귀 기울이고
너의 취미생활을 함께 하려고 애쓰며
너를 있는 그대로 받아들일 수 있는
그런 친구가 될게

내가 네 친구들에게 소개될 때
기꺼이 밝은 표정으로 즐거워하며
네 친구들과도 잘 어울릴 수 있는
그런 친구가 될게

그러나 어느 날 갑자기
네가 날 좋아하지 않는다고 느낄 때
너의 행복을 빌며 떠날 줄 아는
그런 친구가 될게

Dear John Letter

Dear Sweetie;
How have you been so far?
We had long-awaited snow last night.
Everything became white: roads, roofs, and mountains.
The snow is going to thaw and it'll turn into water, though.
With the snow I am influenced by emotion more than reason.
And I become very lonely.

I guess you also had a lot of snow there where you are.
I wonder what you thought about
seeing snow falling on your chopped hair.
Isn't it much colder because you're in the military?

It's been a long time since I wrote a letter to you.
I stopped sending my messages without any reason.
Maybe you feel somewhat colder than I do.
Let me be frank with you today.

You know we are having a second winter?
Rather more than the feeling of loving you,
I felt like I was becoming a part of you.
I would see you routinely and
I thought I was becoming your date.
However, I must really be honest to myself now.

When you went in the military after having your hair chopped,
I thought I was going to miss you so much.
Because I thought love at least is longing.
Looking back at the places you had been,
I thought I was going to cry over your traces.

🔸 절교 편지

자기야, 안녕

그 동안 잘 있었던 거지?

어제 여긴 모처럼 하얀 눈이 내렸어.

온통 세상이 하얘. 길도, 지붕도, 그리고 산도.

모두 녹아버려서 물이 되어버릴 눈이지만.

이렇게 눈이 오면 이성이 감성에 무너지고 만다.

그래서 아주 쓸쓸한 맘이 돼.

네가 근무하는 곳에도 눈이 많이 내렸겠구나.

너의 짧게 자른 머리 위로 쏟아져 내리는 눈을 보며,

넌 무슨 생각을 했을까.

군대라서 더욱 춥진 않았을까?

오랜만에 편지를 하는 것 같아.

아무런 이유도 없이 연락을 하지 않았구나.

너는 아마도 나보다 춥게 느껴지겠지.

오늘 난 너에게 솔직해 지고 싶다.

벌써 우리가 만난 지

두 번의 겨울을 맞는 거 너도 알지?

너를 사랑한다는 감정보다 그저 너의 사랑에 동화되고 감염된 듯

그렇게 널 만나고

그렇게 너에게 적합한 상대가 되어간다고 생각했던

내 맘에 난 이제 정말로 솔직해지려고 해.

네가 머리를 짧게 자르고 군에 갈 때만 해도

난 네가 아주 많이 그리워질 거라고 생각했어.

적어도 사랑이란 건 그리움이라고 생각했으니까.

그래서 난 항상 네가 있었던 자리들을

돌아보며 울고만 있을 줄 알았어.

I got to thinking that the tears I shed
when you entered the military,
were not from love, but were the remains of emotion.

The thing that I would like to share with you
was not a common sharing.
It was rather a one-sided understanding or consideration.
Now I realize that after you left me.

I thought the sky would turn dark without you,
but the sky is clearer without you.
Looking back on our past, I must not have been in love with you.
But now I'm thinking about saying good bye to you.

Whenever I'm with you,
I feel you are from a far better family and environment.
I've tried to overcome the gap,
but it wasn't easy to do.
In fact I've had a very hard time until now.

Seeing you is like running a long race
wearing ill-fitting rubber shoes.
Maybe you didn't realize this.

Whenever I dated you,
I felt shabby or miserable and
I vowed to myself that love could overcome everything.
Don't you know how much I've tried to comfort myself?

네가 군에 갈 때 나의 눈물은
사랑의 이유가 아닌
감성의 잔해였다고 생각된다.

너와 내가 공유하려고 마음먹었던 모든 것들이
사실은 공유가 아니고
한쪽의 이해와 배려 때문이었다는 것,
그것을 난 네가 없는 지금에서야 알게 됐어.

네가 없으면 까맣기만 할 것 같았던 하늘이
이렇게 맑게 내 눈앞에 펼쳐지고 있는 걸.
돌이켜보면 나 널 사랑한 것이 아니었나 봐.
어느새 나 지금
너와의 이별을 생각하고 있는 걸.

너와 만나면서
나와는 비교조차도 할 수 없는 좋은 배경이나 환경에
나 그 동안 극복하려 했지만,
서로 다른 점이 너무 많아서
나 그 동안 참 힘들었어.

너를 만나면 늘 잘 맞지 않는 신을 신고
오래 달리기를 하는 그런 기분이었던 것,
너는 아마 몰랐을 거야.

너를 만날 때마다
느낀 초라함, 비굴함
사랑으로 극복할 수 있다고 다짐했어.
너는 내 스스로 얼마나 위로했는지 알아?

Now I don't like to worry about such things.
I want to be a person who can maintain her dignity.
Without falling in love,
I think that my saying "I love you" habitually
is somewhat miserable for you and me.

You may feel betrayed remembering what you have done for me.
But parting with each other is good for both of us.
I think this moment is the best time to part.
Can you accept this?

You're very thoughtful and considerate to me.
If I say goodbye to you in this situation,
I believe you will get over it.

When I make trouble like this while you're in the military,
I wonder if you might go AWOL.
But I believe you're not such a stupid guy that you can't overcome this matter.
I guess you are leading a good military life.
Can I believe that?

After a long time has passed
and when we can see each other's point of view,
I wish we could be friends talking over our memories.
Am I wrong to think this?

I feel very sorry that I haven't treated you better.
But I'm sure you'll soon find a better girl than me
because you're a nice, good natured man.

How can I say "thank you?"
I feel really grateful and sorry for you.
Good bye…

그런데 이젠

나 그런 고민 그만하고 싶어.

나도 나 자신한테 당당할 수 있는 사람이 되고 싶어.

사랑하지도 않으면서 습관적으로 "사랑해"라는 말은

너와 나에게 불행일 거라고 생각해.

네가 나한테 해준 것을 생각하면 넌 배신감을 느낄 지도 몰라.

하지만 서로 헤어지는 것이 우리 모두에게 좋아.

지금이 돌아서는데 가장 좋은 시간인 것 같아

받아들일 수 있겠어?

넌 충분히 사려 깊고 나를 배려해 주었던 사람이니까.

이런 상황에서 내가 이별을 고한다고 해도

넌 잘 견뎌 내리라 믿어.

군에 있을 때 이러면

군탈할지도 모른다는 생각도 해봤었는데

내가 아는 넌 그토록 널 이기지 못하는 사람이 아니란 걸 잘 알아.

넌 아주 훌륭한 군생활을 할 거라고 믿을게.

나 그렇게 믿어도 되는 거지?

나중에 정말로 많은 시간들이 지난 다음에

서로가 정말로 친구로서의 눈높이로 바라보게 될 때

그땐 웃으면서 지난 일을 얘기하는 친구가 되었음 하는 바람

나쁜 생각일까?

너한테 좀 더 잘 해주지 못한 점들이

맘에 걸리지만 넌 착하고 좋은 사람이니까

나보다 더 좋은 여자를 금방 만나게 될 거야.

너한테 많이 고마워.

정말루 고맙고 그리고 미안해.

안녕…

Advice from senior rubber shoes

PVT (Trainee)	While he is in boot camp, you really want to see him. You may wonder what he is doing all day and all night. If you're overwhelmed with loneliness, other men may come on to you. Try to relieve loneliness by writing him a letter.
PVT	He is in the busiest period in his military life. So, if you don't receive prompt answers or phone calls from him at a proper time, don't beg him to respond quickly. If you really want to grab him as your future husband, this is the best opportunity!
PFC	If you send a letter saying, "I'm very lonely," "I'm dying to see you," it will make him much uneasier. Try to tell him about your college life, your social circle and other interesting topics. When you go to see him, make up properly and don't forget to put on a skirt!
CPL	Being away from him for a long time, you begin to notice that there are other nice men. When you graduate from college and get a job, your boyfriend will be sharply contrasted with the senior male colleagues in your company. Can you really keep the promise you made on his enlisting day? At this point, you begin to understand why many women say "good-bye" to their male friends.
SGT	Although you said, "congratulations!" on his discharge, you may not decide how to develop the relationship with him. Is he just one of my ex-boyfriends, just a friend or my future husband? Now you're old enough to get married. When do you think he will be able to buy a 32 pyong apartment, a Sonata? Love overcomes everything? After 2 or 3 years of your marriage, you come to realize that money overcomes love!

고참 곰신의 충고

훈련병	네가 훈련 중일 때 애인이 가장 보고 싶을 거다. 그래서 너는 그녀에게 보내는 편지에서 나중에 책임지지도 못할 약속을 할 지 모른다. 너의 힘든 처지를 그녀에게 알려 동정을 구하지 말고 오히려 혼자 남아 있는 그녀를 생각해줘라.
이병	애인 생각? 그것은 완전히 사치다! 너는 잠잘 시간조차도 없다. 네가 훈련소에 있을 때만큼 편지를 자주 받지 못할 것이다. 휴가 계획을 잘 짜서 100일 휴가 때 그녀를 사로잡을 수 있도록 해라.
일병	너는 혼자 남겨둔 그녀가 자꾸만 걱정될지 모른다. 하지만 "노파심"에서 그녀를 통제하는 것은 오히려 그녀를 달아나게 한다. 너의 면회 가능한 날짜를 알려주되 너무 강요하지는 마라.
상병	이제 너는 군생활에 적응도 되었고 일하는 요령도 안다. 그래서 이것이 너의 본성을 가끔 드러낸다. 애인과 오래 떨어져 있으니 그녀를 만나는 것도 어색하다. 편지를 쓰는데 어떻게 시작해야 하는지 착상이 떠오르지 않는다. 편지 한 통 쓰는데 시간이 점점 더 걸린다.
병장	비록 지루한 군생활에 서광이 오기 시작했지만 복학, 진로, 그녀로 착잡해진다. 너는 그녀가 너의 인생을 성취하는데 충분히 도움을 줄 것이라고 생각이 되나? 둘이 궁합은 맞아? 네 입대 일에 그녀가 흘린 눈물은 악어의 눈물이 아니었을까?

Military English

Military Wives
(군인의 아내)

◆ **Recipe for a Military Wife**
- 1½ cups patience
- 2 tablespoons elbow grease
- 1 pound courage
- 1 cup tolerance
- dash of adventure

- Author Unknown -

◆ **군인아내의 처방전**
- 1½ 컵의 인내
- 2스푼의 끈기
- 1파운드의 용기
- 1컵의 관용
- 모험심

- 작자 미상 -

Military English

군대생활의
고뇌 추억 지혜
군대
영어

Military Wives
(군인의 아내)

- 말없는 계급
- 군인 아내는 연의꼬리
- 슈퍼우먼이 못돼서
- 생각이 깊은 군인의 아내
- 군인 아내의 헌장★★★
- 군인 마누라는 상팔자
- 여자도 군대 가야 해
- 영진이 엄마 전에★
- 군인 아내의 맹세★★★
- 유연한 비상대기 명단
- 집시 인생★★
- 군인의 아내
- 하나님

Silent ranks

I wear no uniforms, no blues or army greens.
But I am in the military in the ranks that are rarely seen. I have no rank upon my shoulders.
Salutes I do not give,
but the military world is the place where I live.
I am not in the chain of command, orders I do not get, but my husband does this I can not forget.
I am not the one who fires the weapon[1].

- Author unknown

[해설] [1]weapon: a tool used to harm or kill 무기: Knives and guns are dangerous weapons. 칼과 권총은 위험한 무기이다. 여기서 fire가 있으므로 weapon은 총의 의미이다.

말없는 계급

저는 어떤 제복도 입지 않습니다.
하지만 나는 계급이 거의 보이지 않는 군대에 있습니다.
제 어깨 위에 계급도 없습니다.
저는 거수경례를 하지 않지만,
제가 사는 곳은 군대입니다.
저는 지휘 계통 속에 속하지 않아서
명령을 받지 않지만,
남편은 그렇지 않다는 것을 잊을 수 없습니다.
저는 사격을 할 줄도 모르는 사람입니다.

- 작자 미상

◯ A military wife is like the tail of a kite

When the tail of a kite rolls and pitches moderately, the kite can zoom up to the stars. But if it rolls and pitches severely, the kite will definitely crash to the ground. A military wife's fate is nothing but the tail of a kite.

◯ 군인 아내는 연의 꼬리

연 꼬리가 적절히 움직일 때, 그 연은 별까지 올라갈 수 있다.
하지만 연 꼬리가 너무 요동을 치면, 그 연은 틀림없이 땅에 처박게 된다.
군인 아내의 운명은 연 꼬리와 다름없다.

◯ I am not a super woman

I have often heard that a military wife should be a super woman. The woman who wants to be a military wife has unyielding[1] resolution[2]. I don't think I have the disposition[3] to be a military wife. Now I am exhausted trying to adapt myself to the prospect[4] of becoming a military wife. I completely gave up the idea of marrying a career soldier[5].

[해설] [1]unyielding [ʌnjíːldiŋ]: not willing to change your ideas or beliefs 양보하지 않는, 단호한. [2]resolution [rèzəlúːʃ-ən]: a promise that you make to yourself to do sth 결의, 결심: My New Year's resolution is stop smoking and drinking. [3]disposition [dìspəzíʃən]: the way sb tends to behave 성질, 기질: He has such a cheerful/nervous disposition. [4]prospect [práspekt]: the possibility that sth good might happen in the future 가능성. [5]career soldier 직업군인

◯ 군인 아내는 연의 꼬리

저는 군인 아내는 슈퍼우먼이 되어야 한다는 이야기를 종종 들었습니다. 군인아내 되실 분들은 마음을 독하게 먹어야 할 겁니다. 저는 군인 아내로서 소질이 전혀 없는 것 같습니다. 나는 군인 아내가 되려고 적응하는데 지쳤습니다. 저는 직업 군인과 결혼하는 것을 완전히 포기했습니다.

A considerate military wife

"I'm so proud to be a soldier's wife that I don't mind the separations. He's out there in the rain, snow, sleet, or hot sun training to protect what we all treasure[1]: freedom. What can I complain about, sitting in my snug[2] quarters[3]? As the soldiers are told to behave in a responsible, professional manner, so should the wives."

— from a faithful military wife —

[해설] [1]treasure [tréʒəːr]: 1) riches, such as gold and jewels 보물, 2) to value greatly 소중히 하다: She treasures memories of her childhood. 그녀는 유년기의 추억을 소중히 한다. [2]snug: in a small, comfortable place; cozy 아늑한: She lives in a snug little house. 그녀는 아늑한 작은 집에 산다. [3]quarters. housing, esp. for the military 군대의 막사: She lives in the officers' quarters. 그녀는 장교 막사에 산다.

생각이 깊은 군인의 아내

"나는 군인의 아내가 된 것이 무척 자랑스러워요. 그래서 남편과 떨어져 지내는 것을 겁내지 않아요. 남편은 우리가 그토록 소중히 여기는 '자유'를 지키기 위해서 비, 눈, 진눈개비 속에서, 뜨거운 태양 아래서 훈련을 받지요. 우리는 이 아늑한 관사에 앉아서 무엇을 불평해서 되겠어요? 군인들은 책임감을 가지고 프로 정신으로 행동하라고 교육을 받는데, 군인의 아내인 우리도 당연히 그래야 되죠."

— 충실한 군인의 아내로부터 —

The military wife's charter

I married a soldier in the full realization that I had been entrusted with the mission of assisting my husband to defend the nation. Bringing the brilliant spirit of my own family to my husband's family, I will dedicate myself to making my home secure, helping my husband become successful and increasing the reputation of my husband's family.

Hereupon as the wife of a soldier, I will take the following path. I will not refuse to do anything disagreeable and ensure my husband's love by developing my sensuousness[1] and by using my bewitching[2] figure and capacious[3] breasts as stepping stones.

By realizing that assisting my husband's promotion based on my creativity and originality as well as cooperation with neighbors would be the source of my own development, I, as a soldier's wife, will fulfill my responsibilities and obligations and enhance[4] my housewifely spirit of self-sacrifice.

[해설] [1]sensuous[sénʃuəs]: suggesting physical pleasure 미적인, 관능적인: sensuous lips 관능적인 입술. [2]bewitch [biwítʃ]: charm; captivate 매혹하다, 호리다: She is so charming that men are bewitched by her. 그녀는 너무 매력적이어서 남자들이 그녀에게 매혹되었다. [3]capacious [kəpéiʃəs]: having a lot of space to put things in 큼직한, 용량이 큰. [4]enhance [enhǽns]: to improve sth 향상시키다. Winning the award greatly enhanced his reputation. 그 상을 받은 것이 그의 명예를 크게 향상시켰다.

군인 아내의 헌장

우리는 국가방위의 내조적 사명을 띠고 군인에게 시집왔다. 친정의 빛난 얼을 시댁에 되살려 안으로 가정을 공고히 하며 밖으로 남편의 출세와 가문의 명예에 이바지한다.

이제 군인아내로서 나아갈 바를 밝혀 궂은일을 마다 않으며 타고난 저마다의 교예를 계발하고 우리의 요염한 자태와 풍만한 젖가슴을 약진의 발판으로 삼아 남편의 사랑을 독차지한다.

군인아내로서 창의와 이웃 간의 협력을 바탕으로 남편의 진급이 나의 발전에 근본임을 깨닫고 군인 아내로서의 책임과 의무를 다하고 스스로 봉사하는 주부정신을 드높인다.

🟡 A soldier's wife has the best fate

A: A soldier's wife has the best fate[1], huh?

B: I don't think so.

A: You can get an official residence and tax free goods.

B: But think about it, we have to move every two years.

A: You can regard moving as travel.

B: Our children have trouble with making friends because they move frequently and there are very few sons of officers who have entered prestigious[2] universities.

A: Really?

B: When we have to leave the military, we might not even have a house because we have been living in military housing.

A: But soldiers' wives are all beautiful.

B: That's because girls were momentarily blinded by the uniform.

[해설] [1]fate: destiny; fortune 운명: meet/find one's fate 장차 배우자가 될 사람을 만나다.
[2]prestigious [prestídʒiəs]: admired or respected 명성 있는, 유명한

🟡 군인 마누라는 상팔자

A: 군인 마누라 팔자가 제일 좋지?

B: 뭐가 그러니?

A: 관사에 면세품도 나오고.

B: 2년에 한번 꼴로 이사해야 하는 걸 생각해봐.

A: 이사를 여행으로 생각하면 되지.

B: 잦은 전학으로 애들이 친구 사귀기도 힘들고 그리고 장교의 아이들 치고 명문대학 간 애들이 거의 없어.

A: 정말이니?

B: 군대를 떠날 때에는 관사에 살다 보니 집도 한 채 없지.

A: 그래도 군인들의 마누라들은 다 예쁘더라.

B: 그야 여자들이 제복에 순간적으로 눈이 멀었지.

Women have to join the military

A: Women also have to join the military.

B: What the hell are you saying? A woman is as fickle[1] as a reed.

A: Haven't you heard that a man becomes a real man after serving in the military?

B: Women are swarming[2] at restaurants, department stores and hot springs in the daytime.

A: Korean women have the best fate in the world.

B: Are there any Korean women who don't have a "princess syndrome?"

A: If they serve in the military, they become real women.

B: Anyway the women who served in the military may nag their husbands less.

[해설] [1]fickle [fíkəl]: changeable 변하기 쉬운, 흔들리는: Jane is young and fickle, liking one boy this week and a different one next week. 제인은 어리고 마음이 잘 변해서 이번 주에는 이 남자를, 다음 주에는 다른 남자를 좋아한다. [2]swarm [swɔːrm]: a large number of insects or birds 무리, 떼; move in a crowd 많이 모이다, 북적대다: The bar is always swarming with college students. 그 술집은 대학생들로 늘 북적된다.

여자도 군대 가야 해

A: 여자도 군대 가야 돼.

B: 뭔 소리야, 여자는 연약한 갈대야.

A: 남자가 군대 갔다 와야 사람 된다는 소리 못 들었어?

B: 낮에도 레스토랑, 백화점, 온천은 여자들로 꽉 찼어.

A: 세계에서 한국 여자들이 팔자가 제일 좋아.

B: 한국여자 치고 "공주병 증후군" 없는 여자들 어디 있어?

A: 여자도 군대 갔다 와야 정말 여자될 거야.

B: 어쨌든 군대 갔다 온 여자들은 남편에게 잔소리를 덜 할 거야.

Dear Youngjin's Mom

I chased you and you chased me for 2 years.
Now you've become my wife and I am your husband.
Our love bore fruit after two years when we had a son.
You made my mother so delighted with our first son.

Using the excuse that I was a soldier,
I didn't see you in labor in the hospital
and didn't even care for you after our child was born.
What could I say about last night?

You wandered from store to store
to buy groceries that were a little cheaper
six months' pregnant while carrying our first son.
If I hadn't spent that amount of money last night,
you could easily afford to buy groceries for the next 10 years!

Now all of my colleagues have left for their nests,
And I am just scribbling my thoughts thinking about
how soon I will see your smiling face again.
It's getting darker and darker.
My son, Youngjin is flitting before my eyes.
I'm really sorry, dear!

– From your loving husband

* While I was working in the Air Force Boot Camp in the summer of 1986, a master sergeant who worked with me said to me, "Sir, I wish you could help me." "Tell me what the problem is." I said, "I drank too much last night and got home at three o'clock in the morning. She was so angry that she didn't open the door…. I had a big fight with her. I can't find any solution now." He told me the details of what happened to the family and how they met and got married. And I decided to help him to write his wife a letter. I recently heard that the couple have been living happily together and that their marriage is a successful one!

🔸 영진이 엄마 전에

쫓기고 쫓겼던 당신과 나
지금은 나의 아내가 된 당신
그리고 당신의 남편이 된 나
2년간의 사랑으로 태어난 첫아들
시어머니를 흡족하게 했던 당신

군인이라는 미명하에
출산의 고통도 함께 하지 못하고
산후 몸조리도 잘 해주지 못한 내가
어젯밤과 관련해 무슨 할 말이 있겠소

더구나 임신 6개월의 몸에 첫 아이를 업고
몇 십 원 싼 찬거리를 사기 위하여
이 시장 저 시장을 찾아 다녔던 당신
내가 그 돈만 날리지 않았더라면
당신이 10년간 편히 시장을 볼 텐데!

모두들 자기의 둥지로 떠나 버린 지금
해맑은 당신의 모습을 어떻게 찾을까
이렇게 부질없이 낙서도 하면서
자꾸만 어둠만 짙어 가고
아들 영진이가 눈에 아른거려요.
여보 정말 미안해!

- 당신의 사랑하는 남편

---

* 1986년 어느 여름날 내가 공군훈련소에 근무할 때, 나의 부하, 중사 한명이 나에게 와서 말을 건넸다. "중대장님, 이번에 정말 좀 도와주시면 좋겠습니다." "이야기 해봐."라고 내가 말했다. "제가 어제 밤에 과음하고 새벽 3시에 들어가자 아내가 대문도 안 열어주고…, 대판 싸웠습니다. 이번엔 정말 풀릴 기미가 안 보입니다." 나는 그 가족이 문제가 뭔지, 어떻게 만나서 결혼을 했는지 그에게 아내에게 편지 쓰는 것을 도와주었다. 최근에 그가 잘 살고 있으며 그들의 결혼이 성공적이라는 소식을 들었다.

◎ The military wife's pledge

① I'll send my husband anytime at my nation's call.
② I'll be faithful during his temporary duty.
③ I'll serve his parents as if they were my parents.
④ I'll observe his family's happy and sad functions.
⑤ I'll even go by myself to his home at Chusok and Seol.
⑥ I'll take my children to the hospital by myself when they are sick.
⑦ I'll be a good cook and keep him in good health.
⑧ I won't increase our household goods unnecessarily.
⑨ I'll purchase my home in ten years by being frugal.
⑩ I'll never be a burden to my junior military wives.
⑪ I'll gladly relocate[1] tomorrow though I moved in today.
⑫ I'll never ignore him just because he didn't get a promotion.
⑬ I'll try to be sexually attractive so that he won't look elsewhere.
⑭ I'll upgrade my inborn sexual attraction to Hwang Chin-i level.
⑮ I'll offer warm coffee to the troops returning from a 1,000-ri march.
⑯ I'll gladly eat cold boiled rice because of his unexpected social gatherings.
⑰ I'll get out of the **Korean princess syndrome** as soon as possible.
⑱ I'll play my role successfully as wife, mother and daughter-in-law.
⑲ I'll do it immediately though he says "I wish" or "I would like to."
⑳ I'll be honored to be a soldier's wife even though he may die in battle.

* **The Korean princess syndrome** describes "Korean women who are full of vanity." The women with the Korean princess syndrome act as if they are "princesses" without considering their actual looks and real situations. Korean women are the worlds number one in the following: Cosmetic surgery (17%), Caesarian operations (39.9%), abortion (over a million cases per year), stay-at-home housewives (58%), the number of women who blackmail men, male dependence (changing their fortunes by marrying a rich man), not going Dutch, neglecting Korean men, female cigarette consumption (24.8 cigarettes per day per woman). – As of 2003

🟠 군인아내의 맹세

① 국가의 부름에 남편을 언제든지 보내겠습니다.

② 그가 파견근무 중에 바람을 피우지 않겠습니다.

③ 시댁 어른들을 내 부모처럼 모시겠습니다.

④ 시댁의 애경사를 잘 챙기겠습니다.

⑤ 설과 추석에는 혼자서도 시댁에 가겠습니다.

⑥ 애들이 아프면 혼자서도 병원에 데리고 가겠습니다.

⑦ 훌륭한 요리사가 되어 그의 건강에 신경을 쓰겠습니다.

⑧ 불필요하게 짐을 늘리지 않겠습니다.

⑨ 알뜰히 하여 10년 내에 집을 장만하겠습니다.

⑩ 후배 군인 아내들에게 절대로 짐이 되지 않겠습니다.

⑪ 오늘 이사 왔더라도 내일 즐겁게 이사 가겠습니다.

⑫ 남편이 진급이 안 되어도 그이를 무시하지 않겠습니다.

⑬ 색기 관리를 잘하여 남편이 곁눈질하지 않도록 하겠습니다.

⑭ 타고난 색기를 황진이 수준으로 업그레이드 하겠습니다.

⑮ 천리행군을 다녀오는 군인들에게 따뜻한 커피를 대접하겠습니다.

⑯ 남편의 갑작스런 회식에 찬밥을 혼자서 즐겁게 먹겠습니다.

⑰ **한국형 공주 신드롬**에서 하루빨리 벗어나겠습니다.

⑱ 아내, 어머니, 며느리의 역할을 훌륭히 하겠습니다.

⑲ 그가 "나는…하고 싶다." 라는 말을 해도 당장 이행하겠습니다.

⑳ 그가 전사하더라도 군인의 아내가 된 것을 영광으로 알겠습니다.

* **한국형 공주 신드롬**이란 "허영으로 가득 찬 한국 여자"를 말한다. 한국형 공주 신드롬이 있는 여자들은 자신의 용모나 처지를 개의치 않고 "공주"처럼 행동한다. 다음은 한국여성들이 세계 1위이다. 성형수술(17%) 제왕절개(39.9%) 낙태(매년 100만 건), 전업주부(58%), 남자 등쳐먹은 꽃뱀 수, 남자에 기생하기(돈 많은 남자와 결혼해서 팔자 고치기), 더치페이 안하기, 한국남자 무시하기, 여성흡연자 흡연 량(여성 당 1일 24.8개비) – 2003년 기준

Make the alert list more flexible

I used to like military personnel who defend my country. But I began to hate them after I got married. My husband's elder brother is an Air Force captain. Don't you think that he should visit his parent's home at least once at Chuseok or Seol. But he never comes because he has to be "on the alert." And my sister-in-law doesn't come, either.

Once someone in the family becomes a career soldier, his family members become estranged.[1] I think defending our country is important, but also our family is more than that. Our home and family is more important than our country, not vice versa. I hope to see my husband's brother and his wife next Lunar New Year's Day. I wish you, commanders would make a more flexible list of alert members. Please!

From a fan of the ROK-AF ^ ^

[해설] [1] estrange [istréindʒ]: to make unfriendly and distant, (syn.) to alienate: ~의 사이를 나쁘게 하다, 이간하다: She estranges people by her odd behavior. 그녀의 이상한 행동으로 인해서 사람들이 그녀에게서 멀어지게 했다.

유연한 비상대기 명단

저는 나라를 지키는 군인을 예전에는 좋아했습니다. 하지만 결혼하고부터는 싫어지더군요. 저의 시댁 아주버님이 공군 대위인데 추석이나 구정 중 한번은 시댁에 와야 하는 거 아닌가요. 그러나 저의 아주버님은 항상 "비상대기"라며 내려오시지 않더군요. 덩달아 우리 형님도 내려오시지 안구요. 집안에 누가 직업 군인이 되면 형제 사이가 벌어지더군요. 나라를 지키는 것도 중요하지만 내 가정, 내 가족도 소중하지 않은가요. 내년 설에는 꼭 아주버님과 형님을 보고 싶군요. 지휘관님들이 더 융통성 있는 비상대기 명단을 짜주었으면 합니다. 부탁입니다.

대한민국 공군의 팬으로부터 ^ ^

🔵 Gypsy life

Friends are the mortar[1] that helps to hold your life together. Cultivate them, cherish them, and keep them. This gypsy life we live as military wives sometimes makes that difficult, but it also offers us the opportunity to make friends all over the country.

When it comes to move on, remember that it is more difficult to be the friend left behind than to be the friend who leaves. The one who remains must fill a void[2], while the others go on to a new environment. Keeping in touch with them only takes a few letters or phone calls a year.

[해설] [1]mortar [mɔ́ːrtər]: 1) cement, plaster, etc., used to hold stone or brick together 모르타르, 회반, 2) a type of weapon 박격포: Soldiers fired mortars at the enemy. [2]void [vɔid]: an empty feeling 공허한 느낌: Her husband's death left a void in her life. 그녀의 남편의 죽음은 그녀의 인생에 공허감을 남겼다.

🔵 집시 인생

친구들은 너의 삶에 도움을 주는 회반죽이다. 친구들과 친분을 쌓고 그들을 소중히 여기고 그들을 간직하라. 군인의 아내로서 집시 인생은 때로는 힘겹기도 하지만 전국 도처에 있는 친구들을 사귈 수 있는 기회이기도 하다.

이사를 갈 때 명심할 것은 떠나가는 사람보다 남아 있는 친구들이 더욱 힘들다는 것이다. 떠나가는 사람들은 새로운 환경으로 들어가지만, 남아 있는 사람은 그 공허감을 채워야 한다. 그들과 연락을 유지하는 것이 일 년에 몇 통의 편지와 전화통화 만으로도 충분하다.

Military wife　　　　　　　군인의 아내

The backbone of the home you see.	당신은 가정의 주춧돌을 아시지요.
That's what the military wife is to me,	내가 볼 때 그것은 군인의 아내입니다.
Guarding the fort while her husband's away,	남편이 매일 집을 떠나서 나라를 지킬 때
Defending and protecting his country each day.	군인의 아내는 부대를 지킵니다.
Though many forget the importance of her role in his life,	비록 많은 사람들이 그녀의 역할을 잊지 만
Please, Sir, don't forget the military wife.	여러분, 제발 군인 아내를 잊지 마세요.
The woman who primarily raises her children alone,	그녀는 주로 혼자서 아이들을 키우는 사람이고
The one who strives to make a house, a "home."	집을 "가정"으로 만들려고 분투하는 사람이고
The one who sacrifices the time she could share,	할 수 있는 한 많은 시간을 희생하는 사람이고
The one who has many responsibilities to bear.	많은 것을 책임져야 하는 사람입니다.
The woman who is married to a protector of the world,	그녀는 세상의 수호자와 결혼한 여자이고
The one whose life stays fairly unfurled,	그녀의 인생은 바람에 꽤 나부낍니다.
I say again, kind Sir, don't forget the role she plays in his life.	다시 말씀 드리면, 친절하신 남자들이여 그대의 인생에서 그녀의 역할을 잊지 마시오.
Yes, dear Sir, the military wife.	예, 선생님, 그것은 군인의 아내랍니다.
The woman who stands by her husband's side,	그녀는 그녀의 남편 옆에 서 있는 여자이고,
The one who takes life stride by stride.	그녀는 인생을 오는 대로 받아들이고,
The woman who wonders when he's far away,	남편이 멀리 떠났을 때 걱정하고
The one who prays for his safety and sends tender love his way.	남편의 안전을 위해 기도하며, 남편이 가는 길에 부드러운 사랑을 보냅니다.
Next time you look into a soldier's eyes,	다음에 군인의 눈을 들여다보고,
Think of the one who stands by his side.	그의 옆에 서 있는 사람을 생각해 보세요.
The one left behind, the encouragement in his life.	왼쪽 뒤에 서 있는, 그의 인생에 용기를 주는 사람
The woman who's called the MILITARY WIFE.	그 여자의 이름은 군인의 아내랍니다.
－ Author Unknown	－ 작자 미상

🟠 Dear God

So far today,
I've done all right.
I haven't gossiped.
I haven't lost my temper.
I haven't lied or cheated.
I haven't been greedy, grumpy,
nasty, selfish or overindulgent.
I'm very thankful for that.
But in a few minutes, Lord,
I'm going to get out of bed;
and from then on, I'm probably
going to need a lot more help.
Amen

🟠 하나님

오늘까지
저는 잘 해왔습니다.
험담하지 않았습니다.
화내지 않았습니다.
거짓말도, 속이지도 않았습니다.
욕심을 냈거나, 불평을 했거나,
추하거나 이기적이거나 제 멋대로 하지 않았습니다.
그렇게 한데 대해서 감사드립니다.
하지만 하나님, 조금 있으면
저는 잠자리에서 일어날 것입니다.
그리고 계속해서, 저는 아마도
더 많은 도움이 필요할 겁니다.
아멘

Military English!

Final Test

In life everything begins and ends with tests.
Living in this world is not easy as we think.
I wish you good luck!

최종평가

인생은 시험으로 시작해서 시험으로 끝나지요.
세상살이가 생각처럼 만만치 않아요.
여러분의 건투를 빕니다!

◎ **All the questions are based on this book.**

01 If someone gets a draft notice, he has to go into _____.
ⓐ an army boot camp
ⓑ a navy boot camp
ⓒ an air force boot camp
ⓓ a marine corps boot camp

02 At what rank do private soldiers usually get a Dear John letter?
ⓐ private
ⓑ private first class
ⓒ corporal
ⓓ sergeant

03 Who is the busiest soldier, usually doing weeding, cleaning toilets, etc?
ⓐ private
ⓑ private first class
ⓒ corporal
ⓓ sergeant

04 What makes most soldiers dislike summer?
ⓐ heat waves
ⓑ mosquitoes
ⓒ athlete's foot
ⓓ cutting and weeding grass

05 Who cries three times a day?
ⓐ private soldiers
ⓑ soldiers' girlfriends
ⓒ private soldiers' mother
ⓓ sergeants who are going to be discharged

06 Select an item that is not handed down in the US boot camps.
   ⓐ Be a wallflower.
   ⓑ Always be a volunteer.
   ⓒ Do exactly as you are told.
   ⓓ Keep your mouth shut at all times.

07 Which recruits are most welcomed by their senior?
   ⓐ who have sisters.
   ⓑ who have much money.
   ⓒ whose parents have pull.
   ⓓ who are from prestigious colleges.

08 If an O-2 is considered an airplane, _____ is a bird.
   ⓐ a sparrow   ⓑ a mosquito
   ⓒ a butterfly   ⓓ a dung fly

09 In which branch of the armed forces did the ceremony of lighting a cigarette exist?
   ⓐ Army   ⓑ Navy
   ⓒ Air Force   ⓓ Marine Corps

10 Select an item that is not common to both a rifle and a woman.
   ⓐ It should be polished after using.
   ⓑ It takes some time to break them in.
   ⓒ It's sometimes annoying to carry them.
   ⓓ Brand-new ones always guarantee good performance.

11 What do gunbaries get after one week of waiting in the military?

ⓐ a pack of cigarettes

ⓑ a pack of hardtack biscuits

ⓒ an opportunity to go to the PX

ⓓ an opportunity to call their girlfriends

12 Select an item that is not correctly defined.

ⓐ Gibulick means a multi-religious person.

ⓑ To Mark means to have sex to make sure of a virgin girl.

ⓒ AWOL is the abbreviation for absent without official leave.

ⓓ Jody is a gentleman who is loved by all women in the U.S.

13 If a soldier says, "If I go now, when shall I come back? I will not survive the mistreatment," where is he probably serving?

ⓐ Hwachun   ⓑ Wontong

ⓒ Jeju-do   ⓓ Backryeong-do

14 Which unit is often called "the Marine Corps" of the ROK Air Force?

ⓐ Supply Squadron

ⓑ Signal Squadron

ⓒ Civil Engineering Squadron

ⓓ Air Defense Artillery Unit

15 Select an item that you don't need to put on at MOPP 3rd phase?

ⓐ a gas mask   ⓑ a raincoat

ⓒ protective gloves   ⓓ gas proof clothes

16 Select the natural dating sequence.

ⓐ attraction → uncertainty → exclusivity → intimacy → engagement

ⓑ attraction → uncertainty → intimacy → exclusivity → intimacy

ⓒ uncertainty → attraction → intimacy → exclusivity → engagement

ⓓ uncertainty → attraction → exclusivity → intimacy → engagement

17 Which is not the correct answer to each question?

Questions	Men	Women
① Who falls in love faster?	☑	☐
② Who is more idealistic about love?	☑	☐
③ Who usually initiates a breakup?	☐	☑
④ Who suffers more from a breakup?	☐	☑

18 Select an item that is mismatched between a rank and its image as seen by army private soldiers.

ⓐ private first class - quick-witted

ⓑ staff sergeant - talkative

ⓒ first lieutenant - dandy

ⓓ Lt. colonel - authoritative

19 Select a mismatched item between a slang term and its meaning.

ⓐ a ssogari - a platoon leader

ⓑ a hobagssi - a master sergeant

ⓒ a judori - a warrant officer

ⓓ a paecham - a sergeant who is about to be discharged

20 By whom was julbbadda brought into existence in the military?

ⓐ Seoul gunbaries   ⓑ Jella-do gunbaries

ⓒ Jeju-do gunbaries   ⓓ Gyeongsang-do gunbaries

21 Select an item that does not belong to a soldier's seven evils

ⓐ Who is very lazy.

ⓑ Who is poor at marksmanship.

ⓒ Who does not salute to one's seniors.

ⓓ Who emphasizes his age rather than his ability.

22 Select an item that does not belong to an officer's seven evils.

ⓐ Who is ignorant

ⓑ Who cannot drink at all

ⓒ Who gives and takes bribes.

ⓓ Who punishes his men collectively over trivia.

23 Which commanders devastate the armed force the most?

ⓐ The brilliant and industrious commanders

ⓑ The brilliant and lazy commanders

ⓒ The stupid and lazy commanders

ⓓ The stupid and industrious commanders

24 If your seniors give you instruction in something that you already know, that is a compete _____.

ⓐ education ⓑ training

ⓒ nagging ⓓ brainwashing

25 What is not common to both golf and learning English?

ⓐ They need motivation.

ⓑ They can be addictive.

ⓒ They need much time and money.

ⓓ Once you master them, you don't need to practice them anymore.

26 Hitting a homerun in a baseball game is equivalent to going to _____ the hole in playing golf?

ⓐ 18th   ⓑ 19th
ⓒ 20th   ⓓ 21st

27 Select an item that is not common to both election and promotion.

ⓐ It's like a total war.
ⓑ First you must be selected.
ⓒ You must grasp the right rope.
ⓓ Hard work alone guarantees victory.

28 What is the typical menu at social gatherings in the military?

ⓐ beef steak and wine
ⓑ sliced pork and belly and soju
ⓒ roast beef and boiler makers
ⓓ bean curd stew and makkolli(rice wine)

29 When enforcing Gyegeubju at social gatherings, how much soju would a 2nd Lt. have to drink first in order to offer two glasses of soju to a colonel?

ⓐ 5 glasses of soju   ⓑ 8 glasses of soju
ⓒ 10 glasses of soju   ⓓ 15 glasses of soju

30 Who is often called "the tail of kite" in the military?

ⓐ an adjutant   ⓑ an orderly
ⓒ a vice commander   ⓓ a military wife

This is the end of the test.

🔖 시험문제 해설 및 정답

01 누가 영장을 받는다면 그는 _____로 가야 한다.
  ⓐ 육군훈련소   ⓑ 해군훈련소
  ⓒ 공군훈련소   ⓓ 해병대 훈련소

02 사병들은 보통 어느 계급에서 절교편지를 받는가?
  ⓐ 이병   ⓑ 일병   ⓒ 상병   ⓓ 병장

03 보통 잡초사역, 화장실 청소 등으로 가장 바쁜 군인은?
  ⓐ 이병   ⓑ 일병   ⓒ 상병   ⓓ 병장

04 무엇 때문에 군인들이 여름을 그토록 싫어하는가?
  ⓐ 더위   ⓑ 모기   ⓒ 무좀   ⓓ 잡초사역

05 누가 하루에 세 번 우는가?
  ⓐ 이병   ⓑ 병사들의 여자친구
  ⓒ 이병의 어머니   ⓓ 전역예정 병장

06 미군훈련소에서 신송되는 것이 아닌 것은?
  ⓐ 벽에 붙은 꽃이 되어라.   ⓑ 항상 자원하라.
  ⓒ 정확히 들은 대로 하라.   ⓓ 입을 항상 닫고 있어라.

07 어떤 신병이 고참들에게 가장 환영을 받는가?
  ⓐ 누이가 있는 병사   ⓑ 돈이 많은 병사
  ⓒ 부모님이 빽있는 병사   ⓓ 명문대학 출신인자

08 O-2기가 비행기라고 한다면 _____도 새다.
  ⓐ 참새   ⓑ 모기   ⓒ 나비   ⓓ 똥파리

09 어느 군대에 점화식이 존재했었는가?
  ⓐ 육군   ⓑ 해군   ⓒ 공군   ⓓ 해병대

10 총과 여자의 공통점이 아닌 것은?
ⓐ 사용 후에는 닦아줘야 한다.
ⓑ 길들이는데 시간이 좀 걸린다.
ⓒ 때때로 휴대하기에 귀찮다.
ⓓ 새것은 항상 훌륭한 성능을 보장한다.

11 군대에서 군바리가 일주일을 기다려서 얻는 것은?
ⓐ 담배 한 갑   **ⓑ** 건빵 한 봉지
ⓒ PX에 갈 기회   ⓓ 여친에게 전화할 기회

12 올바르게 정의되지 않은 것을 골라라.
ⓐ 기불릭은 다 종교적인 사람을 의미한다.
ⓑ 주기하다는 처녀를 선점하기 위해서 섹스하다는 말이다.
ⓒ AWOL는 무단이탈(absent without official leave)의 약자다.
ⓓ 조우디는 미국에서 모든 여성들에게 사랑 받는 남자이다.

13 만약 어떤 군인이 "인제 가면 언제 오나? 원통해서 못 살겠네"라고 한다면, 아마도 그는 어디서 근무하고 있을까?
ⓐ 화천   **ⓑ** 원통   ⓒ 제주도   ⓓ 백령도

14 "한국 공군의 해병대"라고 종종 불리는 부대는?
ⓐ 보급대대   ⓑ 통신대대   ⓒ 시설대대   **ⓓ** 방공포 부대

15 MOPP 3단계에서 착용할 필요가 없는 것은?
ⓐ 방독면   ⓑ 우의   **ⓒ** 보호 장갑   ⓓ 보호의

16 데이트의 자연스러운 순서는?
ⓐ 매력→ 불확실→ 배제→ 친밀→ 약혼
ⓑ 매력→ 불확실→ 친밀→ 배제→ 약혼
ⓒ 불확실→ 매력→ 친밀→ 배제→ 약혼
ⓓ 불확실→ 매력→ 배제→ 친밀→ 약혼

17 각 질문에 대한 대답이 맞지 않는 것은?

질 문	남자	여자
ⓐ 누가 먼저 사랑에 빠지는가?	☑	☐
ⓑ 누가 사랑에 더 이상주의인가?	☑	☐
ⓒ 보통 누가 먼저 이별을 제안하는가?	☐	☑
ⓓ 이별 후에 누가 더 괴로워하는가?	☐	☑

18 육군 병사들에 비친 계급과 이미지가 잘 못 연결된 것은?
  ⓐ 일병 - 눈치 빠른　　ⓑ 하사 - 말 많은
  ⓒ 중위 - 멋을 아는　　ⓓ 중령 - 권위적인

19 속어와 그 의미가 잘 못 연결된 것은?
  ⓐ 쏘가리 - 소대장　　ⓑ 주도리 - 상사
  ⓒ 호박씨 - 준위　　　ⓓ 패참 - 전역예정 병장

20 누구 때문에 군대에 줄빠따가 생겼는가?
  ⓐ 서울 군바리　　　ⓑ 전라도 군바리
  ⓒ 제주도 군바리　　ⓓ 경상도 군바리

21 군인의 칠거지악에 해당되지 않는 것은?
  ⓐ 매우 게으른 사람
  ⓑ 사격을 잘 못하는 사람
  ⓒ 상관에게 경례를 하지 않는 사람
  ⓓ 자기 능력 보다는 나이를 내세우는 사람

22 장교의 칠거지악에 해당되지 않는 것은?
  ⓐ 무식한 자
  ⓑ 전혀 술을 못하는 자
  ⓒ 뇌물을 수수하는 자
  ⓓ 사소한 것으로 단체로 벌주는 자

23 어떤 지휘관이 군대를 가장 망치는가?
ⓐ 총명하고 부지런한 지휘관　　ⓑ 총명하고 게으른 지휘관
ⓒ 우매하고 게으른 지휘관　　**ⓓ** 우매하고 부지런한 지휘관

24 이미 당신이 아는 것을 교육한다면, 그것은 완전히 _____이다.
ⓐ 교육　　ⓑ 훈련　　**ⓒ** 잔소리　　ⓓ 세뇌

25 골프와 영어를 배우는데 공통점이 아닌 것은?
ⓐ 동기부여가 필요하다.
ⓑ 중독성이 있다.
ⓒ 시간과 돈이 많이 든다.
ⓓ 한번 마스터하면 연습할 필요가 없다.

26 야구에서 홈런은 골프에서 _____번 홀과 같은가?
ⓐ 18홀　　ⓑ 19홀　　**ⓒ** 20홀　　ⓓ 21 홀

27 선거와 진급의 공통점이 아닌 것을 골라라.
ⓐ 총력전과 같다.　　ⓑ 되고 봐야 한다.
ⓒ 옳은 밧줄을 잡아야 한다.　　**ⓓ** 열심히 일만 하면 승리한다.

28 군대 회식에서 전형적인 메뉴는?
ⓐ 쇠고기와 포도주　　**ⓑ** 삽겹살과 소주
ⓒ 쇠고기와 폭탄주　　ⓓ 두부찌게와 막걸리

29 회식에서 계급주를 시행하는데 소위가 대령에게 소주 두 잔을 권하려면 소위는 먼저 몇 잔의 소주를 마셔야 하는가?
ⓐ 5잔　　ⓑ 8잔　　**ⓒ** 10잔　　ⓓ 15잔

30 군대에서 누가 종종 "연 꼬리"라고 불리는 사람은?
ⓐ 부관　　ⓑ 당번　　ⓒ 부지휘관　　**ⓓ** 군인의 아내

시험 끝!

군대영어
Military English

발 행 일 : 2004. 6. 10. 초판
　　　　　2005. 1. 25. 개정 1쇄
　　　　　2008. 7. 10. 개정 2쇄
　　　　　2009. 4. 20. 3쇄(중판)
　　　　　2011. 1. 5. 4쇄(중판)
　　　　　2016. 3. 15. 5쇄(중판)
　　　　　2022. 12. 10. 6쇄(중판)
　　　　　2023. 03. 10. 7쇄(중판)

저　　자 : 진홍대
영문교열 : Martin D. Blignaut
　　　　　Benjamin N. Graham
펴 낸 이 : 이지수
디 자 인 : 최창규

펴 낸 곳 : 도서출판 써(Sir)24
등　　록 : 제321-302000025100200500046호(2005. 7. 18.)
주　　소 : 서울특별시 성북구 성북로10다길 28 (성북동)

본서의 내용을 출판사의 허락 없이 무단 복사는 법률로 금지됩니다.
All right reserved. No part of this book may be reproduced by any means without written permission from the publisher.